CHEMISTRY

GRADUATE RECORD EXAMINATION

CHEMISTRY

Advanced Test

by

Henry T. Bozimo, Ph.D.
Columbia University

Consultant:

Louis Weiss, Ph.D.
New York University

219 Park Avenue South, New York, N.Y. 10003

Second Edition
Fifth Printing, 1979

Published by Arco Publishing, Inc.
219 Park Avenue South, New York, N. Y. 10003

Library of Congress Catalog Card Number 66-30567
ISBN 0-668-01069-X

Printed in the United States of America

WHY USE THIS BOOK?

If you are planning to take the Graduate Record Examination Advanced Test, this book is indispensable for a higher score.

You are well aware that the GRE Advanced Test is one of the most important examinations that you will have ever taken. The results of this test will determine, in great measure, whether you will be admitted to the graduate school of your choice. Your entire future may well depend on the results of the GRE Advanced Test.

There will be many other candidates taking the test — and not all will score well enough to be accepted by the graduate schools of their choice. There simply are not enough places in the nation's better graduate schools to accommodate all applicants, worthy as they may be.

This book is designed to guide you in your study so that you will SCORE HIGH ON YOUR GRADUATE RECORD EXAMINATION ADVANCED TEST. This claim — that you will get a higher rating — has both *educational and psychological validity for these reasons:*

1. YOU WILL KNOW WHAT TO STUDY — A candidate will do better on a test if he knows what to study. The GRE-type questions in this book will tell you what to study.

2. YOU WILL SPOTLIGHT YOUR WEAKNESSES — In using this book, you will discover where your weaknesses lie. This self-diagnosis will provide you with a systematic procedure of study whereby you will spend your time where it will do you the most good.

3. YOU WILL GET THE "FEEL" OF THE EXAM — It is important to get the "feel" of the entire examination. Gestalt (meaning *configuration* or *pattern*) psychology stresses that true learning results in a grasp of the *entire situation*. Gestalists also tell us that we learn by "insight." One of the salient facets of this type of learning is that we succeed in "seeing through" a problem as a consequence of experiencing *previous similar situations*. This book contains hundreds and hundreds of "similar situations" — so you will discover when you take the actual examination.

4. YOU WILL GAIN CONFIDENCE — While preparing for the exam, you will build up confidence, and you will retain this confidence when you enter the exam room. This feeling of confidence will be a natural consequence of reason "3" above (getting the "feel" of the exam).

5. YOU WILL ADD TO YOUR KNOWLEDGE — "The learned become more learned." In going over the practice questions in this book, you will not — if you use this book properly — be satisfied merely with the answer to a particular question. You will want to do additional research on the other choices of the same question. In this way, you will broaden your background to be adequately prepared for the exam to come, since it is quite possible that a question on the exam which you are going to take may require your knowing the meaning of one of these other choices. Thorndike's principle of "identical elements" explains this important phase of learning — particularly as it applies to examination preparation.

CONTENTS

PART ONE

WHAT YOU SHOULD KNOW ABOUT THE GRADUATE RECORD EXAMINATION ADVANCED TEST

PART TWO

GRE ADVANCED TESTS IN CHEMISTRY

CONTENTS continued

PART ONE

What You Should Know
About The
Graduate Record Examination
Advanced Test

The Advanced Chemistry Test

THE PURPOSE

The Advanced Chemistry Test for the Graduate Record Examination is required by many graduate schools as part of their admissions selection program. Colleges may also use it to evaluate the achievements of their seniors who major in chemistry. The test is administered by the Educational Testing Service of Princeton, New Jersey.

Under the title of *National Program for Graduate School Selection,* it is given to graduate or undergraduate students who register individually to take the test. Under the title of *Institutional Testing Program,* it is given to undergraduates under the supervision of the school they attend.

THE NATURE OF THE TEST

The GRE Advanced Chemistry Test consists of approximately *150* questions with a three-hour time limit. Each question is multiple-choice with five lettered choices. The areas covered in the examination follow:

A. Organic Chemistry

1. Structural concepts
   a. basic reaction mechanisms
   b. electronic structures
   c. interpretation of spectral data
   d. stereochemistry and isomers
   e. theoretical concepts

2. Principal reactions
   a. acids
   b. alcohols
   c. amines
   d. carbonyl compounds
   e. diazonium compounds
   f. hydrocarbons
   g. organometallic compounds
   h. phenols
   i. sulfur compounds

3. Special topics
   a. bifunctional compounds
   b. classical reaction types
   c. classical rearrangements
   d. differentiations
   e. laboratory situations
   f. polymerizations
   g. preparation of organic chemicals
   h. reactivity

B. Inorganic Chemistry

1. Atomic theory

2. Extranuclear structures

3. Families of the elements

4. Other topics
   a. acids and bases
   b. anion and cation separations
   c. coordination compounds
   d. parent solvent systems
   e. polymer systems
   f. various compounds (carbonyl, interhalogen, nitrosyl, pseudohalogen)

C. Analytical Chemistry

1. Classical analysis

2. Instrumental analysis

D. Physical Chemistry

1. Kinetics
   a. chemical kinetics
   b. classical kinetic theory
   c. elementary statistical mechanics
   d. photochemistry and radiation chemistry
   e. theoretical interpretation of rate constant

2. Quantum and structural chemistry
   a. atomic structure
   b. crystal structure
   c. dielectrics
   d. liquids
   e. molecular structure
   f. nucleus
   g. quantum concepts

3. Thermal properties and thermodynamics
   a. chemical equilibrium
   b. chemical potentials
   c. electrochemistry
   d. equilibrium conditions
   e. laws
   f. mixtures
   g. phase equilibria
   h. surface chemistry thermodynamics
   i. temperature equations
   j. thermal properties

OTHER ADVANCED TESTS

Advanced Tests are offered for the following subjects:

Biology	Geology	Physical Ed.
Business	Geography	Physics
Chemistry	History	Political Science
Economics	Literature	Psychology
Education	Mathematics	Sociology
Engineering	Music	Spanish
French	Philosophy	Speech

Candidates may take one (but no more than one) of the Advanced Tests on one test date.

HOW QUESTIONS ARE TO BE ANSWERED

The following will help you become familiar with the way in which answers are to be recorded.

30. Chicago is a
(A) state (B) city
(C) country (D) town
(E) village

Sample Answer Spaces:

30 A B C D E (B blackened)

Note that the letters of the suggested answers appear on the answer sheet and that *you are to blacken the space beneath the letter of the answer you wish to give.*

(You will record your answers on special answer sheets. Careful marking of the answer sheet is necessary so that it will be accurately graded by the test scoring machine.)

APPLYING FOR THE EXAMINATION

Requests for information and application forms should be sent to:

The Graduate Record Examination
Educational Testing Service
Princeton, New Jersey 08540

or

1947 Center Street
Berkeley
California 94704

Every candidate is required to file a formal application and pay an examination fee.

You will be sent a ticket of admission giving the exact address of the place to which you should report for assignment to an examination room. Do not expect to receive your ticket until approximately one month before the examination date. You will be required to show your ticket to the supervisor at each session of the examinations. Normally, no candidate will be admitted to the examination room without his ticket of admission.

A candidate who loses his ticket should immediately write or wire the issuing office for a duplicate authorization. If in unusual circumstances a supervisor admits a candidate who does not have proper authorization, Educational Testing Service will review the case and will report the scores only if in its judgment the circumstances warranted the candidate's admission.

RULES FOR CONDUCT OF EXAMINATIONS

No books, slide rules, compasses, rulers, dictionaries, or papers of any kind may be taken into the examination room; you are urged not to bring them to the center at all. Supervisors will not permit anyone found to have such materials with him to continue a test. Anyone giving or receiving any kind of assistance during a test will be asked to leave the room. His testbook and answer sheet will be taken from him and returned to ETS, the answer sheet will not be scored, and the incident will be reported to the institutions named to receive the score report.

Scratch work may be done in the margins of the testbooks. Scratch paper is not permitted.

You must turn in all testbooks and answer sheets at the close of the examination period. No test materials, documents, or memoranda of any sort are to be taken from the room. Disregard of this rule will be considered as serious an offense as cheating.

If you wish to leave the room during a rest period or during a test, you must secure permission from the supervisor.

The examinations will be held only on the day and at the time scheduled. Be on time. Under no circumstances will supervisors honor requests for a change in schedule. You will not be permitted to continue a test or any part of it beyond the established time limit. You should bring a watch.

To avoid errors or delay in reporting scores:

1. Always use the same form of your name in signing your application form, your answer sheets, and on any correspondence with ETS. Do not write "John T. Jones, Sr." one time, and "J. T. Jones" another. Such inconsistency makes correct identification of papers difficult.
2. Write legibly at all times.

TRANSMITTING THE RESULTS

You will receive a report of your scores directly from Educational Testing Service. You may also have your scores reported to as many as three graduate or professional schools without additional fee, provided you designate them in the appropriate place on your application. After registration closes, you may not substitute for or delete institutions already listed on your application. No partial reports will be issued; reports will include scores made on all tests taken on a given date. To avoid duplication of requests, you should keep a record of the institutions to which you have requested that scores be sent.

If you have not applied for admission to any graduate or professional school when you file your application for the tests, you may write "None at this time" in Section 8 on the application. Score reports will be transmitted later by ETS if you request them within four years. The correct additional fee must accompany your request.

In designating on the application the institutions to which reports are to be sent, you should state the school, division, or department of the university or college as well as the name of the parent institution. Although arrangements have been made by most of the institutions for ETS to send all Advanced Test score reports to only one office at each institution, it may be necessary in some instances for ETS to know which school, division, or department has requested you to have your scores submitted.

Score reports requested on the application or by letter before the closing date will be issued within five weeks after your examination date. Although score reports requested after the closing date cannot be sent as quickly, they will be issued as soon as possible.

Scores on all Advanced Tests taken in the National Program for Graduate School Selection are available to any institution requesting them, whether or not the candidate himself has asked that a report be sent.

PART TWO

Advanced Tests in Chemistry

The six Sample Tests which follow are patterned after the actual test. In all fairness, we emphasize that these Sample Tests are not actual tests. All Graduate Record Examinations are secure tests which cannot be duplicated.

ANSWER SHEET TEST (1)

1 A B C D E
2 A B C D E
3 A B C D E
4 A B C D E
5 A B C D E
6 A B C D E
7 A B C D E
8 A B C D E
9 A B C D E
10 A B C D E
11 A B C D E
12 A B C D E
13 A B C D E
14 A B C D E
15 A B C D E
16 A B C D E
17 A B C D E
18 A B C D E
19 A B C D E
20 A B C D E
21 A B C D E
22 A B C D E
23 A B C D E
24 A B C D E
25 A B C D E
26 A B C D E
27 A B C D E
28 A B C D E
29 A B C D E
30 A B C D E
31 A B C D E
32 A B C D E
33 A B C D E
34 A B C D E
35 A B C D E
36 A B C D E
37 A B C D E
38 A B C D E
39 A B C D E
40 A B C D E
41 A B C D E
42 A B C D E
43 A B C D E
44 A B C D E
45 A B C D E
46 A B C D E
47 A B C D E
48 A B C D E
49 A B C D E
50 A B C D E
51 A B C D E
52 A B C D E
53 A B C D E
54 A B C D E
55 A B C D E
56 A B C D E
57 A B C D E
58 A B C D E
59 A B C D E
60 A B C D E
61 A B C D E
62 A B C D E
63 A B C D E
64 A B C D E
65 A B C D E
66 A B C D E
67 A B C D E
68 A B C D E
69 A B C D E
70 A B C D E
71 A B C D E
72 A B C D E
73 A B C D E
74 A B C D E
75 A B C D E
76 A B C D E
77 A B C D E
78 A B C D E
79 A B C D E
80 A B C D E
81 A B C D E
82 A B C D E
83 A B C D E
84 A B C D E
85 A B C D E
86 A B C D E
87 A B C D E
88 A B C D E
89 A B C D E
90 A B C D E
91 A B C D E
92 A B C D E
93 A B C D E
94 A B C D E
95 A B C D E
96 A B C D E
97 A B C D E
98 A B C D E
99 A B C D E
100 A B C D E
101 A B C D E
102 A B C D E
103 A B C D E
104 A B C D E
105 A B C D E
106 A B C D E
107 A B C D E
108 A B C D E
109 A B C D E
110 A B C D E
111 A B C D E
112 A B C D E
113 A B C D E
114 A B C D E
115 A B C D E
116 A B C D E
117 A B C D E
118 A B C D E
119 A B C D E
120 A B C D E
121 A B C D E
122 A B C D E
123 A B C D E
124 A B C D E
125 A B C D E
126 A B C D E
127 A B C D E
128 A B C D E
129 A B C D E
130 A B C D E
131 A B C D E
132 A B C D E
133 A B C D E
134 A B C D E
135 A B C D E
136 A B C D E
137 A B C D E
138 A B C D E
139 A B C D E
140 A B C D E
141 A B C D E
142 A B C D E
143 A B C D E
144 A B C D E
145 A B C D E
146 A B C D E
147 A B C D E
148 A B C D E
149 A B C D E
150 A B C D E

Equating Percentile Ranking with Scaled Score

Some time after you take the actual Graduate Record Examination Advanced Test you will receive a Score Report form which will include your so-called Scaled Score. This score is given on a scale range of 200-990.The following table equates your Sample Test Percentile Ranking with a Scaled Score.

Sample Test Percentile Ranking	Score (200-990 Scale)
99	983-990
98	975-982
97	967-974
96	959-966
95	951-958
94	943-950
93	935-942
92	927-934
91	919-926
90	911-918
89	903-910
88	885-902
87	877-884
86	869-876
85	861-868
84	853-860
83	845-852
82	837-844
81	829-836
80	821-828
79	813-820
78	805-812
77	797-804
76	789-796
75	781-788
74	773-780
73	765-772
72	757-764
71	749-756
70	741-748
69	733-740
68	725-732
67	717-724
66	709-716
65	701-708
64	693-700
63	685-692
62	677-684

Sample Test Percentile Ranking	Score (200-990 Scale)
61	669-676
60	661-668
59	653-660
58	645-652
57	637-644
56	629-636
55	621-628
54	613-620
53	605-612
52	597-604
51	589-596
50	581-588
49	573-580
48	565-572
47	557-564
46	549-556
45	541-548
44	533-540
43	525-532
42	517-524
41	509-516
40	501-508
39	493-500
38	485-492
37	477-484
36	469-476
35	461-468
34	453-460
33	445-452
32	437-444
31	429-436
30	421-428
29	413-420
28	405-412
27	397-404
26	389-396
1-25	200-388

ANSWER SHEET TEST (2)

1 A B C D E
2 A B C D E
3 A B C D E
4 A B C D E
5 A B C D E
6 A B C D E
7 A B C D E
8 A B C D E
9 A B C D E
10 A B C D E
11 A B C D E
12 A B C D E
13 A B C D E
14 A B C D E
15 A B C D E
16 A B C D E
17 A B C D E
18 A B C D E
19 A B C D E
20 A B C D E
21 A B C D E
22 A B C D E
23 A B C D E
24 A B C D E
25 A B C D E
26 A B C D E
27 A B C D E
28 A B C D E
29 A B C D E
30 A B C D E
31 A B C D E
32 A B C D E
33 A B C D E
34 A B C D E
35 A B C D E
36 A B C D E
37 A B C D E
38 A B C D E
39 A B C D E
40 A B C D E
41 A B C D E
42 A B C D E
43 A B C D E
44 A B C D E
45 A B C D E
46 A B C D E
47 A B C D E
48 A B C D E
49 A B C D E
50 A B C D E
51 A B C D E
52 A B C D E
53 A B C D E
54 A B C D E
55 A B C D E
56 A B C D E
57 A B C D E
58 A B C D E
59 A B C D E
60 A B C D E
61 A B C D E
62 A B C D E
63 A B C D E
64 A B C D E
65 A B C D E
66 A B C D E
67 A B C D E
68 A B C D E
69 A B C D E
70 A B C D E
71 A B C D E
72 A B C D E
73 A B C D E
74 A B C D E
75 A B C D E
76 A B C D E
77 A B C D E
78 A B C D E
79 A B C D E
80 A B C D E
81 A B C D E
82 A B C D E
83 A B C D E
84 A B C D E
85 A B C D E
86 A B C D E
87 A B C D E
88 A B C D E
89 A B C D E
90 A B C D E
91 A B C D E
92 A B C D E
93 A B C D E
94 A B C D E
95 A B C D E
96 A B C D E
97 A B C D E
98 A B C D E
99 A B C D E
100 A B C D E
101 A B C D E
102 A B C D E
103 A B C D E
104 A B C D E
105 A B C D E
106 A B C D E
107 A B C D E
108 A B C D E
109 A B C D E
110 A B C D E
111 A B C D E
112 A B C D E
113 A B C D E
114 A B C D E
115 A B C D E
116 A B C D E
117 A B C D E
118 A B C D E
119 A B C D E
120 A B C D E
121 A B C D E
122 A B C D E
123 A B C D E
124 A B C D E
125 A B C D E
126 A B C D E
127 A B C D E
128 A B C D E
129 A B C D E
130 A B C D E
131 A B C D E
132 A B C D E
133 A B C D E
134 A B C D E
135 A B C D E
136 A B C D E
137 A B C D E
138 A B C D E
139 A B C D E
140 A B C D E
141 A B C D E
142 A B C D E
143 A B C D E
144 A B C D E
145 A B C D E
146 A B C D E
147 A B C D E
148 A B C D E
149 A B C D E
150 A B C D E

Advanced Test in Chemistry

(Sample 2)

Time: 3 hours

Directions: Select from the lettered choices that choice which best completes the statement or answers the question. Indicate the letter of your choice on the answer sheet.

1. A compound having a molecular weight of 58 is shown by analysis to consist of 5/29 hydrogen and the rest carbon by weight. The number of hydrogen atoms in one molecule of the compound is
   (A) 5
   (B) 4
   (C) 8
   (D) 10
   (E) 14

2. The maximum number of electrons that may be found in the "L" shell of an atom is
   (A) 6
   (B) 8
   (C) 32
   (D) 18
   (E) 10

3. If strontium and sulfur combine, the formula for the product would most likely be
   (A) Sr_2S_3
   (B) Sr_3S
   (C) SrS
   (D) SrS_3
   (E) SrS_2

4. Of the following, the particle having the least mass is the
   (A) meson
   (B) electron
   (C) hydrogen ion
   (D) neutron
   (E) proton

5. Rutherford's bombardment of gold foil with alpha particles helped to establish the electron theory by
   (A) determining the mass of the atom
   (B) determining the number of particles in a mole
   (C) determining the charge on a single electron
   (D) determining the number of protons in the nucleus
   (E) demonstrating that the atom is largely empty space with a concentrated positive charge

6. The relative abundance of two rubidium isotopes of atomic weights 85 and 87 is 75% and 25% respectively. The average atomic weight of rubidium is
   (A) 75.5
   (B) 85.5
   (C) 87.5
   (D) 86.5
   (E) 86.0

7. Oxidation may be defined as
   (A) the gain of hydrogen
   (B) the loss of electrons
   (C) a loss of mesons from the nucleus
   (D) an increase in negative charge
   (E) the gain of electrons

8. As we go from left to right in period two of the periodic table, the gram atomic volume of the elements
   (A) will change indefinitely
   (B) increases at a constant rate
   (C) remains unchanged
   (D) first increases than decreases
   (E) decreases

9. On the basis of placement in the electromotive force series, it is possible to predict that in a chemical reaction
   (A) hydrogen with a potential of zero is inert
   (B) copper will displace lead from lead salts
   (C) gold is more readily oxidized than aluminum
   (D) tin will displace copper from salts
   (E) copper will displace hydrogen from acids

10. A certain metal will liberate hydrogen from dilute acids. It will react with water to form hydrogen only when the metal is heated, and the water is in the form of steam. The metal is probably
    (A) Fe
    (B) K
    (C) Cu
    (D) Hg
    (E) Na

11. 500 ml. of a 0.1N solution of $AgNO_3$ are added to 500 ml. of a 0.1N solution of KCl. the concentration of nitrate ion in the resulting mixture is
    (A) 0.05N
    (B) 0.1N
    (C) reduced to zero
    (D) 0.2N
    (E) 0.01N

12. The reaction
    $H_2O + C_{12}H_{22}O_{11} \rightarrow 4CO_2 + 4C_2H_5OH$
    is an example of
    (A) fermentation
    (B) esterification
    (C) saponification
    (D) polymerization
    (E) photolysis

13. A deuteron is a(n)
    (A) electron with a positive charge
    (B) neutron plus two protons
    (C) nucleus containing a neutron and two protons
    (D) helium nucleus
    (E) nucleus containing a neutron and a proton

14. The graphite rods in the nuclear pile
    (A) convert fast moving neutrons into thermal neutrons
    (B) react with U^{235} to release energy
    (C) furnish deuterons to fission U^{238}
    (D) undergo combustion which triggers the fission reaction
    (E) furnish alpha particles

15. In the series of active metals (Na, K, Rb, Cs) cesium is the most active because it (its)
    (A) incomplete shell is closest to the nucleus
    (B) exerts the greatest attractive force on valence electrons
    (C) has the largest number of valence electrons
    (D) valence electron has a larger orbit than the orbit of the valence electron of any of the others
    (E) has the highest boiling point

16. The equivalent weight of an element is always
    (A) its atomic weight multiplied by the valence
    (B) one-half its molecular weight
    (C) the weight of 22.4 liters (S.T.P.) of the gaseous element
    (D) one-third of its atomic weight
    (E) the weight of the element which combines with eight parts, by weight, of oxygen

17. The atomic number of a certain element is 83. An atom of this element must contain
    (A) 42 protons and 41 electrons
    (B) 83 neutrons
    (C) 1 neutron, 41 electrons and 41 protons
    (D) 83 electrons
    (E) 42 neutrons and 41 protons

18. A Dewar flask is usually used to
    (A) store liquid air
    (B) measure known quantities of gases
    (C) distill water
    (D) prepare bromine in the laboratory
    (E) measure the amount of liquid

19. The best evidence that electrons are arranged in definite orbits or energy levels is based on the observation that
    (A) atomic spectra consist of discrete lines and not continuous bands
    (B) electrons in the beta-ray have high kinetic energy
    (C) the penetrating power of cathode ray electrons depends on the voltage used to produce them
    (D) electrons revolve around the nucleus
    (E) electrons in metal are almost free

20. The atomic weight of atoms may be determined readily by the use of the
    (A) Wilson cloud chamber
    (B) zinc-sulfide fluorescent screen
    (C) electron microscope
    (D) nuclear magnetic resonance
    (E) mass spectrograph

21. If the principal quantum number of an atom is three, it possesses
    (A) only s and p electrons
    (B) only s electrons
    (C) only s, p, and d electrons
    (D) s,p,d, and f electrons
    (E) only p electrons

22. In order for the chain reaction during the fission of uranium to continue, the particle that is most necessary is the
    (A) positron
    (B) proton
    (C) electron
    (D) meson
    (E) neutron

23. The loss of a neutron from the nucleus of an atom
    (A) changes the chemical nature of the atom
    (B) causes the gain of a proton
    (C) causes the subsequent loss of an electron
    (D) reduces the atomic number of the atom
    (E) changes a physical property of the atom

24. In beta emission from the nucleus, an atom
    (A) increases by one in atomic weight
    (B) decreases by one in atomic number
    (C) decreases by four in atomic weight
    (D) increases by one in atomic number
    (E) remains constant in its atomic number

25. When hydrogen nuclei trap neutrons, they form
    (A) alpha particles
    (B) deuterium
    (C) beta rays
    (D) positrons
    (E) tritium

26. CH_3NH_2 in water will act as a(n)
    (A) acid
    (B) base
    (C) ester
    (D) salt
    (E) ketone

27. The slow partial oxidation of ethyl alcohol results in the formation of
    (A) acetone
    (B) acetic acid
    (C) butyric acid
    (D) propionic acid
    (E) acetaldehyde

28. The weight in grams of nitrogen in 11.2 liters (S.T.P.) of ammonia is
    (A) 7
    (B) 8.5
    (C) 22.4
    (D) 14
    (E) 3.5

29. The general formula for ketones may be expressed as
    (A) RCOOR′
    (B) ROR′
    (C) RCOR′
    (D) RNH_2
    (E) RCHO

30. Gamma rays have
    (A) unit mass and minus charge
    (B) unit mass and zero charge
    (C) zero mass and zero charge
    (D) zero mass and minus charge
    (E) unit mass and positive charge

31. The postulate that, "Equal volumes of gases contain the same number of molecules at the same temperature and pressure," was first proposed by
    (A) Avogadro
    (B) Boyle
    (C) Gay-Lussac
    (D) Dalton
    (E) Henry

32. A reagent used in testing for a carbonate is
    (A) H_2S
    (B) $CaCl_2$
    (C) HCl
    (D) NaOH
    (E) $MgCl_2$

33. When a solid is changed to a gas, without melting, the process is called
    (A) diffusion
    (B) boiling
    (C) sublimation
    (D) osmosis
    (E) fusion

34. Homogenized milk is a colloidal suspension from which fats and proteins may be precipitated by
(A) adding some ethanol
(B) allowing the milk to settle
(C) filtration
(D) pasteurization
(E) adding an acid

35. When KNO_3 dissolves in a beaker of water, it dissociates according to the equation $KNO_3 + 8500\ \text{Cal.} \rightarrow K^+ + NO_3^-$. It follows that
(A) the ions contain less energy than molecular KNO_3
(B) the water will become warmer
(C) 8500 calories will be given off during the ionization of 1 gram molecular weight of KNO_3
(D) the beaker will become cooler
(E) the temperature of the beaker will be kept constant

36. Moseley's name is most closely associated with the discovery of
(A) atomic numbers
(B) neutrons
(C) positrons
(D) atomic weights
(E) deuterons

37. The valence of ruthenium in the compound $K_2Ru(OH)Cl_5$ is
(A) plus 2
(B) minus 2
(C) plus 3
(D) plus 4
(E) minus 4

38. In the reaction:
$Ag + 4HNO_3 \rightarrow AgNO_3 + 2H_2O + 2NO$
some of the nitrogen atoms
(A) gain 2 electrons
(B) lose 2 electrons
(C) lose 3 electrons
(D) gain 3 electrons
(E) gain 1 electron

39. An example of a polar covalent compound is
(A) KCl
(B) NaCl
(C) CCl_4
(D) HCl
(E) CH_4

40. Chlorous acid has the formula
(A) HClO
(B) HCl
(C) $HClO_4$
(D) $HClO_3$
(E) $HClO_2$

41. In the electrolysis of a solution of copper sulfate, the reaction which takes place at the cathode can best be described as
(A) decomposition
(B) reduction
(C) oxidation
(D) ion exchange
(E) catalysis

42. A chemist whose name is closely associated with the determination of ionic radii is
(A) Arrhenius
(B) Pauling
(C) Urey
(D) Nernst
(E) Van't Hoff

43. A radioisotope has a half-life of 20 days; after 40 days the fraction of pure radioisotope which remains is
(A) 1/3
(B) 1/2
(C) 1/4
(D) 1/6
(E) 1/8

44. Of the following gases, the lightest is
(A) carbon monoxide
(B) chlorine
(C) sulfur dioxide
(D) hydrogen sulfide
(E) fluorine

45. The usual valence or oxidation number of the elements in the lanthanide series is
(A) 2
(B) 1
(C) 3
(D) 4
(E) 5

46. Tritium has an atomic number of
(A) 1
(B) 2
(C) 4
(D) 3
(E) 5

47. In the nuclear equation

$$_{52}Te^{130} + {}_1H^2 \rightarrow {}_{53}I^{131} + \overset{?}{\_\_\_\_}$$

the missing term is a(n)
(A) positron
(B) alpha particle
(C) neutron
(D) proton
(E) electron

48. Calomel is the common name for
(A) copper sulfate
(B) calcium fluoride
(C) dextrose
(D) mercurous chloride
(E) calcium chloride

49. Four liters of gas are contained under a pressure of 1140 mm and a temperature of 273°C. The volume of this gas (in liters) at S.T.P. will be
(A) 1.5
(B) 3
(C) 9
(D) 6
(E) 12

50. The normality of a solution of sulfuric acid containing 50 grams of acid in 500 ml of solution is
(A) 0.49
(B) 0.1
(C) 0.98
(D) 0.35
(E) 2.04

51. Which one is not a well-known value for the oxidation number of Mn?
(A) +2
(B) +4
(C) +5
(D) +6
(E) +7

52. Which one of the following cations forms complex ions with ammonia?
(A) Ca^{++}
(B) Fe^{++}
(C) Sc^{+++}
(D) K^{+}
(E) Cu^{++}

53. The Franck-Condon principle is used in the field of
(A) thermodynamics
(B) electrochemistry
(C) radiochemistry
(D) polymer chemistry
(E) quantum chemistry

54. The Miller indices of a face such that it is perpendicular to the a axis is
(A) (1,1,2)
(B) (1,0,0)
(C) (0,1,0)
(D) (0,0,1)
(E) (1,1,1)

55. What is the efficiency of a reversible Carnot cycle having a mass of steel as working substance?
(A) 1%
(B) 10%
(C) 50%
(D) 80%
(E) 100%

Answer Questions 56 and 57 with reference to the following formulas:

Work done isothermally $= nRT \ln (V_2/V_1)$
Adiabatic condition: $P_1V_1^{\gamma} = P_2V_2^{\gamma}$

56. Calculate the work done by 1 liter of hydrogen initially at 0°C and 760 mm. pressure in expanding to a volume of 2 liters isothermally.
(A) 0.1 cal
(B) 0.01 cal
(C) 1.7 cal
(D) 17.0 cal
(E) 1700 cal

57. (For oxygen, $\gamma = 1.4$). Calculate the work done when 5 liters of oxygen at 2 atm expands adiabatically to 20 liters.
(A) 0.1 liter-atm
(B) 1.07 liter-atm
(C) 10.7 liter-atm
(D) 107 liter-atm
(E) 0.01 liter-atm

58. The dissociation energy of H_2 into neutral atoms in kcal/mole is about
(A) 104.0
(B) 10.4
(C) 1040.0
(D) 500.0
(E) 5.0

59. The fundamental vibrational frequency in wave number units(cm^{-1}) of HCl gas is about
(A) 2.99
(B) 29.9
(C) 299
(D) 2990
(E) 29900

60. The room-temperature effective "hard sphere" collision diameter of the HBr molecule in cm is
(A) 1.29×10^{-12}
(B) 3.40×10^{-11}
(C) 1.29×10^{-10}
(D) 3.40×10^{-9}
(E) 2.40×10^{-8}

61. The electrons in the outer orbit of an atom of aluminum can be described as
(A) 2-1p; 1-1s
(B) 2-1s; 1-2s
(C) 2-3s; 1-3p
(D) 2-3p; 1-2d
(E) 2-2s; 1-2p

62. A 0.2 molar solution of formic acid is ionized 3.2%. Its ionization constant is
(A) 9.6×10^{-3}
(B) 2.1×10^{-4}
(C) 1.25×10^{-6}
(D) 4.8×10^{-5}
(E) 2.1×10^{-8}

63. When 0.450 gm of a substance was dissolved in 30.0 gm of water, the freezing point was lowered 0.150°C. The molecular weight of the compound is
(A) 100
(B) 83.2
(C) 186
(D) 204
(E) 50

64. The system $CaCO_3$: CaO: CO_2 has
(A) 2 components, 3 phases, and one degree of freedom
(B) 3 components, 2 phases, and 3 degrees of freedom
(C) 3 components, 3 phases, and zero degree of freedom
(D) 2 compounds, 2 phases, and one degree of freedom
(E) 3 components, 1 phase, and 2 degrees of freedom

65. The reaction: $3O_2 \rightarrow 2O_3$ -69,000 calories, is aided by
(A) higher temperature and lower pressure
(B) higher temperature and higher pressure
(C) lower temperature and lower pressure
(D) lower temperature and higher pressure
(E) adding more ozone

66. A 0.3M HC1 solution contains the following ions:
Hg^{++}, Cd^{++}, Sr^{++}, Fe^{++}, Cu^{++}
The addition of H_2S to the above solution will precipitate
(A) Hg, Sr, Fe
(B) Cd, Fe, and Sr
(C) Hg, Cu, and Fe
(D) Cu, Sr, and Fe
(E) Cd, Cu and Hg

67. In the ion Cu $(NH_3)_4^{++}$, the valence and coordination number of the copper are respectively
(A) zero and 3
(B) + 4 and 12
(C) + 2 and 8
(D) + 2 and 4
(E) + 2 and 12

68. The conjugate base of NH_4^+ is
(A) NH_3
(B) NH_4OH
(C) KOH
(D) OH^-
(E) NH_2

69. An example of a buffer solution is
(A) $HC_2H_3O_2 + NaC_2H_3O_2$
(B) $HC1 + HC_2H_3O_2$
(C) $NaOH + NH_4OH$
(D) HCI + NaCl
(E) NaOH + NaCl

70. The Williamson synthesis is an important means of preparing
(A) alkyl halides
(B) ketones
(C) higher alkynes
(D) mixed ethers
(E) aldehydes

71. A saturated solution of CaF_2 is 2×10^{-4} moles per liter; its solubility product constant is
(A) $2.6x10^{-9}$
(B) $4x10^{-8}$
(C) $3.2x10^{-11}$
(D) $8x10^{-12}$
(E) $8x10^{-10}$

72. The simplest amino acid is
(A) cystine
(B) alanine
(C) glycine
(D) histidine
(E) valine

73. Of the following substances, the one that would cause blue litmus to turn red is
(A) $(C_6H_{10}O_5)x$
(B) CH_3CHO
(C) CH_3CH_2OH
(D) $C_{12}H_{22}O_{11}$
(E) CH_3COOH

74. Lactose has the same molecular formula as
(A) glucose
(B) maltose
(C) levulose
(D) galactose
(E) erythrose

75. An acid that is classified as a hydroxy acid is
(A) oxalic
(B) lactic
(C) succinic
(D) acetic
(E) propionic

76. A fundamental equation in X-ray spectroscopy is
(A) $H = E + pV$
(B) $n\lambda = 2d \sin\theta$
(C) $PV = nRT$
(D) $nFE° = RT \ln K$
(E) $F = H-TS$

77. An element may be defined as a substance, all the atoms of which have the same
(A) atomic weight
(B) atomic number
(C) radioactivity
(D) number of neutrons
(E) number of positrons

78. A solution contains the following ions: Ag^+, Hg^+, Al^{+++}, Cd^{++}, Sr^{++}
The addition of dilute HCl will precipitate
(A) Ag only
(B) Al and Cd
(C) Ag, Cd, and Sr
(D) Al and Sr
(E) Ag and Hg

79. A current of 0.100 amperes is passed through a copper sulfate solution for ten minutes, using platinum electrodes. The number of milligrams of copper deposited at the cathode is
(A) 19.9
(B) 29.0
(C) 39.8
(D) 34.5
(E) 60.0

80. According to the Brönsted definition of acids and bases,
(A) the same substance cannot function both as acid and base
(B) any acid can yield a base by gaining a proton
(C) a base cannot be a cation
(D) a base may be an electrically neutral substance
(E) a base cannot be an anion

81. The cobalt nitrate test for magnesium produces the color
(A) green
(B) blue
(C) pink
(D) brown
(E) yellow

82. A blue color obtained as a result of the borax bead test indicates the presence of
(A) aluminum
(B) cobalt
(C) nickel
(D) magnesium
(E) sodium

83. An element which forms amphoteric compounds is
(A) S
(B) Zn
(C) La
(D) F
(E) Cl

84. Linus Pauling received the Nobel Prize for his work on
(A) atomic structure
(B) chemical bonds
(C) photosynthesis
(D) genetic effects of radiation
(E) thermodynamics

85. Compounds in which electrovalent bonds predominate have liquid forms characterized by
(A) low freezing point and slight electrical conductivity
(B) low freezing point and good electrical conductivity
(C) high freezing point and good electrical conductivity
(D) high freezing point slight electrical conductivity
(E) hydrogen bonding

86. The compound whose water solution has the highest pH is
(A) NaCl
(B) Na_2CO_3
(C) NH_4Cl
(D) $NaHCO_3$
(E) CH_3COOH

87. Different compounds with the same crystalline form are said to be
(A) isogonic
(B) isomorphic
(C) isotropic
(D) isotopic
(S) isoelectronic

88. The most satisfactory way to separate and identify sugars is to use
(A) biuret
(B) Benedict's solution
(C) mass spectroscopy
(D) fractional crystallization
(E) chromatography

89. The inversion of sucrose is catalyzed by the addition of
(A) platinum
(B) Fehling's solution
(C) hydrochloric acid
(D) ptyalin
(E) ethanol

90. Of the following compounds the one that has optical isomers is
(A) CH_3CH_2COOH
(B) $CH_3CHOHCOOH$
(C) $HOOCH_2COOH$
(D) $CH_3COCOOH$
(E) CH_3COOH

91. An example of a much used reducing agent is
(A) $SnCl_4$
(B) HF
(C) $KMnO_4$
(D) Cl_2
(E) $SnCl_2$

92. An element with atomic number 19 will most likely combine chemically with the element whose number is
(A) 16
(B) 18
(C) 21
(D) 20
(E) 17

93. The numerical value of the dipole moment of the molecule Cl_2 is
(A) zero
(B) 1.03
(C) 1.85
(D) 1.67
(E) 1.51

94. Aldehydes may be distinguished from ketones by the use of
(A) concentrated sulfuric acid
(B) Benedict's solution
(C) Schweitzer's reagent
(D) Cadet's liquid
(E) Hoffman's reagent

95. Properties which depend upon the number rather than the nature of the dissolved particles in a solution are called
(A) general
(B) colligative
(C) isotropic
(D) isotonic
(E) isoelectronic

96. The commercial separation of oxygen from nitrogen in liquid air is effected by the differences in
(A) boiling point
(B) color
(C) density
(D) index of refraction
(E) melting point

97. Insoluble rock phosphate is converted into an important fertilizer by treatment with
(A) HNO_3
(B) HCl
(C) H_2SO_4
(D) HF
(E) NaOH

98. When gold is dissolved in aqua regia, the gold compound formed is the
(A) sulfate
(B) nitrate
(C) chlorate
(D) nitrite
(E) chloride

99. Solve the following differential equation:

$$xdy\text{-}ydx + y^2dx = 0$$

(A) $x + y = 3$
(B) $y/x + x = 3/2$
(C) $x/y + y = 2$
(D) $x/y + y = 1$
(E) $\frac{x}{y} - x = -\frac{1}{2}$

100. According to the Maxwell-Boltzman distribution law of gas, the average translational kinetic energy is
(A) kT/2 per molecule
(B) kT per molecule
(C) 3kT/2 per molecule
(D) RT per molecule
(E) 5kT/2 per molecule

101. The molal magnetic susceptibility of HF gas in cm^3/mole is of the order of
(A) 75,000
(B) $3.50x10^{-2}$
(C) 1.00
(D) $-1.05x10^{-3}$
(E) $-25.6x10^{-6}$

102. The element *X* crystallizes in the face centered cubic structure. How many atoms of *X* are in a unit cell?
(A) 1
(B) 2
(C) 3
(D) 4
(E) 6

103. The definition of the epimers is a pair of diastereomeric aldoses that differ only in configuration at the position
(A) C-1
(B) C-2
(C) C-3
(D) C-4
(E) C-5

104. The Ruff degradation is used to reduce the carbon chain in a(n)
(A) alcohol
(B) alkane
(C) alkene
(D) ketose
(E) aldose

105. The compound furan is a five member ring containing, in addition to carbon atoms, an atom of
(A) nitrogen
(B) phosphorus
(C) sulfur
(D) selenium
(E) oxygen

106. The basic unit of the porphyrin system, which occurs in chlorophyll and in hemoglobin, is
(A) pyrrole
(B) furan
(C) thiophene
(D) oxazole
(E) thiazole

107. The ph value of the solution in which a particular amino acid does not migrate under the influence of an electric field is called the
(A) eutectic point
(B) yielding point
(C) neutralization point
(D) effusion point
(E) isoelectric point

108. The Cannizzaro reaction is used to produce an alcohol from a(n)
(A) alkane
(B) acid
(C) ketone
(D) aldehyde
(E) amide

109. Methyl ketones are usually characterized through
(A) the Tollens' reagent
(B) the Benedict's solution
(C) the Schiff test
(D) the bromine test
(E) the iodoform test

110. A compound whose atoms are superimposable on their mirror images even though they contain asymmetric carbon atoms is called
(A) a meso compound
(B) an erythro isomer
(C) a threo isomer
(D) a glycol
(E) an eutectic compound

111. A 1 molal solution of NaCl in water freezes at a temperature somewhat higher than —3.72°C. The best explation for this is
(A) incomplete dissociation of NaCl
(B) hydrogen bonding
(C) increased vapor pressure of the solvent
(D) interionic attraction
(E) interionic repulsion

112. In a chemical reaction equilibrium has been established when the
(A) opposing reactions cease
(B) concentrations of the reactants and the products are equal
(C) reaction ceases to generate heat
(D) order of the reaction is larger than two
(E) velocity of the opposing reaction is the same as that of the forward reaction

113. The lightest metal known is
(A) beryllium
(B) lithium
(C) sodium
(D) magnesium
(E) boron

114. The application of quantum mechanics to atomic structure is based largely on work done by
(A) Fitzgerald
(B) Einstein
(C) Giaque
(D) Schrodinger
(E) Planck

115. In the reaction:
$4P + 3KOH + 3H_2O \rightarrow 3KH_2PO_2 + PH_3$
(A) phosphorus is reduced only
(B) phosphorus is oxidized only
(C) phosphorus is neither oxidized nor reduced
(D) PH_3 is a solid precipitate
(E) phosphorus is both oxidized and reduced

116. In the reaction:
$2KMnO_4 + 16HCl \rightarrow 5Cl_2 + 2MnCl_2 + 2KCl + 8H_2O$
the reduction product is
(A) Cl_2
(B) $MnCl_2$
(C) H_2O
(D) KCl
(E) HCl

117. Raoult's law is concerned primarily with the lowering of the
(A) freezing point
(B) vapor pressure
(C) boiling point
(D) osmotic pressure
(E) electrical conductivity

118. Ernest O. Lawrence is credited with the invention of
(A) the neutron
(B) the cyclotron
(C) nuclear fusion
(D) fluorescence
(E) molecular beams

119. Boyle's and Charles' Laws are readily explained in terms of the
(A) theory of generalized relativity
(B) kinetic-molecular theory
(C) DeBroglie wave theory
(D) Le Chatelier's principle
(E) quantum mechanics

120. The reaction of the type: $RX + 2Na + R^1X \rightarrow 2NaX + RR^1$, is an example of a
(A) Cannizzaro reaction
(B) Friedel-Crafts reaction
(C) Wurtz-synthesis
(D) Grignard reaction
(E) Hoffman's reaction

121. The development of the ultramicroscope makes use of the
(A) Edison effect
(B) Tyndall effect
(C) Stark effect
(D) Raman effect
(E) Zeeman effect

122. The quantitative relationship between reaction rate and concentration was established experimentally in 1867 by
(A) Guldberg and Waage
(B) Arrhenius
(C) LeChatelier
(D) van't Hoff
(E) Faraday

123. Isobars are two nuclei that have
(A) the same atomic numbers, but different numbers of neutrons
(B) the same arrangement of outer electrons
(C) the same number of electrons, but different number of neutrons
(D) the same number of neutrons, but different number of protons
(E) the same mass numbers, but different atomic numbers

124. Radioactive isotopes that have an excesssive neutron-proton ratio generally exhibit which one of the following?
(A) alpha emission
(B) beta emission
(C) positron emission
(D) K-capture
(E) fission

125. Which one of the following is a product of the reaction between copper and hot concentrated sulfuric acid?
(A) hydrogen
(B) oxygen
(C) sulfur dioxide
(D) sulfur trioxide
(E) cuprous ions

126. If a current of 10 amperes is passed through solution of $CuSO_4$ for 16 minutes in an electroplating cell, the weight, in gm, of copper (atomic weight = 64) deposited is closest to which one of the following?
(A) 1.6
(B) 3.2
(C) 6.4
(D) 12.8
(E) 25.6

127. Which one of the following is a man-made element?
(A) actinium
(B) thorium
(C) radon
(D) curium
(E) samarium

128. How many ml of O.lM NaOH are equivalent to 10 ml of O.l M H_2SO_4?
(A) 5.0
(B) 10.0
(C) 20.0
(D) 40.0
(E) 50.0

129. The placement of an iron nail in an aqueous solution of aluminum sulfate and copper sulfate results in
(A) no reaction
(B) the formation of Al°, H_2° and Fe^{++}
(C) the formation of Al° and H_2
(D) the formation of Fe^{++}, Al° and Cu°
(E) the formation of Fe^{++} and Cu°

130. The chemical activity of the metals increases with increasing atomic number *except* in which one of the following groups?
(A) IA
(B) IB
(C) IIA
(D) IIIA
(E) IIIB

131. Which one of the following is *not* soluble in concentrated NH_4OH?
(A) AgF
(B) AgCl
(C) AgBr
(D) AgI
(E) $CuCl_2$

132. Which one of the following reagents is used in testing for magnesium ions?
(A) dimethylglyoxime
(B) dithizone
(C) 8-hydroxyquinoline
(D) salicylaldoxime
(E) urea

133. Of the following, the group that has the greatest effect in directing toward the ortho and para positions in aromatic substitution reactions is
(A) $-NO_2$
(B) -COOH
(C) -OH
(D) -CN
(E) -Cl

134. Of the following, the compound, that will react most readily with gaseous bromine has the formula

(A) C_3H_6
(B) C_4H_{10}
(C) C_4H_8
(D) C_2H_6
(E) C_2H_2

135. When determining the end point in an unknown weak acid determination, the solution is boiled

(A) to expel oxygen
(B) to expel hydrogen
(C) to expel carbon dioxide
(D) because it is easier to see the end point when the solution is hot
(E) boiling makes the titration quicker as a result of the faster dissociation of the weak acid

136. What is the potential of a platinum wire dipped into a solution of 0.1 M in Sn^{+2} and 0.01M in Sn^{+4}?

(A) E_0
(B) $E_0+0.059/2$
(C) $E_0+0.059$
(D) $E_0-0.059$
(E) $E_0-0.059/2$

137. In a standardization of hydrochloric acid with sodium carbonate, a student failed to dry the sodium carbonate completely. The resulting normality will

(A) be too high
(B) be too low
(C) be independent of the amount of water present in the Na_2CO_3
(D) be inversely proportional to the amount of water in Na_2CO_3
(E) be the correct normality

138. If carbon dioxide is dissolved in a solution of sodium hydroxide of known normality,

(A) a precipitate will form
(B) there will be no effect on the normality
(C) the normality will increase
(D) the normality will decrease
(E) the concentration of sodium ions will change

139. 15 grams of salt are dissolved in 60 grams of water. The per cent strength of the solution is

(A) 25
(B) 20
(C) 15
(D) 60
(E) 37.5

140. One mole of SO_3 was placed in a liter reaction vessel at a certain temperature. When equilibrium was established in the reaction, $2SO_3 \rightleftarrows 2SO_2 + O_2$, the vessel was found to contain 0.6 moles of SO_2. The value of the equilibrium constant is

(A) 0.36
(B) 0.68
(C) 0.45
(D) 0.54
(E) 0.18

141. If the dissociation constant of acetic acid is 1.75×10^{-5}m/l, in what proportion should acetic acid and sodium acetate be mixed to produce a buffer of pH 6.2?

(A) 6.3/17.5
(B) 6.3/1.75
(C) 6.3/35
(D) 63/1.75
(E) 6.3/175

142. In the conductometric method of analysis, the electrical resistance between two electrodes is dependent upon all of the following except

(A) kind of electrodes used
(B) distance between the electrodes
(C) the temperature
(D) the type of ions present
(E) the concentration of each type of ion present

143. Which of the following compounds would undergo the Cannizzarro Reaction?

(A) Acetaldehyde
(B) Benzaldehyde
(C) Propionaldehyde
(D) Anisole
(E) Bromobenzene

144. Which of the following reagents would distinguish cis-cyclopenta-1, 2-diol from the trans- isomer?

(A) Acetone
(B) Ozone
(C) Manganese dioxide
(D) Aluminium isopropoxide
(E) Lithium aluminum hydride

145. In the presence of dry HCl, ethylene glycol reacts with acetaldehyde to yield a(n)

(A) ester
(B) acid
(C) ketal
(D) α-dione
(E) acetal

146. Which of the following amino acids would give a colored product when its HCl solution is treated with ninhydrin?

(A) proline
(B) tryptophan
(C) tyrosine
(D) alanine
(E) glycine

147. The product of the reaction:

C_6H_5-CO-CH_2-CH_2-CH_3

$+ 2(NH_4)_2S + S \xrightarrow{160^\circ}$? is

(A) C_6H_5-C(=NH_2)-CH_2-CH_2-CH_3
(B) C_6H_5-CH_2-N(CH_3)CH_2-CH_3
(C) C_6H_5-N=C=O
(D) C_6H_5-CH_2-CH_2-NO-CH_3
(E) C_6H_5-CH_2-CH_2-CH_2-CO-NH_2

148. How many structural isomers [Kekule structures only] does bromodichlorobenzene have?

(A) 3
(B) 4
(C) 5
(D) 6
(E) 7

149. Pyrrole is less basic than pyridine because

(A) pyrrole can give off a proton
(B) pyrrole is smaller than pyridine
(C) pyrrole behaves as a cyclic diene
(D) pyrrole is "anti-aromatic"
(E) pyrrole has its electron pair as part of an "aromatic sextet"

150. In practical organic chemistry tetramethylsilane is used mainly for

(A) making volatile derivatives of alcohols
(B) a spectroscopic standard
(C) a substitute for neopentane
(D) a solvent for infrared spectra
(E) an "anti-knock" in gasolines

END OF ADVANCED TEST (2) IN CHEMISTRY

ANSWER KEY TO ADVANCED TEST 2 IN CHEMISTRY

In order to help pinpoint your weaknesses, the specific area of each question is indicated in parentheses after the answer. Refer to textbooks and other study material wherever you have an incorrect answer.

Area Code

ORGANIC CHEMISTRY = O
INORGANIC CHEMISTRY = I
ANALYTICAL CHEMISTRY = A
PHYSICAL CHEMISTRY = P

1. D(I)
2. B(I)
3. C(I)
4. B(P)
5. E(P)
6. B(I)
7. B(I)
8. E(I)
9. D(I)
10. A(I)
11. A(I)
12. A(O)
13. E(I)
14. A(P)
15. D(I)
16. E(I)
17. D(I)
18. A(P)
19. A(P)
20. E(I)
21. C(P)
22. E(P)
23. E(P)
24. D(P)
25. B(P)
26. B(O)
27. E(O)
28. A(I)
29. C(O)
30. C(P)
31. A(I)
32. C(I)
33. C(I)
34. E(P)
35. D(P
36. A(I)
37. D(I)
38. D(I)
39. D(I)
40. E(I)
41. B(I)
42. B(P)
43. C(P)
44. A(I)
45. C(I)
46. A(I)
47. C(P)
48. D(I)
49. B(P)
50. E(A)
51. C(I)
52. E(I)
53. E(P)
54. B(P)
55. E(P)
56. D(P)
57. C(P)
58. A(P)
59. D(P)
60. E(P)
61. C(P)
62. B(P)
63 C(P)
64. A(P)
65. B(P)
66. E(I)
67. D(I)
68. A(I)
69. A(I)
70. D(O)
71. C(I)
72. C(O)
73. E(O)
74. B(O)
75. B(O)
76. B(P)
77. B(I)
78. E(I)
79. A(I)
80. D(I)
81. C(I)
82. B(I)
83. B(I)
84. B(P)
85. C(I)
86. B(I)
87. B(P)
88. E(O)
89. C(O)
90. B(O)
91. E(I)
92. E(I)
93. A(P)
94. B(O)
95. B(I)
96. A(I)
97. C(I)
98. E(I)
99. E(P)
100. C(P)
101. E(P)
102. D(O)
103. B(P)
104. E(O)
105. E(O)
106. A(O)
107. E(P)
108. D(O)
109. E(O)
110. A(O)
111. D(P)
112. E(P)
113. B(I)
114. D(P)
115. E(I)
116. B(I)
117. B(P)
118. B(P)
119. B(P)
120. C(O)
121. B(P)
122. A(P)
123. E(P)
124. B(P)
125. C(I)
126. B(P)
127. D(I)
128. C(I)
129. E(I)
130. B(I)
131. D(I)
132. C(I)
133. C(O)
134. E(O)
135. C(A)
136. E(A)
137. A(A)
138. D(A)
139. B(A)
140. B(A)
141. E(A)
142. A(A)
143. B(O)
144. A(O)
145. C(O)
146. A(O)
147. A(O)
148. D(O)
149. E(O)
150. B(O)

Explanatory Answers for Advanced Test 2

1. **(D)** 5/29 is equivalent to 10/58. Since the molecular weight of the compound is 58, it must contain 10 atoms of hydrogen. That leaves $\frac{(58-10)}{12} = 4$ atoms of carbon.

2. **(B)** The "L" shell of an atom contains one "s" and three "p" orbitals. According to the Pauli exclusion principle, each of these orbitals can accommodate a maximum of two electrons. Thus, the "L" shell can contain a maximum of 8 electrons.

3. **(C)** Strontium, element #38, belongs in Group IIa of the Periodic Table, and would acquire the stable electronic configuration of Krypton by losing two electrons; that is, its valence is +2. Sulfur, element #16, belongs in Group VIa, and would acquire Argon's electronic configuration by gaining two electrons. It, thus, has a valence of −2. Therefore, one atom of strontium would combine with one atom of sulfur to give SrS.

4. **(B)** A hydrogen ion, a proton and a neutron have similar masses; and each is about 1840 times as heavy as an electron. The mass of the meson has been variously estimated as from 200 to 400 times that of the electron.

5. **(E)** By observing the X-ray scattering pattern of gold foil, Rutherford was able to show in 1912 that the positive charge of an atom was associated with most of the mass at the central core or nucleus, with enough negative charge distributed around the nucleus to render the whole atom neutral. This formulation is known as the nuclear atom model.

6. **(B)** For every rubidium atom with mass 87, there are three with mass 85. Therefore, the average mass of a rubidium atom is:

$$\frac{3\times 85+1\times 87}{4}=85.5$$

7. **(B)** In its original usage, oxidation was simply combination with oxygen. The definition has been progressively extended to include such similar processes as combination with sulfur or other strongly electronegative elements like fluorine and chlorine. In its widest application, oxidation is the removal of electrons from a substance.

8. **(E)** As one goes from left to right in the second period of the Periodic Table, electrons are added to "s" and "p" orbitals which have the same effective radii, and cannot shield each other from the increasing nuclear charge. This progressive increase in the positive charge draws in the orbital electrons and causes a progressive decrease in the effective radius of the elements.

9. **(D)** For the elements under consideration, the order of appearance in the electrochemical series is:
   aluminum-tin-lead-hydrogen-copper-gold.
   Along this list, any element, A, can displace any other element, B, from its (B's) salts if B appears to the right of A. That is, A is more easily oxidized than B if A appears to the left of B. On this basis, the only true statement listed is that tin will displace copper from copper salts.

10. **(A)** Sodium and potassium react violently with cold water to liberate hydrogen. Copper and mercury, being less electropositive than hydrogen, cannot liberate the latter from dilute acids. Iron reacts slowly with dilute hydrochloric acid to liberate hydrogen; and with steam, hot iron reacts according to the equation:

$$3Fe + 4H_2O \rightarrow Fe_3O_4 + 4H_2.$$

11. **(A)** The reaction between $AgNO_3$ and KCl is:

$$AgNO_3 + KCl \rightarrow AgCl + K^+ + NO_3^-$$

Thus the total quantity of NO_3^- remains constant. Since the starting concentration is 0.1N in 500 ml., and the final volume is 1000 ml., the final concentration of NO_3^- is:

$$\frac{0.1 \times 500}{1000} = 0.05N.$$

12. **(A)** Industrial alcohol can be prepared by the fermentation of sucrose from molasses or other suitable sources. The fermentation can be viewed as occurring in two steps:

$$\underset{\text{sucrose}}{C_{12}H_{22}O_{11}} + H_2O \xrightarrow{\text{sucrase}} \underset{\text{glucose}}{C_6H_{12}O_6} + \underset{\text{fructose}}{C_6H_{12}O_6}$$

$$\underset{\text{glucose or fructose}}{C_6H_{12}O_6} \xrightarrow{\text{zymase}} 2CO_2 + \underset{\text{ethanol}}{2C_2H_5OH}$$

13. **(E)** There are three known isotopes of atom #1: hydrogen, deuterium and tritium. Each of these has one orbital electron and one nuclear proton. Deuterium has an additional neutron while tritium has two neutrons in the nucleus. When the orbital electron is removed from the atom, a positively charged core is left which, for hydrogen, is called a proton; and for deuterium, is called a deuteron. The latter is, therefore, a nucleus containing a neutron and a proton.

14. **(A)** A nuclear pile is an assembly designed to sustain and control a neutron chain reaction with a fissionable fuel. Neutrons released by the fission reaction have very large kinetic energies (about 2 MeV). This energy is dissipated as heat by successive scattering collisions of the neutrons with the nuclides of the medium—a process known as neutron moderation. Examples of effective moderators are heavy water, graphite and beryllium.

15. **(D)** The reactivity of the alkali metals is due to the ease with which they can be oxidized; that is, the ease with which they lose the lone electron in the outermost valence orbital. For cesium, this orbital is of higher energy than are the analogous orbitals on the other elements under consideration. In addition, the attractive force between this outermost electron and the nucleus is smaller for cesium because the inner filled shells act as a shield. These two factors render cesium more electropositive than the other elements listed.

16. **(E)** The equivalent weight of an element is often defined as the weight of the element that would react with or displace one equivalent weight of hydrogen. According to this definition, the equivalent weight of oxygen is 8 atomic mass units. Thus, the equivalent weight of an element can also be defined as the weight of the element that would combine with 8 parts by weight of oxygen.

17. **(D)** For a neutral atom, the number of nuclear protons is equal to the number of orbital electrons, and is defined as the atomic number of the element. Therefore, an element with the atomic number 83 would have 83 protons and an equivalent number of electrons.

18. **(A)** A Dewar flask is a vessel that is constructed in such a way as to maintain almost constant temperatures by minimizing heat exchange with the surroundings. Liquid air, which boils at much lower than regular room temperatures, is, therefore, stored in Dewar flasks for laboratory use.

19. **(A)** Rutherford's scattering experiments with alpha particles established the planetary model of atoms, according to which the mass of the atom as well as the positive charge are concentrated in the nucleus, and the electrons are distributed like planets in orbit around the nucleus. However, classical electromagnetic theory demanded that such an arrangement would be inherently unstable, since the revolving electrons would radiate, lose energy and fall into the nucleus. This difficulty was solved by the Bohr model which confined electrons to definite orbitals. Movement from one orbital to another would be accompanied by the absorption or radiation of definite energies, leading to the observation of line, rather than band, spectra.

20. **(E)** A mass spectrograph is an instrument which operates on the principle of accelerating a charged particle by means of a field. Since the amount of acceleration can be correlated with the size of the particle, observation of the molecular ion would give the molecular weight of the substance.

21. **(C)** For any given value, n, of the principal quantum number, the angular momentum quantum number can assume any integral value from zero to $(n-1)$.

    Thus, for $n=3$, l can be 0, 1, or 2. Electrons with $l=0$ are "s" electrons; those with $l=1$ are "p" electrons; and those with $l=2$ are "d" electrons. Therefore, if the principal quantum number of an atom is 3, then the atom possesses "s", "p" and "d" electrons.

22. **(E)** The controlled fission of uranium is carried out in a nuclear reactor which is an assembly of special materials designed to sustain and control a neutron chain reaction, which leads to the ultimate production of lead from the uranium.

23. **(E)** Whereas the chemical behavior of an atom is dependent only on its electronic configuration, the atomic number is dependent only on the number of protons in the nucleus. Loss of a neutron would decrease the atomic weight by one, but would leave the atomic number constant. The resulting change in molecular weight would show up in such physical measurements as the mass spectrum, rate of diffusion, melting and boiling points, and infra-red vibrational frequencies.

24. **(D)** Beta emission involves the loss of an electron from a neutron and results in the production of a proton. The net result of beta emission, therefore, is an increase by one of the number of protons in the nucleus, and, consequently, of the atomic number of the atom.

25. **(B)** When a neutron is captured by a nucleus, the next higher isotopic nucleus is formed. In the case of hydrogen the resulting nucleus is that of deuterium, which has an atomic mass of two on the hydrogen scale.

26. **(B)** In water, CH_3NH_2 undergoes the following equilibration:

$$H_2O + CH_3NH_2 \rightleftarrows CH_3NH_3^+ + OH^-$$

    Examination of this equilibration shows that CH_3NH_2 is acting as a Bronsted base since it combines with a proton to give $CH_3NH_3^+$.

27. **(E)** Ethanol can be oxidized in a step-wise fashion that leads ultimately to the production of CO_2. The first step in this oxidation is the production of acetaldehyde:

$$\underset{\text{ethanol}}{CH_3CH_2OH} + [O] \rightarrow \underset{\text{acetaldehyde}}{CH_3CHO} + H_2O$$

28. **(A)** At S.T.P. one mole of any gas occupies 22.4 liters. Therefore, 11.2 liters of any gas contain ½ mole of that gas. One mole of ammonia, NH_3, contains 14 grams of nitrogen. Therefore, ½ mole of ammonia contains 7 grams of nitrogen.

29. **(C)** Ketones have the general formula, R-CO-R′. The general formula R-CO-OR′ stands for esters; R-O-R′ is the general formula for ethers; RNH_2 is the general formula for primary amines; and R-CHO stands for aldehydes.

30. **(C)** Gamma rays are electromagnetic rays which have higher energy than X-rays. The photon, the unit of electromagnetic radiation, has a rest mass of zero and a charge of zero.

31. **(A)** The hypothesis that equal volumes of all gases at the same temperature and pressure contain the same number of *molecules* was advanced by Avogadro to correct a similar one that had been made earlier by Gay Lussac that equal volumes of all gases at the same temperature and pressure contain the same number of *atoms*. Boyle discovered the relationship between the pressure and volume of a fixed mass of gas at a constant temperature. Dalton is famous for propounding the atomic theory of matter; and Henry worked out the relationship between the solubility of a gas and its pressure.

32. **(C)** With dilute mineral acids, carbonates react to give carbon dioxide. This reaction is used as a test for the carbonate anion:

$$CO_3^{--} + 2H^+ \rightarrow CO_2 + H_2O$$

33. **(C)** Sublimation is the process of transforming a solid to a gas without passing through the liquid phase.

34. **(E)** The particles in a colloidal suspension are of such dimensions that they do not precipitate out merely on standing, and they cannot be separated by ordinary filtration. However, most such particles bear an electrical charge on their surface which helps to keep them apart from one another. Addition of electrolytes, such as acids, would cause neutralization of this surface charge and would result in coagulation.

35. **(D)** According to the equation, 8500 calories are needed to separate the ions from each other. If this energy is not provided from the environment, it would be obtained at the expense of the internal energy of the solution, leading to a lowering of its temperature.

36. **(A)** By studying the X-rays emitted by different elements, Moseley observed a proportionality between the wave numbers of these rays and the squares of a new property which he called the atomic numbers of the elements – the numbers of protons in the nuclei of these elements.

37. **(D)** The compound, as written, is electrically neutral. Since there is a total of six negative charges (five on the chlorines and one on the hydroxyl group) and two positive charges on potassium, there will have to be four positive charges on ruthenium to create electrical neutrality.

38. **(D)** In HNO_3 and $AgNO_3$ the formal oxidation of nitrogen is +5, whereas in NO the formal oxidation of nitrogen is +2. Thus, in going from HNO_3 to NO, nitrogen has gained three electrons.

39. **(D)** Salts such as NaCl and KCl are ionic even in the crystalline state. CCl_4 and CH_4, though covalent, are not polar due to the tetrahedral symmetry around the carbon atom. Because of unequal sharing of the electron pair, HCl gas is both polar and covalent.

40. **(E)** In general, a chlorous compound is one which contains trivalent chlorine. Specifically, the formula for chlorous acid is:

$$HO\text{-}Cl{=}O \text{ or } HClO_2$$

41. **(B)** In an electrolytic cell, the cathode is the electrode from which electrons enter the cell. It is therefore negatively charged and attracts positive ions, to which it imparts electrons; that is, the cathode causes the reduction of positive ions in solution.

42. **(B)** In 1927, L. Pauling used Schrodinger's wave mechanics to devise theoretical expressions for the radii of ions. This treatment has stood as a theoretical standard against which to compare many experimental observations and semi-empirical treatments.

43. **(C)** By definition, the half-life of a first order reaction is the time required for half of a given amount of starting material to react. Therefore, after 20 days, ½ of the radioisotope would be left. After another 20 days, ½ of ½, or ¼, of pure radioisotope would be left.

44. **(A)** Carbon monoxide, with a molecular weight of 28, is the lightest of the gases listed. The molecular weights of the other gases are: chlorine, 71; sulfur dioxide, 64; hydrogen sulfide, 34; and fluorine, 38.

45. **(C)** Although other, less stable, oxidation states exist for some of the elements in the lanthanide series, the characteristic group valency for these elements is the tri-positive state, M^{+++}.

46. **(A)** Like deuterium, tritium is an isotope of hydrogen. Its nucleus contains one proton and two neutrons. Since atomic number is the number of protons in the nucleus of an atom, the atomic number of tritium is also 1.

47. **(C)** Nuclear equations, like chemical equations, are written so as to create a balance of masses and charges on both sides of the arrow. On this criterion, the missing term should have a charge of zero, and a mass of unity. The particle that satisfies these requirements is a neutron; and the complete equation is:

$${}_{52}Te^{130} + {}_{1}H^{2} \rightarrow {}_{53}I^{131} + {}_{0}n^{1}$$

48. **(D)** The standard calomel electrode employs the potential developed by solid mercurous chloride in potassium chloride solution. This should suggest that calomel is mercurous chloride.

49. **(B)** For a given mass of gas, the volume change produced by changes in temperature and pressure can be calculated by the relationship:

$$\frac{P_1V_1}{T_1} = \frac{P_2V_2}{T_2}, \text{ where T is in degrees Kelvin.}$$

Therefore,

$$V_2 = \frac{P_1V_1T_2}{T_1P_2}$$

For the present problem, we have:

$$V_2 = \frac{4 \times 1140 \times 273}{546 \times 760} = 3 \text{ liters.}$$

50. **(E)** A normal solution is one which contains one gram equivalent weight of solute in 1 liter of solution. If 500 ml of the solution contain 50g., then 1 liter would contain 100g. of H_2SO_4. Since each mole of H_2SO_4 contains 2 moles of hydrogen ions, the gram equivalent weight of H_2SO_4 is one half its gram molecular; that is, 49g. Therefore, 49g. of H_2SO_4 in 1 liter of solution is 1 molar; and 100g. of H_2SO_4 in 1 liter is 100/49 = 2.04 molar.

51. **(C)** Few compounds of Mn^{+5} are known, although this oxidation state has often been postulated as an intermediate in the reduction of permanganates.

52. **(E)** The deep-blue complex, $Cu(NH_3)_4^{++}$, which cupric ions form in the presence of excess ammonia, is a well-known analytical test for the cupric ion.

53. **(E)** The Franck-Condon principle states that within the time span that electronic transitions occur (about 10^{-15} sec.), nuclear positions can be assumed to be constant. The principle is used mainly in spectroscopic and quantum mechanical calculations.

54. **(B)** A face that is perpendicular to the a axis would intersect the a axis at a, the b axis at ∞, and the c axis at ∞. Therefore, the Weiss indices of the face are: (a, ∞, ∞). Miller indices are obtained by taking the least common multiples of the reciprocals of the Weiss indices. Thus, the Miller indices of this face are (1, 0, 0).

55. **(E)** The efficiency of a reversible Carnot cycle is independent of the working substance, and is always 100% of the thermodynamic efficiency, which is determined only by the operating temperatures.

56. **(D)** The work done in a reversible isothermal expansion is given by the expression:

$$w = nRT \ln \frac{V_2}{V_1}$$

1 mole of a gas at STP occupies 22.4 liters. Therefore, 1 liter of hydrogen at STP contains 1/22.4 moles.
Therefore, w = 1/22.4 × 2 × 273 ln 2
= 17.0 cal.

57. **(C)** For a reversible adiabatic expansion, the maximum work done can be shown to be:

$$w_m = \frac{nR(T_2 - T_1)}{(1 - \gamma)}$$

However, since $P_1V_1 = nRT_1$ and $P_2V_2 = nRT_2$, this expression reduces to:

$$w_m = \frac{P_2V_2 - P_1V_1}{1 - \gamma}$$

We are given that $P_1 = P_2$ atm.; $V_1 = 5$ liters; and $V_2 = 20$ liters.

Therefore, $P_2 = P_1(V_1/V_2)^{\gamma} = 2(5/20)^{1.4} = 0.286$ liters.

And

$$w_m = \frac{(0.286 \times 20) - (2 \times 5)}{1 - 1.4} = \frac{-4.28}{-0.4}$$

$$= 10.7 \text{ lit-atm.}$$

58. **(A)** The dissociation energy of H_2 is equivalent to the bond strength between two hydrogen atoms. The H-H bond is a relatively strong bond, and has a bond strength of 104.2 k cal/mole.

59. **(D)** The masses of atoms, and the forces that hold them together are of such magnitude that most chemical bonds have their fundamental vibrational frequencies in or near the infrared region of the electromagnetic spectrum. Since this region ranges (in wave-number units) from 650 to 4000 cm^{-1}, it may be guessed that the fundamental vibrational frequency of HCl is 2990 cm^{-1}.

60. **(E)** Remembering that atomic radii are usually measured in Angstrom units, and that one Angstrom unit is equivalent to 10^{-8} cm., the likeliest choice for the room temperature "hard sphere" collision diameter of the HBr molecule is 2.40×10^{-8} cm.

61. **(C)** Aluminum, atom #13, has the electronic configuration: $1s^2$, $2s^2$, $2p^6$, $3s^2$, $3p^1$. The K and L shells are filled, and the open shell is the M shell, which has two electrons in the 3s orbital and one electron in the 3p orbital.

62. **(B)** The ionization constant for formic acid is defined by the equation:

$$K_i = \frac{[H^+]\,[HCOO^-]}{[HCOOH]}$$

If a 0.2 molar solution of formic acid is 3.2% ionized, then the concentrations of the H^+ and $HCOO^-$ ions are 0.2×0.032; and that of formic acid is 0.2×0.968. Therefore, the ionization constant of formic acid is:

$$K_i = \frac{(0.2 \times 0.032)\,(0.2 \times 0.032)}{0.2 \times 0.0968} = 2.1 \times 10^{-4}$$

63. **(C)** The molecular weight of a solute is related to the freezing point depression of a solution of the solute by the equation:

$$\Delta T_f = K_f \frac{(1000 w_2)}{(w_1 M_2)}$$

In this equation, ΔT_f is the observed freezing point depression for a solution containing w_2 g of solute of molecular weight M_2 dissolved in w_1 g of solvent with a freezing point depression constant K_f. For water, $K_f = 1.86$
Substitution of the known values into the above equation gives:

$$M_2 = \frac{1.86 \times 1000 \times 0.450}{0.15 \times 30} = 186 \text{ g.}$$

64. **(A)** For the system, $CaCO_3 \rightleftarrows CaO + CO_2$, there are three phases (solid $CaCO_3$, solid CaO and gaseous CO_2). The system contains two components because its composition is determined by fixing any two of its constituents.

Gibb's phase rule states that F, the number of degrees of freedom, is equal to $C - P + 2$; where C is the number of components and P is the number of phases. Therefore, for this system, the number of degrees of freedom is $2 - 3 + 2 = 1$.

65. **(B)** Since the reaction is endothermic, Le Chatelier's principle would predict that an increase in temperature would drive it from left to right. Also, since three volumes of reactant yield two volumes of product, an increase in pressure would aid the forward reaction.

66. **(E)** The addition of H_2S to an acidic solution of metallic ions leads to the precipitation of ions in Group II of the analytical tables. In the list, cadmium, copper and mercury ions belong in this group. Strontium belongs in Group IV, for which the group reagent is basic ammonium carbonate. The reagent for Group III, the iron group, is H_2S in the presence of NH_3 and NH_4Cl.

67. **(D)** The valence of the ion is the same as the charge on the complex, since the ligands are neutral. The coordination number is defined as the number of ligands around the central ion. In $Cu(NH_3)_4^{++}$, this number is obviously 4.

68. **(A)** The conjugate base of any substance is obtained by the removal of a proton from the substance. Removal of a proton from NH_4^+ leaves NH_3, which is the conjugate base of NH_4^+.

69. **(A)** A buffer solution consists of a weak acid and one of its salts, or a weak base and one of its salts; and possesses the ability to resist pH changes caused by the addition of some acid or base. On this basis, the obvious choice for a buffer solution is $HC_2H_3O_2 + NaC_2H_3O_2$.

70. **(D)** The Williamson synthesis employs alkyl halides and sodium to obtain higher homologues of alkanes:

$$2RX + 2Na \rightarrow R\text{-}R + 2NaX$$

Modification of this reaction, by the use of an alkyl halide and the sodium salt of an alcohol leads to mixed ethers:

$$RX + R'ONa \rightarrow ROR' + NaX$$

71. **(C)** For CaF_2 the solubility product is defined as:

$$K_{sp} = [Ca^{++}]\,[F^-]^2$$

A solution that contains 2×10^{-4} moles of CaF_2 per liter would contain 2×10^{-4} moles of Ca^{++}, and 4×10^{-4} moles of F^-. Therefore,

$K_{sp} = (2 \times 10^{-4})\,(4 \times 10^{-4})\,(4 \times 10^{-4})$
$= 3.2 \times 10^{-11}$

72. **(C)** The expression, amino acid, is a shortened form of α-amino acid, and refers to any compound in which an amino group and a carboxylic acid group are bonded to the same carbon atom, which may or may not carry other substituents. The simplest amino acid is the one which has no other substituents than hydrogens; that is, NH_2-CH_2-COOH. It is called glycine.

73. **(E)** A substance that turns blue litmus red is an acid. In the list, CH_3COOH, acetic acid, is the only acid.

74. **(B)** Lactose is a dissacharide obtained by the condensation of glucose with galactose. It has the same molecular formula as maltose which is obtained by the condensation of two glucose molecules.

75. **(B)** The following are the formulae of the examples:

HOOC-COOH	$CH_3CH(OH)COOH$
oxalic acid	lactic acid

HOOC-CH_2-CH_2-COOH
succinic acid

CH_3-COOH	CH_3-CH_2-COOH
acetic acid	propionic acid.

Examination of these structures shows that lactic acid is the only hydroxy acid in the list.

76. **(B)** The Bragg equation is a fundamental equation in X-ray crystallography. It relates the diffraction angle to crystalline parameters:

$$n\lambda = 2d \sin \Theta.$$

In this equation, n is an integer, λ is the wavelength of the X-rays, d is the separation between atomic planes, and Θ is the diffraction angle.

77. **(B)** All atoms of an element have the same chemical behavior. This behavior is determined only by the number and configuration of the orbital electrons. The number of orbital electrons in a neutral atom is equal to the number of nuclear protons and, thus, to the atomic number. Therefore, all atoms of an element have the same atomic number.

78. **(E)** Addition of HCl to a solution of metallic ions causes the precipitation of the Group I ions, which are Ag^+, Pb^{++} and Hg^+.

79. **(A)** The equation for the reduction is:

$$\tfrac{1}{2}Cu^{++} + e^- \rightarrow \tfrac{1}{2}Cu$$

It can be seen that 1 faraday, or 96,500 coulombs, would cause the deposition of one half the gram atomic weight of copper, or 32 g of copper.

One coulomb is the quantity of electricity obtained by passing 1 ampere for 1 second.

Therefore, 0.100 amperes passing through a solution for 10 minutes is equivalent to $0.1 \times 60 \times 10 = 60$ coulombs.

96,500 coulombs deposit 32,000 milligrams of Cu. Therefore, 60 coulombs deposit $(32{,}000 \times 60)/96{,}500 = 19.9$ milligrams of copper.

80. **(D)** Bronsted defines a base as a substance that can accept a proton. Thus, since such electrically neutral substances as H_2O and NH_3 can accept protons to give H_3O^+ and NH_4^+, they are also defined as bases.

81. **(C)** If magnesium oxide, moistened with cobalt nitrate solution, is ignited, it turns pale pink. This reaction is given by many minerals which contain magnesium oxide, and is due to the formation of the double oxide, magnesium cobaltite, $MgO \cdot CO_2O_3$.

82. **(B)** On heating, borax loses water, swells into a white porous mass, and fuses to give a clear glass—anhydrous borax, $Na_2O \cdot 2B_2O_3$. Because it contains an excess of acidic oxide, borax is able to dissolve metallic oxides and produce characteristic colors—the borax bead test. Thus, cobalt oxide gives a blue bead; and chromium oxide a green one.

83. **(B)** An amphoteric compound is one which can react both as an acid and as a base. Zinc oxide is an example of such a compound. With acids, it forms zinc salts:

$$ZnO + 2HCl \rightarrow ZnCl_2 + H_2O$$

And with alkalis, it forms zincates:

$$ZnO + 2NaOH \rightarrow Na_2ZnO_2 + H_2O$$

84. **(B)** In addition to his many other achievements, Linus Pauling is the well-known founder of the valence-bond approach to chemical bonding. His 1954 Nobel award was given "for his research into the nature of the chemical bond and its application to the elucidation of the structure of complex substances."

85. **(C)** Electrovalent bonding confers high melting points on substances since the ionic particles are held into rigid crystalline structures by strong electrostatic forces. Also, the ionic nature of the particles makes the transport of electricity possible in the liquid state.

86. **(B)** The most basic substance in the group would give the water solution with the highest pH. In general, salts obtained by the neutralization of a strong acid with a strong base give neutral aqueous solutions; those obtained from weak acids and strong bases give basic solutions; and those from strong acids and weak bases give acidic solutions. With this as a guide, it can be seen that NaCl gives a neutral solution; NH_4Cl and CH_3COOH would give acidic solutions. Na_2CO_3 and $NaHCO_3$ are both derived from a strong base and a weak acid. However, the former would hydrolyze to give more NaOH than would the latter. It would, therefore, give the aqueous solution with the highest pH.

87. **(B)** Compounds which have the same crystalline form are said to be isomorphic. The property of isomorphism, as expressed in Mitscherlich's Law—the same number of atoms combined in the same manner produce the same crystalline form—was widely used in the early days of the atomic theory to determine atomic weights.

88. **(E)** Biuret and Benedict's solution are useful only in the classification of pure sugar samples. Mass spectrometry is not only destructive of the sample but it cannot by itself achieve separation into pure components. Sugars do not differ structurally enough for the technique of fractional crystallization to be very useful in their separation. Chromatography is a technique which allows minute changes in the stationary and moving phases, so that separations can be carried out on relatively similar compounds.

89. **(C)** The inversion of sucrose, which in nature is carried out by the enzyme invertase, is a result of the hydrolysis of the disaccharide to give glucose and fructose. This hydrolysis is also catalyzed by mineral acids such as hydrochloric acid. Platinum is useful in the catalytic hydrogenation of multiple bonds; Fehling's solution is used to distinguish aldoses from ketoses; and ptyalin, an enzyme found in saliva, catalyzes the hydrolyses of starch to disaccharides.

90. **(B)** Tetrahedral carbon can be a center of optical dissymmetry only if it is bonded to four different groups. Of the choices provided, only $CH_3\overset{*}{C}H(OH)COOH$ has such an optical center.

91. **(E)** Because tetravalent tin is the more stable oxidation state of the element, divalent tin is easily oxidized; and is frequently used as a good reducing agent.

92. **(E)** Element number 19 would have the electronic configuration: $1s^2$, $2s^2$, $2p^6$, $3s^2$, $3p^6$, $4s^1$. Thus, by giving up the one electron in the unfilled subshell, it can acquire the stable electronic configuration of argon. It would, therefore, most likely combine with an element which needs one electron to fill a shell; that is, a halogen. Such an element is element #17, which by the acquisition of one electron would also attain the configuration of argon.

93. **(A)** Since there is an equal sharing of the electron pair by the two chlorine atoms, there is no charge separation. Consequently, there can be no dipole moment for Cl_2.

94. **(B)** Benedict's solution, which consists of cupric ions complexed with citrate ions, is able to oxidize aldehydes, but not ketones, to carboxylic acids. In the process it is itself reduced to a brick-red precipitate of cuprous oxide:
$RCHO + Cu(citrate)^{--} \rightarrow RCOO^- + Cu_2O$
The formation of this precipitate is used to distinguish aldehydes from ketones.

95. **(B)** With solutions containing non-volatile solutes, such properties as (a) the vapor pressure lowering of the solvent, (b) the boiling point elevation, (c) the freezing point depression, and (d) the osmotic pressure of the solution are found to depend only on the number of particles in solution, and not on their nature. These properties of the solution are referred to as colligative properties.

96. **(A)** Nitrogen and oxygen can be separated by the fractional distillation of liquid air. This method makes use of the difference in boiling points that exists between the elements. Nitrogen first boils off at −195.8°C, and then oxygen at −183°C.

97. **(C)** Treatment of rock phosphate with concentrated sulphuric acid is a long-established process for the production of chemical fertilizers. The product, which is a mixture of calcium sulphate and calcium phosphates (containing varying amounts of the acid salts) is called superphosphate.

98. **(E)** Halogens react fairly readily with gold. As a halogen-generating solution, aqua regia reacts with gold to yield chloroauric acid, $HAuCl_4$, which can be isolated as yellow crystals in the form of $HAuCl_4 \cdot 4H_2O$.

99. **(E)** $xdy - ydx + y^2dx = 0$
Therefore, $xdy = (y - y^2)dx$
Or $dy/y(1 - y) = dx/x$
By integrating both sides, we get:
$\log y - \log(1 - y) = \log x + \text{constant}$.
Which, on rearrangement, gives:
$(x/y) - x = -1/2$

100. **(C)** The Maxwell-Boltzmann distribution law assigns a value of $(1/2)kT$ to each translational and rotational degree of freedom. Since every molecule has three translational degrees of freedom, then the average translational kinetic energy of a molecule is $(3/2)kT$.

101. **(E)** Experimental measurements of the magnetic susceptibility of HF gas have shown it to be of the order of -1.05×10^{-6}cm³/mole.

102. **(D)** Each atom at an angle of a cube is shared by eight unit cells. Thus, toward each unit cell, the angular atoms count as 1/8. There are eight such atoms, giving a total of $8 \times 1/8$ or 1 atom per unit cell from the angular atoms. Each atom on a face is shared by two unit cells. There are six such facial atoms on each cube, or three facial atoms per unit cell. Therefore, there is a total of 4 atoms per unit cell.

103. **(B)** An aldose cannot have an optical center at C − 1, since this is a carbonyl carbon. Aldoses which differ in the configuration at C − 2 are called epimers, and rotate plane polarized light in different directions.

104. **(E)** The Ruff, or Ruff-Fenton, degradation is used to shorten by one the length of the carbon chain of an aldose through its aldonic

acid. The oxidation is carried out with hydrogen peroxide in the presence of ferric salts:
R-CH(OH)-COOH + $H_2O \longrightarrow$
RCHO + CO_2 + $2H_2O$

105. (**E**) Furan is an aromatic analogue of benzene in which an ethylene moiety is formally replaced by an unshared electron pair on oxygen:

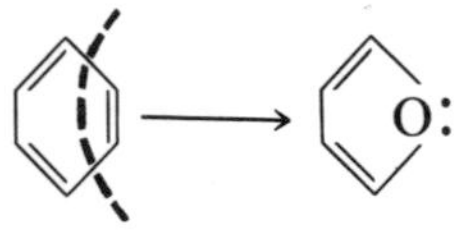

The sulfur analogue of furan is known as thiophene; and the nitrogen analogue as pyrrole.

106. (**A**) Porphyrin is a large heterocyclic ring containing four pyrrole rings whose nitrogen atoms act as ligands for a central metallic ion, which, in the case of chlorophyll, is magnesium.

107. (**E**) Only an electrically charged particle can be accelerated by an electric field. An amino acid can either be positively charged in acidic solutions, or negatively charged in basic solutions. Continuous variation of pH leads to a value at which the amino acid is electrically neutral, and does not migrate under the influence of an electric field. This pH value is known as the isoelectric point of the amino acid.

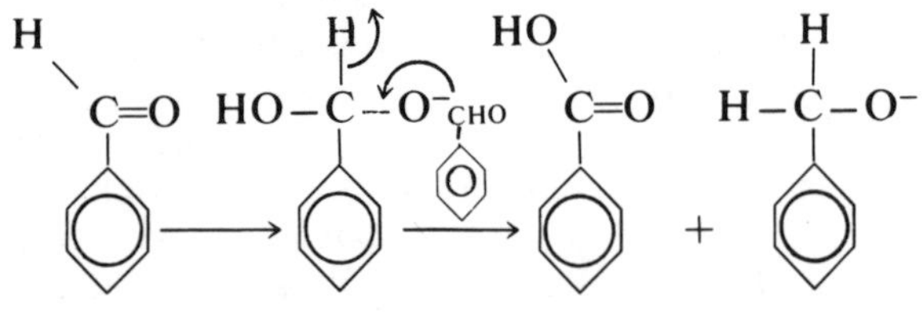

108. (**D**) Aldehydes which have no α-hydrogen atoms, and can, therefore, not undergo aldol condensations, can, in the presence of base, undergo a "disproportionation" to give an alcohol and an acid. Thus, the reaction of benzaldehyde with potassium hydroxide yields benzoic acid and benzyl alcohol:

109. (**E**) Methyl ketones and similar substances, such as acetaldehyde and ethanol, undergo the haloform reaction. This involves the treatment of the substrate with alkaline hypohalite, with the resultant formation of the haloform and alkaline salt of an acid:
$CH_3COR + 3NaOX = CX_3COR + 3NaOH$
$CX_3COR + NaOH = CHX_3 + RCOONa$.

110. (**A**) An optically pure compound which has optical centers but shows no optical activity because of "internal compensation" is known as a meso compound. This "internal compensation" is possible only when there is an even balance of assymmetric centers in the compound.

111. (**D**) The Debye-Hückel extension of the Arrhenius theory of electrolytic dissociation explained deviations from theoretical predictions on the basis of inter-ionic attraction in moderately concentrated solutions. This attraction means that the individual ions are not as free to move about within a concentrated solution as they would be in dilute solutions. Their correction could be compared to the van der Waals correction of the ideal gas equation.

112. (**E**) Chemical equilibrium is dynamic rather than static. This means that the apparent stopping of a reaction at equilibrium is due to equal rates of reaction in the forward and reverse directions.

113. (**B**) Lithium, the smallest member of the alkali metals is the lightest metal known. It has a gram atomic weight of 7 grams, and a specific gravity of 0.53.

114. (**D**) Although many workers contributed to the development of the quantum theory, Schrödinger's development, in 1926, of wave mechanics marked a major step forward. It allowed, for the first time, the extensive application of quantum theory to the solution of problems of atomic structure.

115. (**E**) In KH_2PO_2, phosphorus has a formal oxidation of +1; whereas in PH_3, it has a formal oxidation of −3. Thus, neutral phosphorus has been both oxidized to KH_2PO_2 and reduced to PH_3.

116. (**B**) In going from $KMnO_4$ to $MnCl_2$, manganese has changed its formal oxidation from +7 to +2. That is, it has been reduced; and the product of this reduction is $MnCl_2$.

117. **(B)** Raoult's law states that, in perfect solutions, the vapor pressure of each component is proportional to its mole fraction. It is the solution equivalent to Dalton's law for perfect gas mixtures.

118. **(B)** The cyclotron, a magnetic resonance accelerator, imparts very great velocities to heavy nuclear particles without the necessity of excessive voltages. It was invented by Lawrence and Livingston in 1931.

119. **(B)** The simple assumptions of the kinetic theory of gases can be used to derive both Boyle's and Charles' Laws of perfect gases.

120. **(C)** The synthesis of aliphatic hydrocarbons by the treatment of alkyl halides with metallic sodium is known as the Wurtz reaction. The extension of this reaction to mixed alkyl and aryl halides was effected by Fittig.

121. **(B)** Contrary to what its name suggests, the ultramicroscope is not an instrument of extraordinary magnifying power. The term has reference, rather, to its special system of illumination for very minute objects, such as colloidal particles. It uses the Tyndall effect to create diffraction specks in a dark field. The instrument is especially useful in the study of Brownian motion.

122. **(A)** The law of mass action, which relates reaction rates to concentrations of reactants, was formulated by the Danish chemists, Gulberg and Waage, in 1867. The law states that the rate of any reaction is, at any instant, proportional to the concentrations of the reactants, with each concentration raised to a power equal to the number of molecules of each species participating in the process.

123. **(E)** Isobars are nuclei of different atoms which have the same weight. Atoms which have the same atomic number but differ in their neutron content are known as isotopes.

124. **(B)** By beta emission, the nucleus can convert some of its neutrons to protons, and create a more stable neutron-proton ratio.

125. **(C)** Hot concentrated sulfuric acid is a moderately strong oxidizing agent which can be reduced by such metals as copper to sulfur dioxide. The reaction constitutes a laboratory method of preparing sulfur dioxide:

$$Cu + 2H_2SO_4 = CuSO_4 + 2H_2O + SO_2$$

126. **(B)** The reaction is:

$$(\tfrac{1}{2})Cu^{++} + e^- = (\tfrac{1}{2})Cu.$$

That is, 1 faraday of electricity, or 96,500 coulombs, would deposit one half the gram atomic weight of copper, or 32 g. The flow of 10 amperes for 16 minutes is equivalent to $10 \times 16 \times 60 = 9600$ coulombs. Therefore this quantity of electricity would deposit: $(32 \times 9600)/96{,}500 = 3.2$ g of copper.

127. **(D)** Curium, atom #96, was named in 1944 after Pierre and Marie Curie by Seaborg, James and Ghioso, who created it by the helium ion bombardment of Plutonium-239.

128. **(C)** The neutralization reaction between NaOH and H_2SO_4 is:

$$2NaOH + H_2SO_4 = Na_2SO_4 + 2H_2O$$

Thus, 1 molar equivalent of H_2SO_4 requires 2 molar equivalents of NaOH for neutralization. Therefore, 10 ml. of 0.1M H_2SO_4 require for neutralization,

$$\frac{(2 \times 10 \times 0.1)}{0.1} = 20 \text{ ml of } 0.1\text{M NaOH}.$$

129. **(E)** Iron is more electropositive than copper, but less electropositive than aluminum. Thus it can displace copper from cupric salts, but not aluminum from its salts. Therefore, placing an iron nail into a solution containing copper and aluminum sulfates would lead to the deposition of metallic copper and the formation of iron sulfate in solution.

130. **(B)** The elements, copper, silver and gold constitute the group 1B of the periodic classification of the elements. They each have 18 electrons in their penultimate electronic shells, and 1 electron in the outermost shell. Since loss of this outermost electron does not lead to stable noble gas configurations, these elements do not exhibit the ordered variation of properties that characterizes the group 1A elements—the alkalis.

As transition elements, copper, silver and gold tend to show discontinuities in their properties.

131. **(D)** Although the stability constant sequence for halogen complexes of many metals is F > Cl > Br > I, for Ag^+ and other noble metals, the reverse is true. Thus, AgI is very stable, and does not undergo ligand replacement in the presence of ammonia.

132. **(C)** 8-hydroxyquinoline, for which the trivial name oxine has been proposed, precipitates magnesium completely from ammoniacal solutions containing moderate amounts of ammonium oxalate. This precipitate, Mg $(C_9H_6NO)_2$, is often used for the gravimetric determination of magnesium. Alternatively, it can also be reacted with a known quantity of bromine, and the excess determined by titration.

133. **(C)** $-NO_2$, -COOH, and -CN are strongly electron-withdrawing, and, therefore, meta-directing in electrophilic aromatic substitution. For -Cl, the inductive and resonance effects are opposed to each other and are nearly canceled out. With -OH, the resonance effect is much stronger than the opposing inductive effect, and it is strongly ortho-para-directing.

134. **(E)** Bromine is added more readily to a triple bond than to a double bond.

135. **(C)** Carbon dioxide forms carbonic acid when in water. Boiling the solution removes the carbon dioxide and consequently prevents the formation of the carbonic acid which would interfere with the titration.

136. **(E)** the potential is given by

$$E = E_0 + \frac{0.059}{M} \log \frac{[\text{oxid.}]}{[\text{reduct.}]}$$

$$\text{Therefore, } E = E_0 + \frac{0.059}{2} \log \frac{[0.01]}{[0.1]}$$

$$= E_0 + \frac{0.059}{2} \log [10^{-1}]$$

$$= E_0 + \frac{0.059}{2} [-1]$$

$$= E_0 - \frac{0.059}{2}$$

137. **(A)** Since NV = number of milliequivalents of sodium carbonate used, and the number of milliequivalents is equal to

$$\frac{\text{\# mg. of sample}}{\text{molecular weight of pure sample}}$$

we can then see that if we have water in our sodium carbonate, then our normality will be too high because the number of milliequivalents with water present is greater than the number when the water is not present. So that for the same amounts of sodium carbonate

$$\frac{\text{\#mg. } Na_2CO_3\cdot(H_2O)_3}{\text{molecular weight}} > \frac{\text{\# mg. } Na_2CO_3}{\text{molecular weight}}$$

and since NV is the same for both, then N must be greater for the sample with water in it.

138. **(D)** When CO_2 is added to a water solution, it forms carbonic acid. If this CO_2 is then added to a basic solution, it also forms carbonic acid which will neutralize some of the base so that the normality of the base will be decreased.

139. **(B)** The per cent strength is given by (weight of solute/weight of solution) × 100. Therefore we have (15gm./75gm.) × 100 = 20%.

140. **(B)** The equilibrium constant for the reaction is given by $K = \frac{[SO_2]^2 [O_2]}{[SO_3]^2}$. Since there are 2 moles of SO_2 for one of O_2 the concentration of the O_2 is 1/2 that of the SO_2. The concentration of SO_3 is 1−.6 = 0.4 moles, so that $K = \frac{[0.6]^2 [0.3]}{[0.4]^2} = 0.68$

141. **(E)** pH = 6.2. Therefore $[H^+] = 6.3 \times 10^{-7}$ $HAc \rightleftarrows H^+ + Ac^-$ and $Ka = \frac{[H^+][Ac^-]}{[HAc]}$

Therefore

$$\frac{[Ac^-]}{[HAc]} = \frac{Ka}{[H^+]}$$

$$\text{or } \frac{[HAc]}{[Ac]} = \frac{[H^+]}{Ka} = \frac{6.3 \times 10^{-7}}{1.75 \times 10^{-5}} = \frac{6.3}{175}$$

142. **(A)** The electrical resistance of a solution is not dependent on the type of electrode used but only on the distance between them, the temperature, the type of ions present in solution, and the concentration of these ions.

143. **(B)** In the presence of base, aldehydes which lack α-hydrogens undergo a "disproportion" reaction to yield alcohols and carboxylic acids—the Cannizzarro reaction. Benzaldehyde is the only aldehyde in the list that lacks α-hydrogens.

144. **(A)** With a cis-diol, a ketone can form a five-membered cyclic ketal, which is sterically impossible for the trans isomer. Thus acetone can be used to distinguish the cis-diol from the trans-isomer.

145. **(C)** The condensation product between the carbonyl group of a ketone and two alcoholic O-H groups is known as a ketal. When, the condensation involves only one -OH group, the product is referred to as a hemiketal. Analogously, aldehydes form acetals and hemiacetals.

146. **(A)** Hydrochloric acid solutions of proline and hydroxyproline undergo a unique and characteristic reaction with ninhydrin according to the following scheme:

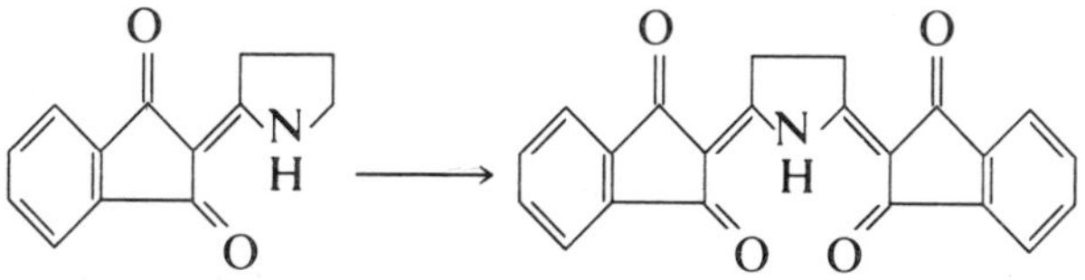

Proline yellow → Proline red

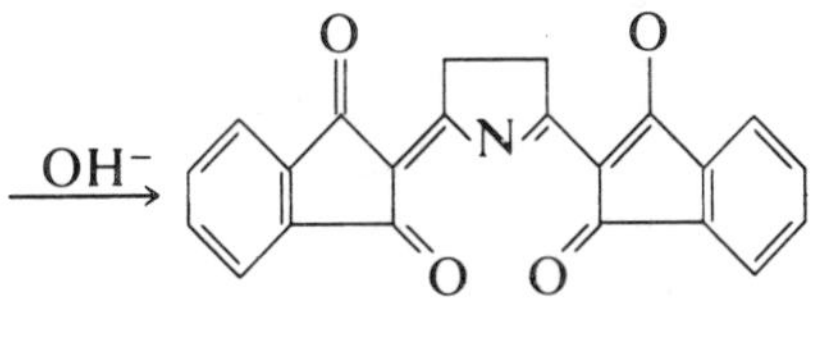

$\xrightarrow{OH^-}$

Blue anion

The amino acid is converted to proline yellow and then to proline red. The latter can be extracted from water with butanol, and when this solution is shaken with alkali containing a reducing agent, a blue anion passes into the water phase.

147. **(A)** The reaction between aryl alkyl ketones and ammonium sulfide and sulfur to produce ω-aryl amides is known as the Willgerodt reaction. The rearranged product always has the carbonyl group on the terminal carbon atom of the side chain.

148. **(D)** There are only six structural isomers of bromodichlorobenzene:

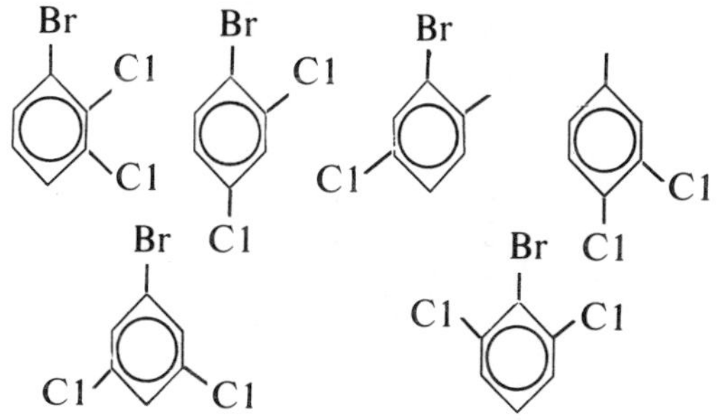

149. **(E)** It has long been known that the properties of benzene could be explained in terms of the six conjugated π-electrons in its cyclic structure—the "aromatic sextet"—an explanation incorporated in the Hückel (4n + 2) rule. In pyridine, the lone pair of electrons on nitrogen is not involved in the cyclic conjugation, and is available for basic bonding in the Lewis sense. In pyrrole, however, the nitrogen lone pair is needed to complete the "aromatic sextet" and is not available for such bonding.

150. **(A)** For practical utility, NMR absorbances have to be referred to a "standard". Tetramethylsilane has many properties that fit it out to play the role of such a "standard," and it is used as such in NMR spectroscopy.

ANSWER SHEET TEST (3)

1 A B C D E
2 A B C D E
3 A B C D E
4 A B C D E
5 A B C D E
6 A B C D E
7 A B C D E
8 A B C D E
9 A B C D E
10 A B C D E
11 A B C D E
12 A B C D E
13 A B C D E
14 A B C D E
15 A B C D E
16 A B C D E
17 A B C D E
18 A B C D E
19 A B C D E
20 A B C D E
21 A B C D E
22 A B C D E
23 A B C D E
24 A B C D E
25 A B C D E
26 A B C D E
27 A B C D E
28 A B C D E
29 A B C D E
30 A B C D E
31 A B C D E
32 A B C D E
33 A B C D E
34 A B C D E
35 A B C D E
36 A B C D E
37 A B C D E
38 A B C D E
39 A B C D E
40 A B C D E
41 A B C D E
42 A B C D E
43 A B C D E
44 A B C D E
45 A B C D E
46 A B C D E
47 A B C D E
48 A B C D E
49 A B C D E
50 A B C D E
51 A B C D E
52 A B C D E
53 A B C D E
54 A B C D E
55 A B C D E
56 A B C D E
57 A B C D E
58 A B C D E
59 A B C D E
60 A B C D E
61 A B C D E
62 A B C D E
63 A B C D E
64 A B C D E
65 A B C D E
66 A B C D E
67 A B C D E
68 A B C D E
69 A B C D E
70 A B C D E
71 A B C D E
72 A B C D E
73 A B C D E
74 A B C D E
75 A B C D E
76 A B C D E
77 A B C D E
78 A B C D E
79 A B C D E
80 A B C D E
81 A B C D E
82 A B C D E
83 A B C D E
84 A B C D E
85 A B C D E
86 A B C D E
87 A B C D E
88 A B C D E
89 A B C D E
90 A B C D E
91 A B C D E
92 A B C D E
93 A B C D E
94 A B C D E
95 A B C D E
96 A B C D E
97 A B C D E
98 A B C D E
99 A B C D E
100 A B C D E
101 A B C D E
102 A B C D E
103 A B C D E
104 A B C D E
105 A B C D E
106 A B C D E
107 A B C D E
108 A B C D E
109 A B C D E
110 A B C D E
111 A B C D E
112 A B C D E
113 A B C D E
114 A B C D E
115 A B C D E
116 A B C D E
117 A B C D E
118 A B C D E
119 A B C D E
120 A B C D E
121 A B C D E
122 A B C D E
123 A B C D E
124 A B C D E
125 A B C D E
126 A B C D E
127 A B C D E
128 A B C D E
129 A B C D E
130 A B C D E
131 A B C D E
132 A B C D E
133 A B C D E
134 A B C D E
135 A B C D E
136 A B C D E
137 A B C D E
138 A B C D E
139 A B C D E
140 A B C D E
141 A B C D E
142 A B C D E
143 A B C D E
144 A B C D E
145 A B C D E
146 A B C D E
147 A B C D E
148 A B C D E
149 A B C D E
150 A B C D E

ANSWER SHEET TEST (4)

No.						No.						No.						No.						No.					
1	A	B	C	D	E	31	A	B	C	D	E	61	A	B	C	D	E	91	A	B	C	D	E	121	A	B	C	D	E
2	A	B	C	D	E	32	A	B	C	D	E	62	A	B	C	D	E	92	A	B	C	D	E	122	A	B	C	D	E
3	A	B	C	D	E	33	A	B	C	D	E	63	A	B	C	D	E	93	A	B	C	D	E	123	A	B	C	D	E
4	A	B	C	D	E	34	A	B	C	D	E	64	A	B	C	D	E	94	A	B	C	D	E	124	A	B	C	D	E
5	A	B	C	D	E	35	A	B	C	D	E	65	A	B	C	D	E	95	A	B	C	D	E	125	A	B	C	D	E
6	A	B	C	D	E	36	A	B	C	D	E	66	A	B	C	D	E	96	A	B	C	D	E	126	A	B	C	D	E
7	A	B	C	D	E	37	A	B	C	D	E	67	A	B	C	D	E	97	A	B	C	D	E	127	A	B	C	D	E
8	A	B	C	D	E	38	A	B	C	D	E	68	A	B	C	D	E	98	A	B	C	D	E	128	A	B	C	D	E
9	A	B	C	D	E	39	A	B	C	D	E	69	A	B	C	D	E	99	A	B	C	D	E	129	A	B	C	D	E
10	A	B	C	D	E	40	A	B	C	D	E	70	A	B	C	D	E	100	A	B	C	D	E	130	A	B	C	D	E
11	A	B	C	D	E	41	A	B	C	D	E	71	A	B	C	D	E	101	A	B	C	D	E	131	A	B	C	D	E
12	A	B	C	D	E	42	A	B	C	D	E	72	A	B	C	D	E	102	A	B	C	D	E	132	A	B	C	D	E
13	A	B	C	D	E	43	A	B	C	D	E	73	A	B	C	D	E	103	A	B	C	D	E	133	A	B	C	D	E
14	A	B	C	D	E	44	A	B	C	D	E	74	A	B	C	D	E	104	A	B	C	D	E	134	A	B	C	D	E
15	A	B	C	D	E	45	A	B	C	D	E	75	A	B	C	D	E	105	A	B	C	D	E	135	A	B	C	D	E
16	A	B	C	D	E	46	A	B	C	D	E	76	A	B	C	D	E	106	A	B	C	D	E	136	A	B	C	D	E
17	A	B	C	D	E	47	A	B	C	D	E	77	A	B	C	D	E	107	A	B	C	D	E	137	A	B	C	D	E
18	A	B	C	D	E	48	A	B	C	D	E	78	A	B	C	D	E	108	A	B	C	D	E	138	A	B	C	D	E
19	A	B	C	D	E	49	A	B	C	D	E	79	A	B	C	D	E	109	A	B	C	D	E	139	A	B	C	D	E
20	A	B	C	D	E	50	A	B	C	D	E	80	A	B	C	D	E	110	A	B	C	D	E	140	A	B	C	D	E
21	A	B	C	D	E	51	A	B	C	D	E	81	A	B	C	D	E	111	A	B	C	D	E	141	A	B	C	D	E
22	A	B	C	D	E	52	A	B	C	D	E	82	A	B	C	D	E	112	A	B	C	D	E	142	A	B	C	D	E
23	A	B	C	D	E	53	A	B	C	D	E	83	A	B	C	D	E	113	A	B	C	D	E	143	A	B	C	D	E
24	A	B	C	D	E	54	A	B	C	D	E	84	A	B	C	D	E	114	A	B	C	D	E	144	A	B	C	D	E
25	A	B	C	D	E	55	A	B	C	D	E	85	A	B	C	D	E	115	A	B	C	D	E	145	A	B	C	D	E
26	A	B	C	D	E	56	A	B	C	D	E	86	A	B	C	D	E	116	A	B	C	D	E	146	A	B	C	D	E
27	A	B	C	D	E	57	A	B	C	D	E	87	A	B	C	D	E	117	A	B	C	D	E	147	A	B	C	D	E
28	A	B	C	D	E	58	A	B	C	D	E	88	A	B	C	D	E	118	A	B	C	D	E	148	A	B	C	D	E
29	A	B	C	D	E	59	A	B	C	D	E	89	A	B	C	D	E	119	A	B	C	D	E	149	A	B	C	D	E
30	A	B	C	D	E	60	A	B	C	D	E	90	A	B	C	D	E	120	A	B	C	D	E	150	A	B	C	D	E

Advanced Test in Chemistry

(Sample 4)

Time: 3 hours

Directions: Select from the lettered choices that choice which best completes the statement or answers the question. Indicate the letter of your choice on the answer sheet.

1. When chlorine and carbon tetrachloride are added to a solution of an iodide and shaken, the color produced is
(A) brown
(B) orange
(C) red
(D) yellow
(E) violet

2. If an eudiometer tube was filled with 26 ml of hydrogen and 24 ml of oxygen and the mixture exploded, there would remain uncombined
(A) 2 ml hydrogen
(B) 14 ml hydrogen
(C) 23 ml hydrogen
(D) 11 ml oxygen
(E) 12 ml oxygen

3. In sulfuric acid the valence or oxidation number of sulfur is
(A) plus 2
(B) minus 2
(C) minus 4
(D) plus 6
(E) plus 4

4. In the fractional distillation of liquid air, the gas among the following which boils off last is
(A) argon
(B) helium
(C) nitrogen
(D) oxygen
(E) hydrogen

5. Of the following, an example of a transition element is
(A) aluminum
(B) astatine
(C) nickel
(D) rubidium
(E) selenium

6. An oxide whose water solution will turn litmus red is
(A) BaO
(B) Na_2O
(C) Al_2O_3
(D) CaO
(E) P_2O_5

7. If twenty-five ml of an acid are needed to neutralize exactly 50 ml of a 0.2N solution of a base, the normality of the acid is
(A) 0.1
(B) 0.2
(C) 0.4
(D) 2.0
(E) 0.5

8. At about 4°C., water has its maximum
(A) density
(B) vapor pressure
(C) specific heat
(D) volume
(E) specific conductivity

9. The electronic configuration of the element xenon is
(A) 2-8-8
(B) 2-8-18-18-1
(C) 2-8-18-18-8
(D) 2-8-18-28-8-2
(E) 2-8

10. After 40 days, the weight in grams of the pure radioisotope which remains of eight grams of a pure radioisotope with a half-life of 10 days is
(A) 0.5
(B) 4.0
(C) 2.0
(D) 6.0
(E) 1.0

11. If a container is filled with hydrogen and another container of the same size is filled with carbon dioxide, both containers will, under normal air pressure, contain the same
(A) number of atoms
(B) number of electrons
(C) weight of gas
(D) number of neutrons
(E) number of molecules

12. Which one of the following weights of nickel metal would be closest to the weight deposited by the passage of 24,125 coulombs through an aqueous solution of NiI_2?
(Atomic wt. of Ni = 58.7)
(A) 7.3g
(B) 14.6g
(C) 29.2g
(D) 3.7g
(E) 58.7g

13. Of the following elements to which one does the plastic "Teflon" owe many of its unique properties?
(A) chlorine
(B) nitrogen
(C) sulfur
(D) fluorine
(E) phosphorus

14. The total number of types of water that can be made from
$_1H^1$, $_1H^2$, $_1H^3$ and $_8O^{16}$, $_8O^{17}$ and $_8O^{18}$ is
(A) 3
(B) 9
(C) 6
(D) 27
(E) 18

15. Assume that air is 21.0% oxygen and 79.0% nitrogen by volume. If the barometric pressure is 740 m.m., the partial pressure of oxygen is closest to which one of the following?
(A) 155 m.m.
(B) 310 m.m.
(C) 580 m.m.
(D) 740 m.m.
(E) 320 m.m.

16. To which one of the following can the relatively great stability of the HCl molecule be attributed?
(A) ability of chlorine to support combustion
(B) ability of hydrogen gas to burn
(C) non-ionic type of bonding
(D) ionic bonding
(E) unequal sharing of the electron pair

17. If seven milliequivalents of a base exactly neutralize 40 ml. of an acid, the normality of the acid is
(A) 0.700
(B) 0.280
(C) 1.750
(D) 7.000
(E) 0.175

18. The fact that carbon dioxide has no dipole moment indicates that the molecule is
(A) covalently bonded
(B) ionically bonded
(C) angular
(D) linear and symmetrical
(E) nonlinear

19. Assume that a mole of gas "X" weighs 70 grams at S.T.P. The weight of 300 ml of this gas at 27°C and 760 m.m. pressure is
(A) 0.853 grams
(B) 0.938 grams
(C) 1.030 grams
(D) 2.330 grams
(E) 3.310 grams

20. If the analysis of a hydrocarbon is 83.6% carbon and 16.4% hydrogen, the most probable empirical formula is (Atomic Weights: C = 12; H = 1).
(A) C_3H_6
(B) C_3H_8
(C) C_6H_{14}
(D) C_7H_{16}
(E) C_6H_{12}

21. Which one of these following elements belongs to the family of elements that also includes the element gallium?
(A) carbon
(B) aluminum
(C) arsenic
(D) iron
(E) oxygen

22. In the reaction given in unbalanced form below, the number of moles of $KClO_3$, needed to react with one mole of $C_{12}H_{22}O_{11}$ is
$KClO_3 + C_{12}H_{22}O_{11} \rightarrow KCl + CO_2 + H_2O$
(A) 2
(B) 4
(C) 6
(D) 8
(E) 5

23. Silver chloride was precipitated by adding HCl to a solution of a silver salt until the concentration of chloride ions is 0.20 mole/liter. Ideally, the concentration of silver ions in this case should be:
(K_{sp}AgCl $1.56x10^{-10}$)
(A) $\sqrt{1.56x10^{-5}}$
(B) $\sqrt{7.8x10^{-10}}$
(C) $7.8x10^{-9}$
(D) $1.56x10^{-10}$
(E) $7.8x10^{-10}$

24. If a 0.1 M solution of HCN is 0.01% ionized, the ionization constant for hydrocyanic acid is
(A) 10^{-2}
(B) 10^{-3}
(C) 10^{-7}
(D) 10^{-9}
(E) 10^{-6}

25. If solid sodium acetate is added to a dilute solution of acetic acid the pH will
(A) increase
(B) be unaffected
(C) decrease
(D) first decrease, then increase
(E) first increase then decrease

26. A colloidal solution of arsenious sulfide is most rapidly coagulated by the addition of a normal solution of which one of the following?
(A) NaCl
(B) $CaCl_2$
(C) Na_3PO_4
(D) $Al_2(SO_4)_3$
(E) $MgCl_2$

27. The molality of a glucose solution containing 22.5 grams of glucose (atomic weights: C = 12; O = 16; H = 1) in 500 grams of water is closest to which one of the following?
(A) 0.13
(B) 0.75
(C) 0.38
(D) 0.50
(E) 0.25

28. In the following incomplete nuclear equation,
${}_{29}Cu^{64} \rightarrow ? + {}_{28}Ni^{64}$,
the missing term is
(A) an electron
(B) a neutron
(C) a positron
(D) a proton
(E) a muon

29. An isotone is a nucleus identical with a reference nucleus in
(A) number of electrons
(B) weight
(C) number of protons
(D) atomic number
(E) number of neutrons

30. Which one of the following is an equivalent term to *mass-defect?*
(A) average atomic weight
(B) binding energy
(C) crystal dislocation
(D) Brillouin zone
(E) atomic number

31. Assuming equal mole of radioactive elements, the most dangerous to approach immediately would be one having a half life of
(A) 4.5 billion years
(B) 65 years
(C) 12 days
(D) 0.001 minute
(E) 1 minute

32. When a radioactive atom emits a beta particle from the nucleus, the new substance produced
(A) has the same atomic number
(B) gains one unit in atomic mass
(C) gains one atomic number unit
(D) gains one neutron
(E) lost one unit in atomic mass

33. Nuclear particles which are presently thought to hold the nucleus together are
(A) protons
(B) neutrons
(C) electrons
(D) mesons
(E) positrons

34. The half-life of U-238 is approximately
(A) 0.3×10^{-6} second
(B) 2.5 minutes
(C) 5580 years
(D) 4.5×10^{9} years
(E) 4 hours

35. In the equation $E = mc^2$, when m is measured in grams and c is measured in centimeters per second, E is expressed in
(A) volts
(B) BTU's
(C) ergs
(D) degrees, centigrade
(E) dynes

36. The initial step in the conversion of uranium to plutonium involves the process of
(A) neutron capture
(B) proton bombardment
(C) fission
(D) alpha emission
(E) beta emission

37. Of the following particles, the one whose discovery was announced most recently is the
(A) meson
(B) neutron
(C) anti-proton
(D) positron
(E) muon

38. For hydrogen gas, the ratio $\frac{C_p}{C_v}$ is approximately
(A) 1.25
(B) 1.00
(C) 2
(D) 1.67
(E) 1.41

39. The maximum number of p electrons in any shell is
(A) 2
(B) 6
(C) 14
(D) 8
(E) 10

40. The nickel ion is usually identified by
(A) cupferron
(B) dimethylglyoxime
(C) p—nitrobenzene azo resorcinol
(D) diphenyl benzidine
(E) thiourea

41. When an electron moves from the K level to the L level, there is an accompanying
(A) absorption of energy
(B) emission of a beta particle
(C) emission of x-rays
(D) emission of gamma rays
(E) absorption of a proton

42. The atom with the electronic structure:
2 - 1s, 2 - 2s, 6 - 2p, 2 - 3s, 1 - 3p is
(A) Mg
(B) Na
(C) Cr
(D) He
(E) Al

43. In a solution containing 1 mole of alcohol and 4 moles of water, the mole fraction of alcohol is
(A) 1/5
(B) 1/4
(C) 4/5
(D) 3/4
(E) 0.1

44. Of the following, four of the groups are meta directing when present on a benzene ring. The one which is not meta directing is
(A) – COOH
(B) – NO_2
(C) – CHO
(D) – NH_2
(E) – $COOCH_3$

45. An example of a ketohexose is
(A) fructose
(B) mannose
(C) galactose
(D) glucose
(E) ribose

46. Ozonolysis of fatty acids is a technique used for determining
(A) number of OH groups
(B) average molecular weights
(C) number of COOH groups
(D) ability to form soaps
(E) position of double bonds

47. Gabriel's synthesis is used for the preparation of
(A) primary amines
(B) aldehydes
(C) tertiary amines
(D) phthalimides
(E) secondary amines

48. When butene–1 is mixed with excess bromine the reaction product to be expected is
(A) hydrobromic acid
(B) butylene gas
(C) 1, 2–dibromo butane
(D) perbromo butane
(E) 1–bromo butane

49. The compound n-butyl magnesium iodide when reacted with water will produce
(A) magnesium iodide
(B) n-butyl alcohol
(C) n-butyl ether
(D) n-butane
(E) n-butene

50 The Geneva name for the alkane represented by the following structure
$CH_3 \cdot CH_2 \cdot C\ (CH_3)_2 \cdot CH\ (CH_3)_2$ would be
(A) 2, 3, 3 – trimethy – 1 pentane
(B) 1, 1 dimethyl – 2, 2 dimethyl – butane
(C) tetramethyl butane
(D) 3, 3 dimethyl – isohexane
(E) 1 — methyl 2, 2 — dimethyl hexane

Questions 51—52

51. Using arbitrary energy units, we can calculate that 864 arbitrary units (a.u.) are required to transfer an electron in a hydrogen atom from the most stable Bohr orbit to a large distance from the nucleus. (See diagram)

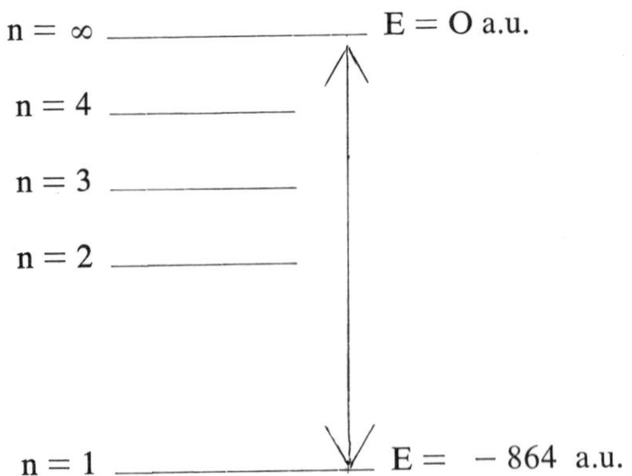

Energy required to excite an electron from the 3rd Bohr orbit to the n = ∞ orbit.
(A) 96 a.u.
(B) 192 a.u.
(C) 288 a.u.
(D) 384 a.u.
(E) 432 a.u.

52. From the above charts we know the energy of the light emitted (in same arbitrary units) when an electron falls from 4th orbit to the second orbit is
(A) 96 a.u.
(B) 54 a.u.
(C) 81 a.u.
(D) 324 a.u.
(E) 162 a.u.

53. If a normal hydrogen molecule is 2.2 Å in diameter when both electrons are in the most stable Bohr orbit, the size of a hypothetical molecule in which the electrons were each in the third Bohr orbit is

H H
←2.2→

(A) 4.4Å
(B) 6.6Å
(C) 8.8Å
(D) 19.8Å
(E) 13.2Å

54. Electronic configurations for the atoms of the five elements are indicated in the table below. Which of the configurations in one of its states of oxidation would be colorless in an aqueous solution?

(A)	2	8	18	1
(B)	2	8	14	2
(C)	2	8	16	2
(D)	2	8	18	2
(E)	2	8	13	1

55. From quantum mechanical treatment, the degree of degeneracy for a rigid rotator in an energy level with quantum number J = 5 is
(A) 5
(B) 1
(C) 11
(D) 12
(E) 10

56. Hydrogen bonding is shown most strongly in which one of the following?
(A) NH_3
(B) H_2O
(C) H_2S
(D) HCl
(E) HF

57. From Boltzmann distribution law, the velocity of an atom in the room temperature 25°C is most probably in the order of
(A) 10 meter/sec
(B) 1 meter/sec
(C) 10 cm/sec
(D) 1000 meter/sec
(E) 0.1 cm/sec

58. The Planck constant h is a fundamental constant of nature. Its value is
(A) 6.02 x 10^{23} ergs
(B) 6.625 x 10^{-30} erg-sec
(C) 1.38 x 10^{-16} erg-sec
(D) 6.02 x 10^{-24} ergs
(E) 6.26 x 10^{-27} erg-sec

59. The infrared spectra of molecules give us some information about molecular structures. The origin of the spectra is due to
(A) electronic excitation
(B) nuclear excitation
(C) electron spin excitation
(D) vibrational modes
(E) rotational modes

60. The wavelength of the infrared spectra is usually in the range of
(A) 1Å—100Å
(B) 1000Å—2000Å
(C) 3000Å—6000Å
(D) 1cm—3 meter
(E) 10^{-4}cm – 10^{-3}cm

61. The fundamental sub-atomic particle called the neutron was discovered by
(A) E. Rutherford
(B) H. J. Moseley
(C) H. Yukawa
(D) J. Chadwick
(E) M. Planck

62. To a large extent, radium has been replaced in radiotherapy by an isotope of
(A) iron
(B) uranium
(C) plutonium
(D) palladium
(E) cobalt

63. Radiocarbon dating makes use of the isotope of carbon with atomic weight:
(A) 13
(B) 12
(C) 14
(D) 15
(E) 11

64. In the nuclear equation:

$$_{15}P^{30} \rightarrow ? + {}_{14}Si^{30}$$

the missing term is:
(A) a neutron
(B) an electron
(C) a positron
(D) gamma rays
(E) a proton

65. Thermal neutrons have energies in the range of
(A) one electron volt
(B) hundreds of electrons volts
(C) millions of electron volts
(D) thousands of electron volts
(E) .1 electron volt

66. A certain atom has the symbol $_{67}X^{139}$. This symbol tells us that
(A) there are 206 protons in the nucleus
(B) it has 139 electrons
(C) it has 139 protons
(D) its atomic weight is 67
(E) there are 72 neutrons in the nucleus

67. A radioactive atom having atomic No. 82 and atomic mass 214 loses a beta particle. The element which is the product of this nuclear change has

	ATOMIC NO.	ATOMIC MASS
(A)	80	212
(B)	81	213
(C)	82	213
(D)	83	214
(E)	84	214

68. $CH_3CO\text{-}OC_2H_5$ is an example of which one of the following?
(A) alcohol
(B) soap
(C) acid
(D) ester
(E) ketone

69. The Kolbe-Schmitt reaction is used commercially to produce
(A) perfumes
(B) phenol
(C) salicylic acid
(D) alcohol
(E) aldehydes

70. The iodine number of an oil is the number of
(A) grams of iodine reacting per mole of oil
(B) moles of iodine reacting per mole of oil
(C) millimoles of iodine reacting per millimole of oil
(D) millimoles of iodine reacting per mole of oil
(E) percent by weight of iodine absorbed

71. Which one of the following substances is produced when ethyl alcohol in dilute solution is oxidized by action of "mother of vinegar" bacteria?
(A) glucose
(B) carbon monoxide
(C) acetaldehyde
(D) acetic acid
(E) acetone

72. Of the following, the formula which represents an unsaturated organic compound is
(A) C_6H_{14}
(B) C_4H_8
(C) C_3H_7OH
(D) $C_2H_4Cl_2$
(E) CH_3OH

73. Because of dangers inherent in the process, special precautions should be taken in diluting concentrated
(A) HNO_3
(B) HCl
(C) H_2SO_4
(D) H_2CO_4
(E) NaOH

74. As the atomic number of the halogens increases, the halogens
(A) lose their outermost electrons less easily
(B) become less dense
(C) become lighter in color
(D) gain electrons less easily
(E) are more active

75. Hydrogen that is used commercially is frequently obtained from which one of the following?
(A) marsh gas
(B) coal gas
(C) producer gas
(D) water gas
(E) electrolysis

76. In general, a plastic shows greater strength and rigidity as the polymer molecules show more
(A) polymorphous nature
(B) amorphous nature
(C) random arrangement
(D) atactic nature
(E) crystallinity

77. When a 0.1N solution of an acid of 25°C has a degree of ionization of 1%, the concentration of hydroxyl ions present is
(A) 10^{-3}
(B) 10^{-11}
(C) 10^{-12}
(D) 10^{-13}
(E) 10^{-5}

78. A saturated solution of Ag_2SO_4 is $2.5 x 10^{-2}$ M. The value of its solubility product is
(A) $6.25 x 10^{-7}$
(B) $1.6 x 10^{-5}$
(C) $6.25 x 10^{-5}$
(D) $1.25 x 10^{-3}$
(E) $1.25 x 10^{-4}$

79. When the specific heat of a metallic element is 0.214 calories/gram, the atomic weight will be closest to which one of the following?
(A) 6.6
(B) 12
(C) 30
(D) 45
(E) 66

80. The most probable valence number for the atom with the total electron configuration, $1s^2 2s^2 2p^6 3s^2 3p^6 3d^{10} 4s^2 4p^5$, is
(A) -1
(B) -3
(C) $+1$
(D) $+3$
(E) $+5$

81. A solution of 4.5g of a pure nonelectrolyte in 100.0g of water was found to freeze at -0.465°C. The molecular weight of the solute is closest to which one of the following?
(A) 135
(B) 172.4
(C) 90
(D) 86.2
(E) 180

82. Eight liters of 0.86 N HBr solution contain
(A) 6800 millimoles of HBr
(B) 0.688 moles of HBr
(C) 3.44 moles of HBr
(D) 8000 millimoles of HBr
(E) 6.88 moles of HBr

83. When a gas expands adiabatically,
(A) the temperature remains constant
(B) energy is liberated
(C) the pressure increases
(D) the environment remains unchanged
(E) the temperature decreased

84. The Fahrenheit and Centigrade scales of temperature have the same numerical reading at a temperature of
(A) $-40°$
(B) 0°
(C) 32°
(D) 212°
(E) $-10°$

85. Of the following, the element which in solution will form a white precipitate with chloride ion which will turn black on the addition of aqueous ammonia is
(A) lead
(B) silver
(C) tin
(D) sodium
(E) mercury

86. When 27 grams of Al are added to one liter of 3N $CuSO_4$, the number of grams of Cu that will be displaced is (atomic weights: Cu = 64; Al = 27).
(A) 32
(B) 64
(C) 192
(D) 128
(E) 96

87. An application of Stokes' law is in the determination of
(A Avogadro's number
(B) activity coefficients
(C) rate of K-electron capture
(D) transference numbers
(E) molecular structures

88. Entropy may be expressed as
(A) joules
(B) calories
(C) dynes/cm^2
(D) calories/degree
(E) calories/degree-mole

89. The Clausius-Clapeyron equation may be used to calculate
(A) the angle between two crystal faces
(B) the heat of vaporization of a liquid
(C) the half-life of a radioisotope
(D) the solubility product of a slightly soluble salt
(E) the angle of diffraction

90. The unit "poise" is used as a measure of
(A) surface tension
(B) adiabatic expansion
(C) osmotic pressure
(D) force of electrical attraction
(E) viscosity

Questions 91—94

The velocities of the molecules depend upon the temperature of the gas. The average velocity is proportional to the square root of the temperature measured from absolute zero (-273°C.). At the absolute zero of temperature, the molecules have no velocity. They are all brought to rest.

Physicists have been able to reach temperatures within a fraction of a degree of the absolute zero, but the zero itself has never been reached. The average velocity at the temperature of boiling water (100°C.) is, for instance, 17 per cent greater than the average velocity at the freezing point of water (0°C.). By means of this relationship, the average velocity at any temperature can readily be found if its value at some given temperature is known.

In a mixture of gases, the molecules of different kinds move at different speeds. The lighter the molecules, the faster they move on the average. There is a simple law, known as the law of equipartition of energy, which governs the distribution of velocities amongst the different kinds of molecules. The law of equipartition of energy states that in a mixture of gases the average energy of each kind of molecule is the same.

Since the energy of a molecule is proportional to its molecular weight multiplied by the square of its velocity, it follows that the average speed of each kind of molecule is inversely proportional to the square root of its molecular weight. In a mixture of oxygen and hydrogen, for instance, the average speed of the molecules of oxygen will only be one-quarter of that of the molecules of hydrogen, because oxygen is sixteen times as heavy as hydrogen.

91. In a mixture of a light gas and a heavy gas in a closed container, the light gas will
(A) have a higher absolute temperature than the heavier gas
(B) have a higher average velocity per molecule than the heavier gas
(C) have a lower average energy per molecule than the heavier gas
(D) rise to the top of the container
(E) have a lower absolute temperature than the heavier gas

92. The average velocity of water molecules
(A) can be found by solving
$$\frac{\sqrt{273}}{\sqrt{373}} = \frac{x}{1.17x}$$
(B) can be found by solving
0 : x : : 100 : 117x
(C) can be found by solving
273 : 373 : : x : (.17)x
(D) cannot be found from the information given
(E) can be found by solving
0 : x = 100z − 273

93. According to the paragraphs, for a single gas which equation is incorrect? m.w. = molecular weight, v = average velocity, t = absolute temperature, and e = energy per molecule.
(A) $\text{m.w.} = \frac{Ke}{v^2}$
(B) $t = Kv^2$
(C) $v = Kt^2$
(D) $v = K\sqrt{\frac{e}{\text{m.w.}}}$
(E) PV = RT

94. The average velocity of carbon dioxide molecules at 0°C. is 0.25 mi./sec. What is the average velocity at 127°C.?
(A) 0.015 mi./sec
(B) 0.30 mi./sec
(C) 0.32 mi./sec
(D) 31.75 mi./sec
(E) 317.5 mi./sec

95. The possible results for the measurement of the z component of the orbital angular momentum for a hydrogen atom in a 3d state are
(A) 1
(B) 2
(C) 3
(D) 4
(E) 5

96. The radius of the first orbital for a hydrogen atom is
(A) $0.53\text{x}10^{-8}$cm
(B) $0.53\text{x}10^{-9}$cm
(C) $0.53\text{x}10^{-10}$cm
(D) 0.53 cm
(E) 0.53 meter

97. From classical statistical thermodynamics, each degree of freedom of a molecule has (at temperature T) energy of
(A) kT
(B) 3/2 kT
(C) 1/2 kT
(D) RT
(E) 5/2 kT

98. If we assume that the ideal gas law is valid for both gases, the entropy change during the mixing of 0.8 moles of nitrogen with 0.2 moles of oxygen is
(A) zero
(B) 0.1 cal/deg
(C) 0.2 cal/deg
(D) 1.0 cal/deg
(E) 10 cal/deg

Questions 99 and 100 make use of the following information:

R = 1.987cal/mole-deg
dF = VdP-SdT
dA = − PdV-SdT

99. What is the change in Gibb's free energy during isothermal expansion of 1 mole of ideal gas from a pressure of 10 atm to a presure of 1 atm at a temperature of 25°C?
(A) 10 cal
(B) − 2980 cal
(C) 298 cal
(D) − 1365 cal
(E) 250 cal

100. To what extent does the work function change during the above conditions?
(A) zero
(B) − 250 cal
(C) − 1365 cal
(D) − 2980 cal
(E) − 10 cal

101. LeChatelier's Principle applies
(A) only to reactions among gases
(B) to all chemical reactions
(C) only to chemical reactions at equilibrium
(D) to all systems at equilibrium
(E) to all physical equilibrium only

102. A compound whose dipole moment equals zero is
(A) H_2O
(B) HCl
(C) NH_3
(D) HF
(E) C_6H_6

103. The molar gas constant, R, equals
(A) 22.41 liters
(B) 0.0821 liter-atm./degree
(C) 8.3142 calories/degree
(D) 1.987 joules/degree
(E) 1.987 erg/degree

104. To a solution of 0.06 M acetic acid enough sodium acetate is added to make the solution 0.2 M with respect to the sodium acetate. The ionization constant of acetic acid is $1.8 x 10^{-5}$. The hydrogen ion concentration will be approximately
(A) $10.8 x 10^{-7}$
(B) $5 x 10^{-8}$
(C) $3.6 x 10^{-6}$
(D) $5 x 10^{-6}$
(E) $3 x 10^{-4}$

105. The number of ml of a stock solution of 2M sodium hydroxide which is needed to make 80 ml of a 0.1M sodium hydroxide solution is
(A) 0.2
(B) 40
(C) 20
(D) 8
(E) 4

106. The standard electromotive force, in volts, produced by the cell

$$Zn; Zn^{++} // Ag^{+}; Ag$$

where E° for Zn^{++} = — 0.761 volts and E° for Ag^{+} = 0.799 volts, is
(A) 1.180
(B) 0.038
(C) 0.076
(D) 2.359
(E) 1.560

107. The number of coulombs required for the liberation of 128 grams of copper (atomic weight = 64) by the electrolysis of a solution of copper sulfate is
(A) 96,500
(B) 48,250
(C) 193,000
(D) 386,000
(E) 24,125

108. The number of degrees of freedom at the eutectic point of a mixture of two metals is
(A) four
(B) one
(C) three
(D) two
(E) zero

109. A molal solution is one that contains one mole of solute per
(A) liter of solvent
(B) liter of solution
(C) 1000 g of solvent
(D) 1000 g of solution
(E) 22.4 liters of solution

110. By applying the Dulong and Petit Law, we find that the approximate specific heat of lead (atomic weight = 207) is
(A) 0.031
(B) 0.094
(C) 0.214
(D) 0.168
(E) 0.060

111. In chemical kinetics a zero order reaction is recognized as being one in which the rate of decrease in concentration of reactants (is)
(A) varies inversely with initial concentration
(B) varies as the square root of initial concentration
(C) varies as the square of initial concentration
(D) varies linearly with initial concentration
(E) unaffected by the initial concentration

112. The Debye and Huckel theory differs from that of Arrhenius in that the first theory
(A) holds that ions are not strictly independent units
(B) applies only to ions of non-transition elements
(C) applies only to saturated solutions
(D) applies only to ions of transition elements
(E) applies only to aqueous solutions

113. Lead is dissolved most readily in dilute
(A) acetic acid
(B) sulfuric acid
(C) phosphoric acid
(D) hydrochloric acid
(E) sodium hydroxide

114. The specific resistance of a 0.1N NaCl solution was found to be 93.6 ohms at 25°C. Its specific conductance will be
(A) 6.4 reciprocal ohms
(B) 0.936 ohms
(C) 9.36 reciprocal ohms
(D) 93.6 ohms
(E) 0.011 reciprocal ohms

115. The per cent of gold in 14-carat gold is approximately
(A) 40
(B) 78
(C) 70
(D) 83
(E) 58

116. The kinetic theory of gases predicts that the viscosity of gases will
(A) vary with the square root of the density
(B) decrease with decreased density
(C) increase with decreased density
(D) vary with the square of the density
(E) be independent of density

117. A liter of carbon dioxide gas is compared to a liter of hydrogen gas, both gases at 50 deg. Centigrade and 5 atmospheres. Of the following statements, the correct one is:
(A) CO_2 molecules are on the average moving slower than H_2 molecules.
(B) There are more molecules of H_2 than CO_2 present.
(C) The average kinetic energy of the CO_2 molecules is greater than that of the H_2 molecules.
(D) CO_2 molecules are, on the average, moving faster than the H_2 molecules.
(E) There are more molecules of CO_2 than H_2 present.

118. A quantity of a gas has a volume of 100 ml when the barometric pressure is 740 mm and the temperature is 27°C. The volume of the gas under standard conditions of temperature and pressure, in ml, is approximately
(A) 90
(B) 126
(C) 110
(D) 105
(E) 60

119. 2.00 grams of a univalent metal dissolved in an acid produced 0.11 gram of hydrogen. The conclusion that may be correctly drawn is that the
(A) equivalent weight of the metal is 11 g
(B) equivalent weight of the metal is 18.2 g
(C) equivalent weight of the metal is 36.4 g
(D) atomic weight of the metal is 18.2 mass units
(E) equivalent weight of the metal is 30.49

120. A series of salt solutions was added to equal portions of a negatively charged colloid. Assuming the salt solutions to be of equal concentration, the least volume of solution required for coagulation would be that of
(A) $AlCl_3$
(B) $BaCl_2$
(C) KCl
(D) NH_4Cl
(E) $MgCl_2$

121. One liter of a certain gas, under standard conditions, weighs 1.16 grams. A possible form for the gas is
(A) C_2H_2
(B) CO
(C) O_2
(D) NH_3
(E) CH_4

122. An isomer of ethanol is
(A) methanol
(B) dimethyl ether
(C) diethyl ether
(D) ethylene glycol
(E) acetone

123. In cis-trans isomerism, the compound generally
(A) rotates the plane of polarized light
(B) exhibits enantiomorphism
(C) possesses an asymmetric carbon atom
(D) contains a triple bond
(E) contains a double bond

124. The degree of unsaturation in an organic compound may be found by shaking a specified weight of the substance with a standard solution of which one of the following?
(A) sulfuric acid
(B) potassium hydroxide
(C) acetone
(D) iodine
(E) chloroform

125. The Hinsberg test, one of the most important reagents in organic chemistry, is used to test
(A) alcohols
(B) ketone
(C) alkynes
(D) alkenes
(E) amines

126. A mixture of one mole of carbon dioxide and one mole of hydrogen attains equilibrium at a temperature of 25°C and a total pressure of 0.1 atm. The following reaction takes place:

$$CO_2 + H_2 \leftrightarrows CO + H_2O$$

Analysis of the final reaction mixture shows 0.16 vol. percent of carbon monoxide. The equilibrium constant is about
(A) $1.00x10^{-3}$
(B) 1.00
(C) $1.00x10^{-7}$
(D) 100
(E) $1.00x10^{-5}$

127. If the above reaction would have taken place at 10 atm, the equilibrium constant would
(A) change to a smaller value
(B) change to a larger value
(C) remain constant
(D) change with the total pressure
(E) change indeterminably

128. Liquid butyl methacrylate has a density of 0.88 g/cm³ at 30°C. The change in work function (or Gibbs free energy) during the isothermal compression of 1 mole of this substance from 1 atm to 20 atm is about the order of
(A) 10 cal
(B) 1 cal
(C) 1000 cal
(D) 75 cal
(E) 0.1 cal

129. The heat of fusion of ice is 79 cal/g. The entropy change of the transformation of 1 g of water at 0°C into ice at the same temperature is
(A) zero
(B) − 79 cal/g
(C) − 0.29 cal/g-deg
(D) + 79 cal/g
(E) + 273 cal/g-deg

130. From the above transformation, water into ice, the Gibb's free energy change is
(A) zero
(B) − 79 cal/g
(C) − 0.29 cal/g
(D) + 79 cal
(E) + 273 cal

131. The numerical value of the equilibrium constant for any chemical change is affected by changing the
(A) concentration of the products
(B) catalyst
(C) concentration of reacting substances
(D) volume
(E) temperature

132. At 10°C, the reaction between CO and Cl_2 occurs at a rate which converts 5 g. of CO per hour. If the temperature is raised to 30°C, the approximate number of grams of CO converted per hour should be
(A) 10
(B) 5
(C) 15
(D) 20
(E) 30

133. One mole of a compound AB reacts with one mole of compound CD according to the equation

$$AB + CD \rightarrow AD + CB$$

When equilibrium had been established it was found that ¾ mole of each of reactants AB and CD had been converted to AD and CB. There is no change in volume. The equilibrium constant for the reaction is
(A) 9/16
(B) 1/9
(C) 16/9
(D) 9
(E) 16

134. Bromine can be extracted from 75 ml. of a water solution most efficiently by
(A) three 25 ml. portions of $CHCl_3$
(B) one 75 ml. portion of $CHCl_3$
(C) fifteen 5 ml. portions of $CHCl_3$
(D) five 15 ml. portions of $CHCl_3$
(E) twenty-five 3 ml. portions of $CHCl_3$

135. Given a solution of silver chromate. A student adds one mole of sulfide ion. The temperature is raised and more chromate is added simultaneously. What can we say about the precipitate that results?

(A) It is dependent upon temperature only.
(B) It is dependent upon concentration of chromate only.
(C) It is dependent upon both temperature and concentration of chromate.
(D) It will depend upon neither temperature nor concentration of chromate.
(E) There will be no precipitate.

136. In a solution there is dissolved equimolar amounts of silver bromide, $K_{sp} = 10^{-13}$, and silver chloride, $K_{sp} = 10^{-10}$. Also in the solution is a silver colloid. We can say that

(A) Br^- will be adsorbed preferentially
(B) Cl^- will be adsorbed preferentially
(C) both will be adsorbed in equal amounts
(D) much more bromine will be adsorbed than chlorine
(E) neither ion will be adsorbed preferentially

137. With regard to the phenomenon of isomorphous replacement of barium sulfate by potassium, we can say that it is most dependent upon

(A) temperature
(B) pH
(C) volume
(D) pressure
(E) none of the above

138. An agent that is ideal for homogeneous precipitation is

(A) H_2SO_4
(B) H_2CO_3
(C) Ag_2S
(D) $(NH_2)_2CO$
(E) none of the above

139. An impure oxalic acid sample weighing 0.7500 g is titrated with 21.37 ml of 0.5066 N base solution. What is the percentage oxalic acid, $H_2C_2O_4 \cdot 2HOH$ (MW 126), in the sample?

(A) 95
(B) 11
(C) 63
(D) 84
(E) none of the above

140. Which reagent will transform acetic acid to a strong electrolyte?

(A) HOH
(B) H_2SO_4
(C) $NaC_2H_3O_2 \rightarrow (NaC_2H_3O_2)$
(D) $C_4H_9NH_2$
(E) There is no such reagent.

141. The turbidimetric method of analysis depends upon

(A) the pH of the unknown's parent solution
(B) the scattering of light properties of the unknown
(C) the color of the precipitate of the unknown
(D) the absorption of the unknown in the far microwave region
(E) none of the above

142. Which reagent plays the same role in the thio acid system that water plays in the oxygen acids?

(A) H_2SO_4
(B) HOH
(C) H_2S
(D) HSCN
(E) none of the above

Questions 143-144 are based on the following reaction scheme.

$$CH_3\text{-}CO\text{-}NH_2 \xrightarrow{NaOH + Br_2}$$

$$CH_3\text{-}CO\text{-}NHBr \xrightarrow[-H_2O]{NaOH}$$

$$[CH_3\text{-}CO\text{-}NBr]^-Na^+ \xrightarrow{-NaBr} [CH_3\text{-}CO\text{-}\ddot{N}:] \; (1)$$

$$\rightarrow CH_3\text{-}N{=}C{=}O \; (2) \xrightarrow{2NaOH} CH_3\text{-}NH_2$$

143. Compound (2) is known as a(n)

(A) nitroketene
(B) cyanate
(C) isocyanate
(D) oxymine
(E) imone

144. In addition to methylamine, the final hydrolysis yields

(A) Na_2O
(B) Na_2CO_3
(C) CO_2
(D) $NaNH_2$
(E) HCO_2Na

145. The correct structure of diketene is

(A) 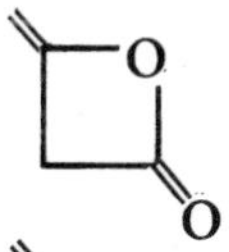
(B) 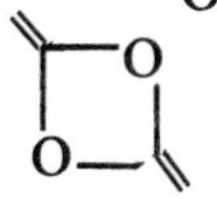
(C) 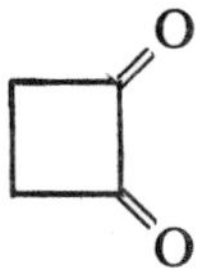
(D) 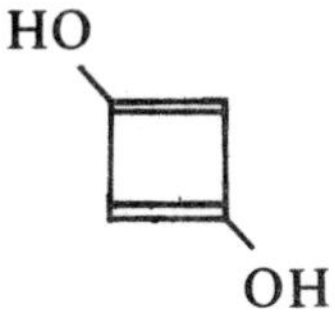 HO OH
(E) CH_3-CO-CH=C=O

146. The Hell-Volhard-Zelinsky Reaction is used to

(A) synthesize primary amines
(B) distinguish secondary from tertiary alcohols
(C) synthesize α-bromoacids
(D) determine the proportion of nitrogen in a compound
(E) protect the N-terminal group of a peptide

147. Which of the following would react with one mole of a Grignard reagent to yield a ketone?

(A) R-CO-NR′R″
(B) R-CO-NHR′
(C) R-CO-NH_2
(D) R-CO-OH
(E) R-O-R′

(*Questions* 148 *and* 149)

A mixture of benzene; 2, 4-hexadiene; hexane; 1-hexanol; and butyl acetate is adsorbed on a column of neutral alumina, and eluted with solvents of increasing polarity.

148. The compound that would be eluted first is

(A) benzene
(B) 2, 4-hexadiene
(C) hexane
(D) 1-hexanol
(E) butyl acetate

149. The last compound out of the column would be

(A) benzene
(B) 2, 4-hexadiene
(C) hexane
(D) 1-hexanol
(E) butyl acetate

150. How many canonical forms without charge separation are there for

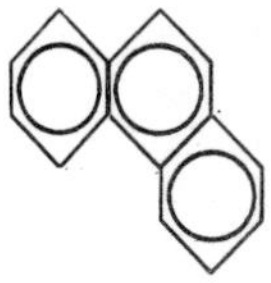

(A) 2
(B) 3
(C) 4
(D) 5
(E) 6

END OF ADVANCED TEST (4) IN CHEMISTRY

ANSWER KEY TO ADVANCED TEST 4 IN CHEMISTRY

In order to help pinpoint your weaknesses, the specific area of each question is indicated in parentheses after the answer. Refer to textbooks and other study material wherever you have an incorrect answer.

Area Code

ORGANIC CHEMISTRY = O
INORGANIC CHEMISTRY = I
ANALYTICAL CHEMISTRY = A
PHYSICAL CHEMISTRY = P

1. E(I)
2. D(I)
3. D(I)
4. D(I)
5. C(I)
6. E(I)
7. C(I)
8. A(I)
9. C(I)
10. A(P)
11. E(P)
12. A(I)
13. D(O)
14. E(I)
15. A(P)
16. E(I)
17. E(A)
18. D(P)
19. A(I)
20. D(I)
21. B(I)
22. B(I)
23. E(A)
24. D(I)
25. A(I)
26. D(P)
27. E(I)
28. C(P)
29. E(P)
30. B(P)
31. D(P)
32. C(P)
33. D(P)
34. D(P)
35. C(P)
36. A(P)
37. C(P)
38. E(P)
39. B(I)
40. B(I)
41. A(P)
42. E(I)
43. A(P)
44. D(O)
45. A(O)
46. E(O)
47. A(O)
48. C(O)
49. D(O)
50. A(O)
51. A(P)
52. E(P)
53. D(P)
54. D(I)
55. C(P)
56. B(I)
57. D(P)
58. E(P)
59. D(P)
60. E(P)
61. D(P)
62. E(P)
63. C(P)
64. C(P)
65. E(P)
66. E(I)
67. D(P)
68. D(O)
69. C(O)
70. E(O)
71. D(O)
72. B(O)
73. C(I)
74. D(I)
75. D(I)
76. E(P)
77. B(I)
78. C(I)
79. C(I)
80. A(I)
81. E(I)
82. E(I)
83. E(P)
84. A(I)
85. E(I)
86. E(I)
87. E(P)
88. D(P)
89. B(P)
90. E(P)
91. B(P)
92. D(P)
93. C(P)
94. B(P)
95. E(P)
96. A(P)
97. C(P)
98. D(P)
99. D(P)
100. C(P)
101. B(P)
102. E(P)
103. B(P)
104. D(I)
105. E(I)
106. E(I)
107. D(I)
108. E(P)
109. C(I)
110. A(I)
111. E(P)
112. A(P)
113. A(I)
114. E(P)
115. E(I)
116. E(P)
117. A(P)
118. A(I)
119. B(I)
120. A(P)
121. A(I)
122. B(O)
123. E(O)
124. D(O)
125. E(O)
126. E(P)
127. C(P)
128. D(P)
129. C(P)
130. A(P)
131. E(P)
132. D(P)
133. D(I)
134. E(P)
135. C(A)
136. E(A)
137. B(A)
138. D(A)
139. E(A)
140. D(A)
141. B(A)
142. C(A)
143. C(O)
144. B(O)
145. A(O)
146. C(O)
147. A(O)
148. C(O)
149. D(O)
150. D(O)

Explanatory Answers for Advanced Test 4

1. **(E)** Because chlorine is more electronegative than iodine, it is able to oxidize iodide ions to iodine, according to the equation:
$$2I^- + Cl_2 \rightarrow I_2 + 2Cl^-$$
The iodine produced from the reaction gives a violet solution.

2. **(D)** $2H_2 + O_2 \rightarrow 2H_2O$
Two volumes of hydrogen react with one volume of oxygen. Therefore, 26 ml of H_2 react with 13 ml of O_2, leaving behind (24 − 13) ml = 11 ml of oxygen.

3. **(D)** A double bond between sulfur and oxygen confers a formal valence of +2 on the sulfur, whereas a single bond between sulfur and the hydroxyl radical confers a formal valence of +1 on sulfur. Since sulfuric acid has the structure HO-S(=O)(=O)-OH, the formal valence of sulfur is +6.

4. **(D)** The following is a listing of the gases in the order of increasing boiling points: Helium [−268.6°C], Hydrogen [−252.5°C], Nitrogen [−195.8°C], Argon [−185.7°C] and Oxygen [−183°C]. Thus in the fractional distillation of liquid air, oxygen would boil off last in the list.

5. **(C)** Because they possess unfilled inner electronic orbitals, transition elements form coordination complexes. Such popular examples $Ni(CO)_4$ and nickelocene should help to decide between nickel and astatine. The latter is the largest known member of the halogen family. Aluminum is a Group III element, rubidium belongs in the same family as sodium and potassium, and selenium is in the family of oxygen and sulfur.

6. **(E)** An acid turns blue litmus red. The oxide should, therefore, give an acidic solution in water. BaO, Na_2O and CaO are basic, Al_2O_3 is amphoteric, and P_2O_5 dissolves in water to yield phosphoric acid.

7. **(C)** In acid-base neutralizations, the product of the normality and volume of the acid is equivalent to the analogous product for the base; i.e., $V_AN_A = V_BN_B$.

Therefore, $25N_A = 50 \times 0.2N$

and $$N_A = \frac{50 \times 0.2}{25} = 0.4N$$

8. **(A)** Unlike the situation with most other liquids, the volume of water does not decrease monotonically with a decrease in temperature. The volume of a given mass of water, when cooled, decreases to a minimum at 4°C and begins to increase with further cooling. Since density is mass per unit volume, the point of minimum volume would be associated with maximum density.

9. **(C)** The inert gases, including xenon, are characterized by their closed electronic configurations. Only A, C and E meet this requirement. In the order of increasing atomic number, the inert gases are Helium, Neon, Argon, Krypton, Xenon and Radon. E is the configuration for Neon, A is that of Argon, and C is that of Xenon.

10. **(A)** For a first order radioactive decay, the mass after each half-life period is half what it was at the beginning of the period. Starting with 8g, we will have 4g after 10 days, 2g after 20 days, 1g after 30 days, and 0.5g after 40 days.

11. **(E)** Avogadro's hypothesis states that, under the same conditions of temperature and pressure, equal volumes of different gases contain the same number of molecules. Stated differently, equal moles of different gases under the same temperature and pressure occupy the same volume.

12. **(A)** From Faraday's laws, it is known that 96,500 coulombs cause the chemical alteration of one gram equivalent of matter at each electrode. For Ni in NiI_2, the reaction is

$$\frac{1}{2}Ni^{++} + e^{-} \rightarrow \frac{1}{2}Ni$$

Thus the gram equivalent weight of Nickel is one half its gram atomic weight.
Therefore, 96,500 coulombs will deposit $\frac{1}{2}(58.7)g = 29.4g$
Therefore, 24,125 coulombs will deposit $29.4 \div 4 \approx 7.3g$

13. **(D)** "Teflon" is a polymer of tetrafluoroethylene. The inertness of the paraffins is usually explained in terms of the strength of the C-H bond (98.7k cal/mole). The C-F bond is even stronger (116k cal/mole) and this explains many of the unique properties of teflon.

14. **(E)** Water is H_2O. There are 6 different combinations of hydrogens from a mixture of $_1H^1$, $_1H^2$, $_1H^3$ [$_1H^1{}_1H^1$, $_1H^2{}_1H^2$, $_1H^3{}_1H^3$, $_1H^1{}_1H^2$, $_1H^1{}_1H^3$, $_1H^2{}_1H^3$ – the ordering is immaterial]. Each of these combinations can combine with any of the three oxygen isotopes giving a total of 18 different types of water.

15. **(A)** From Avogadro's hypothesis, equal volumes of different gases contain the same number of molecules. Thus 21% of the molecules in air are oxygen. The partial pressure of any constituent in a gas mixture is the product of the total pressure and the mole fraction of that constituent. Therefore, partial pressure of Oxygen is:

$$\frac{21}{100} \times 740 = 165.4$$

16. **(E)** The HCl molecule is held together by the strong electrostating forces created by the unequal sharing of the electron pair between the two atoms as a result of the difference in their electronegativities. This unequal sharing does not strictly satisfy the requirement of ionic bonding which demands complete charge separation.

17. **(E)** The general rule is that a given number of milliequivalents of acid neutralize an equal number of milliequivalents of base. By definition, volume in ml × Normality = milliequivalents.

Therefore, $7 = 40 \times N$
And $N = 7 \div 40 = 0.175$

18. **(D)** Since oxygen and carbon differ in electronegativities, any bond between them will have unequal sharing of electrons and would consequently be polar. The only way for the molecule to show no polarity is for the polarity of one C=O to be exactly balanced by the other, and this can happen only if the molecule is linear and symmetrical.

19. **(A)** A mole of any gas at S.T.P. occupies 22400 ml. 22400 ml at S.T.P. is $22400 \times \frac{300}{273}$ at 27°C and 760 mm

Therefore, $\frac{22400 \times 300}{273}$ ml weigh 70g

Therefore, 300 ml weigh $\frac{70 \times 300 \times 273}{22400 \times 300}$

$= 0.853$ g

20. **(D)** Number of C atoms $= \frac{83.6}{12} \approx 7$

Number of H atoms $= \frac{16.4}{1} \approx 16.4$

Therefore, empirical formula = C_7H_{16}

21. **(B)** Gallium is the metal that was anticipated by Mendeleyev as eka-aluminum. Thus, it belongs in Group III of the Periodic Table. Aluminium is the only one in the list that belongs in Group III.

22. **(B)** A balanced equation for the oxidation of the carbohydrate is

$$4KClO_3 + C_{12}H_{22}O_{11} \rightarrow KCl + 12CO_2 + 11H_2O$$

From the above, it can be seen that four moles of $KClO_3$ are required per mole of carbohydrate.

23. **(E)** K_{sp}, the solubility product, is the product of the concentrations of the ions in solution. Therefore, $K_{sp}AgCl = [Ag^+][Cl^-]$
If $[Cl^-] = 0.20 = [2.0 \times 10^{-1}]$
Then $[Ag^+] = \frac{K_{sp}}{[Cl^-]} = \frac{1.56 \times 10^{-10}}{2.0 \times 10^{-1}}$

$$= \frac{1.56 \times 10^{-10} \times 10}{2} = 0.78 \times 10^{-9}$$

$$= 7.8 \times 10^{-10}$$

24. **(D)** Ionization constant for HCN is

$$\frac{[H^+][CN^-]}{[HCN]}$$

If a 0.1M solution of HCN is 0.01% ionized, then the concentration of ions is

$$0.1 \times \frac{0.01}{100} = 0.00001$$

$$K_i = \frac{0.00001 \times 0.00001}{0.1}$$

$$= 1 \times 10^{-9}$$

25. **(A)** Sodium acetate is a salt derived from a strong base and a weak acid. In water, hydrolysis of NaOAc gives a basic solution. Thus, the addition of NaOAc to a dilute solution of HOAc is equivalent to adding a base to an acid solution and the pH would rise since the resulting solution would become less acidic.

26. **(D)** The ability of an electrolyte to precipitate a charged colloid depends generally on the valence of the electrolyte ion that bears the charge opposite to that of the colloid. Arsenious sulfide produces a negatively charged colloid. The electrolyte which has the largest cationic charge will be the most efficient precipitant.

27. **(E)** A molal solution contains one mole per 1000g of solvent. If 500g of water contain 22.5g, then 1000g of water contain 55g of glucose. Glucose, $C_6H_{12}O_6$, has a molecular weight of 180.
Therefore, the molality of a solution containing 55g per 1000g of water is $\frac{55}{180} = 0.3$.

28. **(C)** In going from $_{29}Cu^{64}$ to $_{28}Ni^{64}$, the atomic number, or the number of protons in the nucleus, has decreased by 1 whereas the atomic weight, which is the sum of nuclear protons and neutrons, has remained constant. In other words, a proton in the nucleus has been transformed to a neutron. This can be achieved by having the proton give up a positive electron or positron.

29. **(E)** Two elements with an identical number of neutrons are known as isotones. Isobars are two or more atoms with identical atomic weights. For neutral atoms, the number of electrons is equal to the number of protons, which determines the atomic number. Two or more atoms with the same atomic number are known as isotopes.

30. **(B)** In 1815, Prout put forth the suggestion that all atoms were built up from hydrogen. Although his contemporaries scoffed at the idea, later chemists came to conclusions analogous to Prout's. However, atomic masses have been found to deviate from integral multiples of the mass of hydrogen. This deviation is postulated to be the energy involved in binding the hydrogen nuclei together, and is known as the mass defect. The connection between mass defect and binding energy is Einstein's famous equation, $E = mc^2$.

31. **(D)** The rate of radioactive decay is inversely proportional to the half-life. Thus the element with the shortest half-life will produce the greatest amount of radiation, and would be most dangerous to approach immediately.

32. **(C)** The transformation resulting from the emission of an α or β particle from a nucleus is epitomized in the Fajans-Soddy-Russell displacement law. Whenever a parent nucleus emits an α-particle, its atomic number is decreased by *two units* and the new element is shifted two positions *to the left* in the periodic table from that of the parent. On the other hand, emission of a β-particle from a parent nucleus yields a nucleus that is one unit higher in atomic number and shifted, on the periodic table, one place *to the right* of the parent nucleus.

33. **(D)** Mesons, which have masses between those of the proton and the electrons, are currently thought to bind the other nuclear particles together. Their existence was first predicted by Yukawa in 1935.

34. **(D)** U-238 is the most stable isotope of Uranium from which the nuclear fuel U-235 is separated. The former has the relatively long half-life of 4.5×10^9 years.

35. **(C)** Energy is measured in units of work and it has dimensions of ml^2t^{-2}. The dyne is a unit of force, and when a force of 1 dyne moves through 1 cm, 1 erg of work has been done.
In $E = mc^2$
The dimensions of E are $m \times \frac{l}{t} \times \frac{l}{t} = ml^2t^{-2}$

36. **(A)** The following is the process involved in the conversion of U-238 to Plutonium:

$$_{92}U^{238} \text{ neutron} \rightarrow {}_{92}U^{239} + \gamma$$
$$_{92}U^{239} \rightarrow {}_{93}N_p{}^{239} + \text{electron}$$
$$_{94}N_p{}^{239} \rightarrow {}_{94}P_n + \text{electron}$$

37. **(C)** The experimental discovery of the anti-proton was announced by Segre and his colleagues at the University of California in 1955. The neutron and the positron were observed in 1932 by Chadwick and Anderson, respectively.

38. **(E)** From the kinetic theory of gases, it can be shown that $C_p - C_v = R$ (the universal gas constant). Since C_v depends on the number of atoms in the gas molecule it can be seen that the ratio $\frac{C_p}{C_v}$ or γ can be used to determine the number of atoms per molecule of gas. In general, $\gamma = 1.67$ for monoatomic gases; $\gamma = 1.4$ for diatomic gases; and $\gamma = 1.29$ for triatomic gases.

39. **(B)** There can be only three p orbitals in any sub-shell, and each of these, in accordance with the Pauli Principle, can contain only two electrons.

40. **(B)** Among common chemicals, dimethyl glyoxime is the closest approach to a specific precipitant. This reagent would precipitate only palladium from acidic solution. In a neutral or ammoniacal solution containing the proper complexing and masking agents, it is also quite specific for nickel.

41. **(A)** The L level is higher in energy than the K, and energy is, therefore, needed to promote an electron from the lower K level to the higher L level.

42. **(E)** The element has three electrons in the unfilled M shell. It belongs in Group III and is Al.

43. **(A)** The mole fraction of any constituent in a mixture is the number of moles on that constituent divided by the total number of moles in the mixture.
Therefore, mole fraction of alcohol is

$$\frac{1}{1+4} = \frac{1}{5}$$

44. **(D)** By means of resonance, the electron-donating or electron-withdrawing effect of a substituent can be transmitted to the ortho and para positions on a benzene ring. For electrophilic substitutions, the incoming substituent is electron deficient and would be directed to the ortho and para positions by a previous electron-donating substituent, and to the meta position by an electron-withdrawing one. The N of NH_2 has an unshared electron pair which it can share with the aromatic ring. It is the only one is the group that is orth-para directing.

45. **(A)** Ribose is a pentose. Glucose, mannose and galactose are aldohexoses and thus able to reduce Benedict's and Fehling's solutions. Fructose is a ketohexose.

46. **(E)** Ozone is a reagent used to oxidize organic molecules at double bonds. Through the intermediacy of ozonides, the molecule is broken at the double bonds yielding fragments which are either aldehydes or ketones.

$$R_1R_2C{=}CR_3R_4 \xrightarrow{O_3} R_1R_2C(O{-}O)(O)CR_3R_4 \rightarrow R_1R_2C{=}O + O{=}CR_3R_4$$

Thus ozonolysis gives the position of double bonds.

47. **(A)** Gabriel's synthesis is used for the preparation of primary amines by the reaction of a halo compound with potassium phthalimide followed by hydrolysis of the resulting N-substituted phthalimide

$$C_6H_4(CO)_2NK + ClCH_2\text{-}\phi \longrightarrow C_6H_4(CO)_2N\text{-}CH_2\text{-}\phi + KCl$$

$$\xrightarrow[H^+]{2H_2O} C_6H_4(CO_2H)_2 + H_2N\text{-}CH_2\text{-}\phi$$

48. **(C)** Bromine adds to double bonds to give vicinal dibromides. With butene − 1, the expected product is 1, 2-dibromobutane

$$CH_2{=}CH\text{-}CH_2\text{-}CH_3 \xrightarrow{Br_2} CH_2Br\text{-}CHBr\text{-}CH_2\text{-}CH_3$$

49. **(D)** Grignard reagents react with water and acids to yield a hydrocarbon and a magnesium salt.
$CH_3\text{-}CH_2\text{-}CH_2\text{-}CH_2\text{-}Mg\text{-}I + H_2O$
$\rightarrow CH_3\text{-}CH_2\text{-}CH_2\text{-}CH_2\text{-}H + HOMgI$
In this particular case, the hydrocarbon produced would be n-Butane.

50. **(A)** The Geneva or IUPAC system of nomenclature adopts the name of the longest chain of carbon atoms, and assigns substituents along the chain in such a manner that the number of the substituents adds up to a minimum. By this criterion, the given hydrocarbon is seen to be 2, 3, 3-trimethylpentane.

51. **(A)** Bohr's derivation gives the energy of any orbit as $E = \frac{-2\pi^2me^4}{n^2h^2}$ Thus the energy is inversely proportional to $\frac{1}{n^2}$. The energy of the 3rd orbit is $\frac{1}{9}$ that of the first one.

52. **(E)** The energy of the 4th orbit is $\frac{1}{16}$ that of the 1st orbit; whereas that of the 2nd is $\frac{1}{4}$ that of the first. Therefore the energy difference between the 4th and the 2nd orbits is

$$864\left[\frac{1}{4}-\frac{1}{16}\right]=864\left[\frac{3}{16}\right]=162 \text{ a.u.}$$

53. **(D)** The Bohr radius for the hydrogen atom is given by the relationship:

$$r=\frac{n^2h^2}{4\pi^2me^2}$$

Thus r is proportional to n^2. If atomic radius for n = 1 is 1.1, then for n = 3, atomic radius would be 9.9; and the required radius would be 2 × 9.9 = 19.8

54. **(D)** The atoms listed are respectively
A = Copper
B = Iron
C = Nickel
D = Zinc
E = Chromium
Looking at the list, we find that the only one that forms colorless ions is zinc, since it is the only one that is not a transition element.

55. **(C)** From quantum mechanical treatment, there are, for each value of J, [2J + 1] different states having the same energy but differing in the spatial orientation of the axis of rotation. Thus the degree of degeneracy is 2J + 1.

56. **(B)** The strength of hydrogen bonding depends on the atom to which the hydrogen atom is bound. On the one hand, it must be electronegative enough to weaken the primary bond to hydrogen by polarization, and on the other hand it must have electron pairs available to share with a proton-like hydrogen bound primarily to another atom. Oxygen has these two features in such a balance that it forms very strong bonds. That is why water has such a high mp and bp in comparision to analogous substances like H_2S.

57. **(D)** According to the Maxwell-Boltzmann theory of distribution of molecular velocities, the most probable velocity is given by the expression $U_{mp}=\sqrt{\frac{2RT}{M}}$ where M is the molecular weight of the gas, R is the universal gas constant, and T is measured in degrees absolute. Plugging in values for a gas like oxygen gives

$$U_{mp}=\sqrt{\frac{2\times 8.315\times 10^7 \text{ ergs/mole/degree}\times 298 \text{ degree}}{32}}$$

$$\approx 3.2\times 10^4 \text{ cm/sec.}$$

58. **(E)** A common equation which might help here is the famous $E = h\nu$. Since ergs are units of energy and the dimension of frequency is sec^{-1}, h has to be measured in erg-sec., thus limiting and simplifying the choice to 3 alternatives. Planck's constant is 6.625×10^{-27} erg-sec.

59. **(D)** The masses of atoms and the forces holding them together are of such magnitude that the usual vibrations of organic molecules interact with electromagnetic radiation so as to absorb and radiate in the infrared region. The general requirement for infrared activity of a vibration is that the vibration must produce a periodic change in the dipole moment.

60. **(E)** Before the recent popularity of reciprocal centimeters (cm^{-1}) as a unit of infrared measurement, infrared spectral frequencies were given in the range $2\mu - 15\mu$. Since 1μ is equal to 10^{-6}m, this range is equivalent to 10^{-4}cm to 10^{-3}cm.

61. **(D)** Although the possible existence of neutrons was suggested by Rutherford in 1920, it was Chadwick who first observed them experimentally in 1932.

62. **(E)** The γ radiators, C_o^{60} and C_s^{137}, have largely displaced radium in radiotherapy. The elements can be obtained more cheaply and abundantly and with any desired intensity from atomic piles.

63. **(C)** The two major isotopes of carbon are C^{12} and C^{13}, the latter being 1.08% of the former. Another isotope of carbon C^{14} is produced by cosmic ray bombardment of nitrogen atoms in the upper atmosphere. This isotope is radioactive, reverting by β-decay to N^{14} with a half-life of 5568 ± 30 years. This is the isotope of carbon used in radiocarbon dating.

64. **(C)** In the equation, the atomic mass of the starting atom is the same as that of the product atom. Thus neither a neutron nor a proton has been given up. But the number of protons in the nucleus has been decreased by 1, suggesting that a proton in the phosphorus has given up a positron to become a neutron, thus leaving the mass constant while decreasing the atomic number by 1.

65. **(E)** The steady state energy distribution of neutrons diffusing through matter contains a component that is strongly peaked about the energy kT, where k is Boltzmann's constant and T is the Kelvin temperature. These are known as thermal neutrons and have energies extending to about 0.3 ev.

66. **(E)** The symbol $_{67}X^{139}$ means that X has atomic number 67 and atomic mass 139. Since the atomic number of an element is the number of protons in the nucleus, and the atomic weight is the sum of the neutrons and protons in the nucleus, then the number of neutrons for X is $139-67=72$.

67. **(D)** A beta particle is produced by the loss of an electron from a neutron, which becomes a proton. Therefore, the net result of the emission of a beta particle from a nucleus is the increase by one of the number of protons in the nucleus and, thus, its atomic number; whereas its atomic weight remains constant since the loss of an electron makes a negligible change to this latter property.

68. **(D)** An ester is a substance obtained by the condensation of an organic acid with an alcohol.

$CH_3COOC_2H_5$, ethyl acetate, is the ester obtained by the condensation of acetic acid with ethyl alcohol:

$$CH_3\text{-}\overset{\overset{\displaystyle O}{\|}}{C}\text{-}OH + HO\text{-}CH_2\text{-}CH_3$$

$$\xrightarrow{H^+} CH_3\text{-}\overset{\overset{\displaystyle O}{\|}}{C}\text{-}O\text{-}CH_2\text{-}CH_3 + H_2O$$

69. **(C)** The Kolbe-Schmitt reaction is used in the production of phenolic carboxylic acids by heating an alkali phenolate with carbon dioxide:

$$2\ C_6H_5ONa \xrightarrow{CO_2} C_6H_5OH + C_6H_4(ONa)(CO_2Na)$$

The structure of salicylic acid is $C_6H_4(OH)(CO_2H)$

70. **(E)** The iodine number, commonly used with respect to fatty acids, is the percent by weight of iodine absorbed by a sample of an unsaturated material.

71. **(D)** Vinegar is a 6% aqueous solution of acetate acid. The latter can be obtained by air oxidation of ethanol using the mold, "mother of vinegar."

72. **(B)** An unsaturated organic compound is one in which all the four valences of each carbon is not satisfied by hydrogen or some other substituent with the result that multiple bonds have to be formed between adjacent carbon atoms. The requirement for saturation is that for each n carbon atoms, there be 2n + 2 substituents, showing that C_4H_8 is unsaturated.

73. **(C)** Concentrated sulfuric acid is extremely hygroscopic and produces considerable heat on dilution. To dilute it, one must always add small amounts of the acid to large amounts of water rather than reverse this procedure.

74. **(D)** As atomic weights increase, the outermost valence shells are progressively shielded by the filled inner shells, thus making them less attractive to electrons.

75. **(D)** Water gas is the mixture of gases obtained by burning coke in the presence of steam to give $CO + H_2$

$$C + H_2O \rightarrow CO + H_2$$

Hydrogen can easily be separated from the mixture by condensing out CO.

76. **(E)** Crystallinity in a plastic allows regular arrangement of the atoms in the polymeric chain thus making maximum use of the factors such as hydrogen bonding which lead to structural rigidity.

77. **(B)** If concentration of acid is 0.1N and degree of ionization is 1%, then concentration of $[H^+]$ is $0.1 \times \frac{1}{100} = 10^{-3}$ For a water solution, the product of $[H^+]$ and $[OH^-]$ is 10^{-14}

$\therefore$ If $[H^+] = 10^{-3}$

Then $[OH^-]\ 10^{-14} \div 10^{-3} = 10^{-11}$

78. **(C)** Ag_2SO_4 ionizes as follows: $Ag_2SO_4 \rightarrow 2Ag^+ + SO_4^{=}$ The solubility product $K_{sp} = [Ag^+]^2\ [SO_4^-]$ For a solution that is $2.5 \times 10^{-2}M$, the concentration of Ag^+ is 5×10^{-2} and that of SO_4^{--} is 2.5×10^{-2}

$$\begin{aligned}\therefore K_{sp} &= [5 \times 10^{-2}]^2\ [2.5 \times 10^{-2}] \\ &= 25 \times 10^{-4} \times 2.5 \times 10^{-2} \\ &= 62.5 \times 10^{-6} \\ &= 6.25 \times 10^{-5}\end{aligned}$$

79. **(C)** Dulong and Petit's Law states that the product of the specific heat in calories/gm and the atomic weight of a metallic element is approximately equal to 6.4 calories. Therefore, if the specific heat of the element is 0.214 cal/gm, then its atomic weight is $\frac{6.4}{0.214} \approx 30$

80. **(A)** The outermost 4p orbital has five electrons in it and needs one more electron to complete the shell. It is, therefore, likely to acquire the extra electron, leading to a valence of −1.

81. **(E)** The equation used in calculating molecular weights from freezing point depressions is:

$$M_2 = K_f \cdot \left[\frac{1000\ W_2}{\Delta T_f W_1}\right]$$

Where M_2 is molecular weight of solute, W_2 is weight of solute dissolved in W_1 grams of solvent, ΔT_f is the observed freezing point depression, and K_f is the cryoscopic constant for the solvent. For water, K_f is 1.86 C.

Therefore, $M_2 = 1.86\left(\frac{1000 \times 4.5}{0.465 \times 100}\right) = 180.$

82. **(E)** A normal solution is one which contains a gm. equivalent weight of the solute in 1 litre of solution. For HBr, the equivalent weight is the same as the molecular weight. Thus 1 litre of a normal solution of HBr solution contains 1 mole of HBr.

1 litre of 0.86N HBr solution contains 0.86 moles HBr

8 litres of 0.86N HBr solution contain 0.86×8 moles of HBr

6.88 moles of HBr.

83. **(E)** Adiabatic expansion for an enclosed gas is one in which no heat is allowed into the system from the environment. Gas molecules have a natural gravitational attraction for one another. Thus energy is needed to separate them from one another, as happens in expansion. If this energy is not provided from the environment, then it is removed from the internal energy associated with the gas, leading to a decrease in temperature.

84. **(A)** The conversion formula between the Fahrenheit and Centigrade scales is:

$$C = (F - 32) \times \frac{5}{9}$$

For C and F to be the same, then

$$C = (C - 32) \times \frac{5}{9}$$

Therefore, $C = \frac{5C - 160}{9}$

Therefore, $9C = 5C - 160$

$$4C = -160$$
and $C = -40$

85. **(E)** Mercurous ion forms a white precipitate of Hg_2Cl_2 with chloride ion which, on addition of aqueous ammonia, is oxidized according to the following equation:
$Hg_2Cl_2 + 2NH_3 \rightarrow HgNH_2Cl + Hg + NH_4Cl$
The finely divided particles of Hg appear as a black deposit.

86. **(E)** The equation for the displacement of Cu by Al is:

$$2Al + 3CuSO_4 \rightarrow Al_2(SO_4)_3 + 3Cu$$

Thus, two gm atoms of Al displace 3 gm atoms of copper; and 1 gm atom will displace 1½ gm atoms of Cu. Therefore, since the atomic weight of Cu is 64 g, 27 g of Al will displace $64 \times \frac{3}{2} = 96$ g of Cu.

87. **(E)** Stokes law, which is concerned with the fall of bodies through fluid media, is used in the falling sphere viscometer for the determination of fluid viscosities. Viscosities, in turn, can be correlated with various structural features of fluids, and thus, Stokes law is used, ultimately, in structure determination.

88. **(D)** Entropy is measured in units of the quotient of heat and temperature:

$$ds = \frac{dq}{T}$$

Since q, the quantity of heat, is measured in calories, entropy is measured in calories/degree.

89. **(B)** The Clausius-Clapeyron equation is a fundamental relationship between the temperature of a phase change, its latent heat, and the resultant volume change. It may be written in the form:

$$\frac{dp}{dT} = \frac{\Delta H}{T\Delta V}$$

90. **(E)** The "poise" is named after I. L. Poiseuille, a French scientist, who established an equation for determining the viscosity of a fluid by the use of a capillary tube. The poise is the unit of viscosity and is defined as the tangential force per unit area (dynes/im^2) required to maintain unit difference in velocity (1 cm/sec. between two parallel planes separated by 1 cm of fluid. 1 poise = 1 dyne sec/cm^2 = 1 gm/cm.sec.

91. **(B)** Although for a given gas the average velocity is proportional to the square root of the temperature, the converse is not true for a mixture of gases since the molecular weight of the gas also determines the velocity of the molecule. The total energy E is proportional

to the product of the mass of the molecule and half the square of its velocity. It is this energy that determines the temperature, which is constant for each component of a mixture (from the equipartition principle).

92. **(D)** The equipartition law for molecular velocities refers only to gases and does not contain the information required to calculate the velocity of liquids.

93. **(C)** The first paragraph says that "the average velocity is proportional to the *square root* of the temperature measured from absolute zero." Thus, velocity cannot also be proportional to the square of the temperature, as required by $V = Kt^2$.

94. **(B)** $V = Kt^{\frac{1}{2}}$

Therefore, if V = 0.25 at t = 273° A

Then K $\frac{0.25}{\sqrt{273}}$

Therefore, at 400° A, $V = K\sqrt{400} = \frac{0.25}{273}$

$\times 20 \equiv \frac{5.0}{16.5} \approx 0.30$ mi./sec.

95. **(E)** A d orbital has an angular quantum number, l, of 2. According to quantum mechanics an electron with an orbital angular momentum generates a magnetic moment around the nucleus. This magnetic momentum can be oriented in a total of (2l + 1) directions in an applied field.

96. **(A)** From the Bohr equation for the hydrogen atom, the Bohr radius can be defined as:

$$r = \frac{n^2h^2}{mZe^2}$$

Substitution of the accepted values into this equation gives

$$r = \frac{h^2}{me^2} = 0.528 \times 10^{-8} \text{ cm. for } n = 1$$

97. **(C)** In classical mechanics, the rule for predicting the thermal energy of molecules is the principle of the equipartition of energy. According to this principle, each translational and rotational degree of freedom in a molecule contributes ½kT to the thermal energy, and each vibrational degree of freedom contributes kT to the thermal energy.

98. **(D)** The general equation for calculating the entropy change resulting from mixing gases is:

$\Delta S = -R\sum_i X_i \ln X_i$ where X_i are the mole fractions of the constituents in the mixture. For this mixture

Therefore, $\Delta S = -R[0.8 \ln 0.8 + 0.2 \text{ in } 0.2]$

$= -2[0.8\times(-0.22) + 0.2\times(-1.6)] = -2 \times (-0.5) = 1.0$ cal/deg.

99. **(D)** For an ideal gas, the change in Gibb's free energy is:

$$\Delta F = \int_{P_1}^{P_2} VdP = \int_{P_1}^{P_2} \frac{nRTdP}{P}$$

$$= nRT \ln \frac{P^2}{P_1}$$

Therefore, $\Delta F = -2 \times 298 \times 2.303 \log 10$

$= -1365$ cal.

100. **(C)** By definition, $A = E - TS$

Therefore, at constant T, $\Delta A = -T\Delta S$

$\Delta S = nR \ln \frac{P_1}{P_2} = +2 \times 2.303 \log 10 = 4.6$

Therefore, $\Delta A = -298 \times 4.6 = -1365$ cal.

101. **(B)** Le Chatelier's principle states that a system at equilibrium reacts to an applied stress in such a way as to reduce the effect of that stress. It is applicable to all chemical reactions.

102. **(E)** Benzene is a flat symmetrical molecule, and all local C-H polarizations are balanced out in the entire molecule, yielding a dipole moment of zero.

103. **(B)** One mole of gas at STP occupies 22.4 liters. Since PV = nRT, then for one mole, R = PV/T

$$= 1 \text{ atm.} \times 22.4 \text{ liter}/273 \text{ deg.}$$
$$= 0.0821 \text{ liter-atm/deg.}$$

104. **(D)** Sodium acetate is completely ionized. It can be assumed, therefore, that the concentration of acetate ion is 0.2 molar.

For CH_3COOH, the ionization constant,

$$K = \frac{[H^+][CH_3COO^-]}{[CH_3COOH]}$$

$$= 1.8 \times 10^{-5} = \frac{[H^+][0.2]}{0.06}$$

$$\text{Therefore, } [H^+] = \frac{1.8 \times 10^{-5} \times 6.0 \times 10^{-2}}{2.0 \times 10^{-1}}$$

$$= 5.4 \times 10^{-6}$$

105. **(E)** In general, for a dilution, $V_1N_1 = V_2N_2$. Therefore, $V_2 = V_1N_1/N_2$
$= (80 \times 0.1)/2 = 4$ ml.

106. **(E)** At standard conditions, the emf developed by the cell is the difference in potential between the two electrodes. For this case, E = 0.761 − (−0.799)
= 1.560 volts.

107. **(D)** For cupric sulfate, the equation for the reduction is:

$$\tfrac{1}{2}Cu^{++} + e^- \rightarrow \tfrac{1}{2}Cu.$$

That is, ½ gram atom of Cu is liberated by 1 faraday, or 32g of Cu is liberated by 96,500 coulombs. Therefore, 128g of Cu require (96,500 × 128)/32 = 386,000 coulombs.

108. **(E)** A eutectic is the lowest melting mixture of two or more constituents which melts completely at a definite temperature to form a single liquid. The coordinates of temperature and composition, at which this mixture is in equilibrium with melt, constitute an invariant point; i.e., there are no degrees of freedom with respect to temperature or composition.

109. **(C)** A molal solution is one which contains one mole of solute in 1000g of solvent; whereas one which contains a mole of solute in one liter of solution is said to be a molar solution.

110. **(A)** The Dulong and Petit rule states that the product of the specific heat and atomic weight of a metallic element is approximately equal to 6.4.

Thus for lead, since the atomic weight is 207, its specific heat would be approximately 6.4/207 = 0.031.

111. **(E)** When a chemical reaction is zero order with respect to any parameter, then its rate is independent of that parameter.

112. **(A)** The Debye-Hückel theory for ionic solutions is an extension of the simple Arrhenius theory in that it made, among others, the following assumptions: (a) strong electrolytes are completely dissociated in aqueous solutions; (b) all deviations from ideality result from the electrostatic interactions between the ions separated by a solvent which can be regarded as a structureless dielectric continuum.

113. **(A)** Lead dissolves most readily in acetic acid because it can be complexed by the solvent. Because it is not strongly electropositive, the metal does not displace hydrogen from HCl or H_2SO_4. It is slowly oxidized by nitric acid.

114. **(E)** By definition, the specific conductance of a conductor is the reciprocal of its specific resistance, and is measured in reciprocal ohms or mhos.

If specific resistance is 93.6 ohms, then specific conductance is 1/93.6 reciprocal ohms = 0.011 reciprocal ohms.

115. **(E)** The carat is used as a measure of purity for gold and represents 1/24 of pure gold. Therefore, 14-carat gold contains 14/24 gold, or 58%.

116. **(E)** The simple kinetic theory expression for the viscosity of a gas is: $\eta = \frac{1}{3} n \bar{u} \lambda m$ where η is the viscosity, n is the number of molecules per cubic centimeter, $\bar{u}$ is the average velocity of the molecules, λ is the mean free path and m is the molecular weight. Since n is proportional to the density and λ is inversely proportional to the density, the above equation suggests that the viscosity is independent of the density of the gas.

117. **(A)** According to Avogadro's hypothesis, under identical conditions of temperature and pressure, equal volumes of different gases contain the same number of molecules. Also, the average speed of movement of molecules is directly proportional to the square root of the absolute temperature and inversely proportional to the square root of its molecular weight. Since the temperature is the same for both gases, the only factor that would determine the average speed of movement is the molecular weight. From the principle stated above, the average speed of the carbon dioxide molecules should be less than that of the hydrogen molecules.

118. **(A)** From the kinetic theory for ideal gases, the volume of a given mass of gas is inversely proportional to its pressure and directly proportional to its absolute temperature. If a gas occupies 100 ml at 740 mm and 27°C (or 300°A) it would, at STP, occupy

$$\frac{100 \times 740 \times 273}{760 \times 300}$$

$$= 88.6$$

119. **(B)** Atomic weight = Equivalent weight × valence If 0.11 g of hydrogen is displaced by 2.0 g of metal, then 1.00 g of hydrogen would be displaced by

$$\frac{2.0 \times 1.00}{0.11} = 18.2 \text{ g of metal.}$$

∴ Equivalent weight of metal = 18.2 g. And its atomic weight = 18.2 × 1 = 18.2 g

120. **(A)** Although small quantities of electrolytes enhance the stability of colloids, larger quantities lead to precipitation. Essentially, the ability of the electrolyte to cause precipitation depends on the valence of the electrolyte ion carrying a charge opposite to that of the colloid. In this instance, the most highly charged cation would be the most effective.

121. **(A)** At STP, one mole of a gas occupies 22.4 liters. Therefore one liter of the gas contains 1/22.4 mole. If 1/22.4 mole weighs 1.16 g, then 1 mole weighs 1.16 × 22.4 = 26. C_2H_2 is the only compound in the list that has a molecular weight of 26.

122. **(B)** Isomers are molecules which have the same molecular formula but different structures. Ethanol is C_2H_6O or [CH_3-CH_2-OH], Methanol is CH_4O or [CH_3-OH], Dimethyl ether is C_2H_6O or [CH_3-O-CH_3], Diethyl ether is $C_4H_{10}O$ or [CH_3CH_2-O-CH_2CH_3], Ethylene glycol is $C_2H_6O_2$ or [HO-CH_2-CH_2-OH], and Acetone is C_3H_6O or [CH_3-CO-CH_3]

123. **(E)** Cis-trans or geometrical isomerism is exhibited only by molecules in which rotation of substituents about two adjacent atomic centers is hindered either by the presence of a double bond between the centers or by the presence of a rigid ring involving these centers.

124. **(D)** A standard solution of iodine, when shaken with an unsaturated compound, gives additional products of the iodine to the multiple bond. The degree of unsaturation is expressed as the iodine number, which is the percent by weight of iodine that is absorbed by the unsaturated compound.

125. **(E)** The Hinsberg test is used to distinguish between primary, secondary and tertiary amines. It consists of shaking the amine with benzenesulfonyl chloride in the presence of aqueous NaOH. Primary amines form a clear solution which, upon acidification, yields an insoluble sulfonamide; a secondary amine yields an insoluble sulfonamide which is unaffected by acidification; and a tertiary amine does not react, and dissolves only on acidification.

126. **(E)** $H_2 + CO_2 \rightleftarrows CO + H_2O$. Assuming that x is the amount of starting material that reacted, then we have at equilibrium, $(1-x)H_2 + (1-x)CO_2 \leftrightarrows x\,CO + x\,H_2O$; at 25°C, the volume of H_2O can be neglected.
Therefore the fractional volume of CO is

$$\frac{x}{(1-x)+(1-x)+x} = \frac{x}{2-x} = 0.0016.$$

$\therefore$ x = 0.0032. But equilibrium constant is

$$\frac{[CO]\,[H_2O]}{[H_2]\,[CO_2]} \approx \frac{x^2}{1} = 0.0032 \times 0.0032 = 10^{-5}$$

127. **(C)** The equilibrium constant of a reaction is independent of pressure and volume and depends only upon temperature. Since the product occupies a smaller volume than the reactants, Le Chatelier's principle would predict an increase in the *rate* of the reaction.

128. **(D)** For liquids and solids, changes in pressure have negligible effects on their volumes. Thus, at constant temperature, the change in Gibb's free energy is:

$$\Delta G = V\Delta P.$$

If the density of the ester is 0.88 g/cm³ and its molecular weight is 142, then its molar volume is 142/0.88 = 161 cm³ = 0.161 liter. Therefore, ΔG = 0.161 (20 − 1) = 3.04 liter atm. From the fact that R = 2 cal/deg. mole, and R = 0.082 lit atm./deg. mole, 3.04 lit atm

$$= \frac{3.04 \times 2}{0.082} = 74.1 \text{ cal.}$$

129. **(C)** By definition, $\Delta S = \frac{\Delta H}{T} = \frac{-79}{273}$

$$= -0.29 \text{ cal/g deg.}$$

130. **(A)** The Gibb's Free Energy is defined as G = H − TS. Therefore, at constant temperature, ΔG = ΔH −TΔS. But ΔS = ΔH/T. Therefore, at constant temperature,

$$\Delta G = T\Delta S - T\Delta S = 0$$

131. **(E)** The equilibrium constant for a reaction is independent of concentration and pressure, but varies usually with temperature.

132. **(D)** On the average, the rate of a chemical reaction doubles for every 10°C rise in temperature. If the turn-over rate is 5g per hour at 10°, then it would double at 20°C, and double again at 30°C; giving a total turnover rate of 20g/hr.

133. **(D)** For the reation, AB + CD = AD + CB, the equilibrium constant is defined as:

$$K = \frac{[AD]\,[CB]}{[AB]\,[CD]}$$

For the given reaction, [AD] = [CB] = 3/4; and [AB] = [CD] = 1/4.
Therefore, K = (3/4) (3/4) ÷ (1/4) (1/4) = 9.

134. **(E)** According to the Distribution Law, the weight of solute extracted by a volume, V_2, of a solvent from a given volume, V_1, of solution is given by the equation:

$$x = w\left[1 - \left(\frac{KV_1}{KV_1 + V_2}\right)^n\right]$$

where w is the initial weight of solute in solution, K is the distribution constant, and n is the number of extractions.

Examination of the above equation shows that, if a given volume of solvent is available for the extraction, greater extracting efficiency is obtained by keeping V_2 small and n large than the other way around. That is, it is better to extract several times with small volumes than once with a large volume.

135. **(C)** The solubility of a precipitate tends to increase as the concentration of diverse ions in the solution increases. However the solubility is also dependent upon temperature.

136. **(E)** Since this is a silver colloid it will adsorb whichever lattice ion is present in excess in the surrounding liquid. Since silver is the most abundant, it will be adsorbed preferentially.

137. **(B)** pH is the only factor which is related to the sulfate–bisulfate equilibrium. Co-precipitation of potassium is negligible at pH 5 where there are very few bisulfate ions, while potassium ion co-precipitation is appreciable at pH1 where most of the sulfate exists as bisulfate.

138. **(D)** $(NH_2)_2CO$, commonly called urea, is ideal for homogeneous precipitation since it hydrolyzes very slowly in aqueous solution upon heating. In this method the precipitating agent is not added directly but rather is generated slowly by a homogeneous chemical reaction within the solution at a rate comparable to crystal growth.

139. **(E)** In any acid base neutralization

$$M_{eq\ acid} = M_{eq\ base}$$

Now

$$M_{eq\ acid} = \frac{\text{wt. oxalic acid in sample}}{\text{equivalent wt. oxalic acid}}$$

$M_{eq\ base} = N \times ml_{base}$

Therefore

wt. oxalic acid in sample
$= (0.5066)(21.37)(63) = 682.13$ mg

$$\text{Then } \frac{682.13}{750.00} \times 100\% = 91\%$$

140. **(D)** The effect of a solvent that is more basic than water upon the acidic strength of weak acids dissolved in it is to ionize the acids completely.

141. **(B)** In both turbidimetric and nephelometric methods the unknown is not in solution but rather in a colloidal suspension. Thus we can measure the light-scattering properties of the unknown.

142. **(C)** Water will turn anhydrides into acids. In the thio-acid system, H_2S will transform the sulfides into acids.

143. **(C)** The compound HN=C=O is known as isocyanic acid, and compounds containing the –N=C=O linkage are known as isocyanates.

144. **(B)** The hydrolysis of methyl isocyanate with NaOH goes according to the following scheme:

$$CH_3{-}N{=}C{=}O + 2NaOH \rightarrow CH_3{-}NH_2 + Na_2CO_3$$

Thus, in addition to methylamine, sodium carbonate is obtained.

145. **(A)** For many years, the structure of diketene was thought to be $CH_3{-}CO{-}CH{=}C{=}O$. However, the fact that diketene pyrolyses to give ketene, allene and carbon dioxide, as well as NMR and IR evidence has shown without a doubt that its structure is CH_2 O O

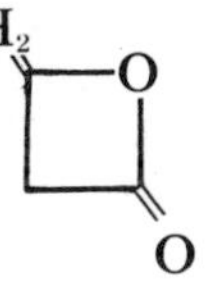

146. **(C)** In the presence of phosphorus, bromine reacts smoothly with carboxylic acids to form α-bromocarboxylic acids. This reaction is known as the Hell-Volhard-Zelinsky reaction.

147. **(A)** Since Grignard reagents react as carbanions, they generally produce hydrocarbons with any proton acid, such as amines and amides. With fully substituted amides, however, the following reaction occurs with one mole of Grignard:

$$R{-}CO{-}NR'R'' + R'''MgX \longrightarrow R{-}CO{-}R''' + XMg{-}NR'R''$$

148. **(C)** The usual order of elution from an alumina column is: alkanes - alkenes - dienes - aromatics - ethers - esters - ketones - alcohols - diols - acids.

It can be seen, therefore, that hexane would be first eluted.

149. **(D)** From the above order (answer 148) 1-hexanol would be eluted last from the column.

150. **(D)** There are five canonical forms for phenanthrene:

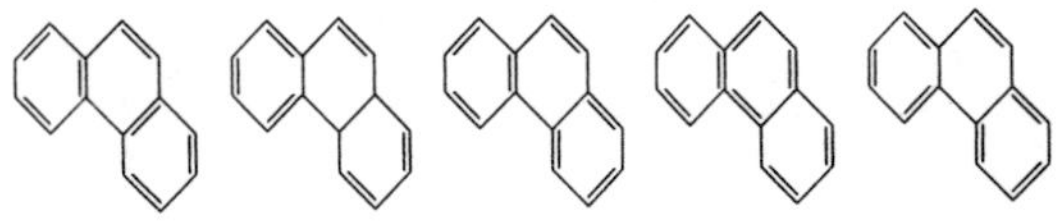

ANSWER SHEET TEST (5)

1	A B C D E	31	A B C D E	61	A B C D E	91	A B C D E	121	A B C D E
2	A B C D E	32	A B C D E	62	A B C D E	92	A B C D E	122	A B C D E
3	A B C D E	33	A B C D E	63	A B C D E	93	A B C D E	123	A B C D E
4	A B C D E	34	A B C D E	64	A B C D E	94	A B C D E	124	A B C D E
5	A B C D E	35	A B C D E	65	A B C D E	95	A B C D E	125	A B C D E
6	A B C D E	36	A B C D E	66	A B C D E	96	A B C D E	126	A B C D E
7	A B C D E	37	A B C D E	67	A B C D E	97	A B C D E	127	A B C D E
8	A B C D E	38	A B C D E	68	A B C D E	98	A B C D E	128	A B C D E
9	A B C D E	39	A B C D E	69	A B C D E	99	A B C D E	129	A B C D E
10	A B C D E	40	A B C D E	70	A B C D E	100	A B C D E	130	A B C D E
11	A B C D E	41	A B C D E	71	A B C D E	101	A B C D E	131	A B C D E
12	A B C D E	42	A B C D E	72	A B C D E	102	A B C D E	132	A B C D E
13	A B C D E	43	A B C D E	73	A B C D E	103	A B C D E	133	A B C D E
14	A B C D E	44	A B C D E	74	A B C D E	104	A B C D E	134	A B C D E
15	A B C D E	45	A B C D E	75	A B C D E	105	A B C D E	135	A B C D E
16	A B C D E	46	A B C D E	76	A B C D E	106	A B C D E	136	A B C D E
17	A B C D E	47	A B C D E	77	A B C D E	107	A B C D E	137	A B C D E
18	A B C D E	48	A B C D E	78	A B C D E	108	A B C D E	138	A B C D E
19	A B C D E	49	A B C D E	79	A B C D E	109	A B C D E	139	A B C D E
20	A B C D E	50	A B C D E	80	A B C D E	110	A B C D E	140	A B C D E
21	A B C D E	51	A B C D E	81	A B C D E	111	A B C D E	141	A B C D E
22	A B C D E	52	A B C D E	82	A B C D E	112	A B C D E	142	A B C D E
23	A B C D E	53	A B C D E	83	A B C D E	113	A B C D E	143	A B C D E
24	A B C D E	54	A B C D E	84	A B C D E	114	A B C D E	144	A B C D E
25	A B C D E	55	A B C D E	85	A B C D E	115	A B C D E	145	A B C D E
26	A B C D E	56	A B C D E	86	A B C D E	116	A B C D E	146	A B C D E
27	A B C D E	57	A B C D E	87	A B C D E	117	A B C D E	147	A B C D E
28	A B C D E	58	A B C D E	88	A B C D E	118	A B C D E	148	A B C D E
29	A B C D E	59	A B C D E	89	A B C D E	119	A B C D E	149	A B C D E
30	A B C D E	60	A B C D E	90	A B C D E	120	A B C D E	150	A B C D E

Advanced Test in Chemistry

(Sample 5)

Time: 3 hours

Directions: Select from the lettered choices that choice which best completes the statement or answers the question. Indicate the letter of your choice on the answer sheet.

Questions 1 to 6 are based on the following paragraphs:

It was discovered by the Dutch physicist P. Zeeman that spectral lines may be split into two or more components when a magnetic field is applied to the atoms that are emitting or absorbing the radiation. This effect is called the Zeeman effect. The splitting of the spectral lines is due to the splitting of the energy levels as a result of the interaction of the magnetic moments associated with the spin of the electrons and their orbital motion with the magnetic field. The Paschen-Back effect is that the magnetic field becomes so strong that the Zeeman splittings of a Russell-Saunders state approximate to the separation of the states with different values of total angular momentum J. These effects may also be applied to the molecules and free radicals.

The magnetic moment of an atom can be expressed in a simple way in terms of its angular momentum. The Bohr unit of angular momentum is $h/2\pi$, and the Bohr unit of magnetic moment is $he/4\pi mc$. An electron moving in an orbital with x units of angular momentum has orbital magnetic moment equal to x Bohr magnetons. This can also be expressed by the g factor for orbital motion of the electron which is 1.

1. The g factor of the spin of the electron is
   (A) 1
   (B) 0
   (C) 1/2
   (D) 2
   (E) indefinite

2. The nuclear magneton is $he/4\pi Mc$. Its value is
   (A) the same as the Bohr magneton of the electron
   (B) about 100 times the Bohr magneton of the electron
   (C) about 1/2000 of the magneton of the proton
   (D) about 100 times the magneton of the proton
   (E) about 1/1840 of the electron magneton

3. The g value of the free radical is about
   (A) 1
   (B) 1.5
   (C) 2
   (D) 5/2
   (E) 3

4. The electron spin resonance is an example of
   (A) Stark effect
   (B) Russell-Saunders state
   (C) Paschen-Back effect
   (D) g factor equals to 1
   (E) vibration effect

5. How many lines are in the spectrum of the CH_3 radical?
   (A) 1
   (B) 2
   (C) 6
   (D) 4
   (E) 3

6. For a electron moving in the s orbital, its total angular momentum is
   (A) 0
   (B) 1/2
   (C) 1
   (D) 3/2
   (E) 2

7. All the terpenes have carbon skeletons made up of
(A) isoprene units
(B) allenes
(C) methyl groups
(D) vinyl units
(E) ethylene units

8. Organic chemists often use the Rast method for the molecular weight determination. This method takes advantage of the unusually large cryoscopic constant of
(A) benzene
(B) ethanol
(C) acetone
(D) carbon disulfide
(E) camphor

9. The melting point of organic compounds depends on the molecular weight and molecular shape. Which, among the following, is the compound that has the highest melting point?
(A) Methane
(B) Butane
(C) o-Xylene
(D) p-Xylene
(E) m-Xylene

10. Which is the compound called benzal chloride?
(A) ClC_6H_5
(B) $C_6H_5CH_2Cl$
(C) $ClC_6H_4CH_3$
(D) $C_6H_5CCl_3$
(E) $C_6H_5CHCl_2$

11. The compound that dehydrates most readily is
(A) R_3COH
(B) R_2CHOH
(C) CH_3OH
(D) RCH_2OH
(E) phenol

12. The Lucas test is used to determine the types of
(A) alcohols
(B) amines
(C) acids
(D) amino acids
(E) phenols

13. The iodoform test is used to show one particular structural unit in
(A) aliphatic alcohols
(B) aromatic alcohols
(C) aliphatic amines
(D) aromatic amines
(E) unsaturated acids

14. In the alpha-halogenation of aliphatic acids, the catalyst is
(A) $FeCl_3$
(B) $AlCl_3$
(C) Zn
(D) Ni
(E) P

15. In esterification of acids, the nucleophilic reagent is the
(A) acid
(B) alcohol
(C) water
(D) hydroxyl ion
(E) hydride ion

16. The Haworth synthesis is a synthesis method for
(A) carbohydrates
(B) benzene derivatives
(C) amino acids
(D) naphthalene derivatives
(E) glycols

In answering questions 17-23 refer to the following information:

Standard free energies of formation

SUBSTANCE	ΔF AT 298° K (KCAL/MOLE)
CO (g)	− 32.8
CO_2 (g)	− 94.3
H_2O (g)	− 54.6
C_4H_6 (g)	+ 36.0
n-C_4H_{10} (g)	− 4.1

Standard entropies

SUBSTANCE	S AT 298° K (CAL/DEG-MOLE)
H_2 (g)	31.2
H_2O (g)	45.1
O_2 (g)	49.1

17. The standard free energy change for the reaction
$CO\ (g) + H_2O\ (g) \rightarrow CO_2\ (g) + H_2(g)$
at 25°C and 1 atm is
(A) 94.3 kcal
(B) 61.3 kcal
(C) -13.6 kcal
(D) -54.6 kcal
(E) -6.9 kcal

18. If the standard free energy change is negative in sign, the reaction
(A) will take place spontaneously
(B) will be exothermic
(C) will be endothermic
(D) will not take place
(E) is in its equilibrium state

19. If the standard free energy change is zero for a certain reaction, then the reaction
(A) will take place spontaneously
(B) will be endothermic
(C) will be exothermic
(D) will not take place
(E) is in its equilibrium state

20. What is the free energy change for the following reaction at 25°C and 1 atm?
$$C_4H_{10} \rightarrow C_4H_6 + 2H_2(g)$$
(A) 36.0
(B) 4.1
(C) -40.1
(D) 40.1
(E) 0

21. The standard entropy change of gaseous water formation at 25°C and 1 atm is about (in cal/mole-deg)
(A) 45.1
(B) 13.9
(C) 49.1
(D) -54.6
(E) -10.6

22. The enthalpy of formation for H_2O at 25°C and 1 atm is about
(A) 10.6 kcal/mole
(B) -57.8 kcal/mole
(C) 5.78 kcal/mole
(D) 45.1 kcal/mole
(E) -54.6 kcal/mole

23. The standard entropy of all elements at absolute zero temperature is
(A) zero
(B) about 10 cal/mole-deg
(C) 1 cal/mole-g
(D) positive
(E) negative

24. The neutron diffraction is an excellent technique in determining the positions of
(A) carbon atoms
(B) hydrogen atoms
(C) oxygen atoms
(D) nitrogen atoms
(E) halogen atoms

25. Acrylic acid is
(A) a saturated aliphatic acid
(B) an unsaturated aliphatic acid with four carbon atoms
(C) an aromatic acid
(D) an unsaturated acid with five carbon atoms
(E) an unsaturated acid with three carbon atoms

26. How can you account for the fact that the addition of HBr to 3,3-dimethyl-1-butene yields some 2,3-dimethyl-2-bromobutane?
(A) 1,2-shifts
(B) 1,3-shifts
(C) 1,4-shifts
(D) free radical reaction
(E) carbanion ion

27. Of the interhalogen AX_3 compound, ClF_3 is the most reactive but BrF_3 has higher conductance in the liquid state. The reason is that
(A) BrF_3 has high molecular weight
(B) ClF_3 is more volatile
(C) BrF_3 dissociates into BrF^+_2 and BrF^-_4 more easily
(D) ClF_3 is the most reactive
(E) electrical conductance is independent of the concentration

28. The structure of ClO_3F is
(A) linear
(B) nonlinear
(C) square planar
(D) trigonal plane
(E) tetrahedral

29. The least polarized anion is
(A) SO_4^{-2}
(B) $C_2O_4^{-2}$
(C) NO_3^-
(D) ClO_4^-
(E) IO_4^-

30. The formula of the isocyanate ion is
(A) OCN^-
(B) SCN^-
(C) ONC^-
(D) CN^-
(E) N_3^-

31. With hydrogen, the pseudohalogens
(A) do not react
(B) react to form very strong acids
(C) react to form bases
(D) react to form weak acids
(E) react to form salts

32. The lanthanides have electron configuration with $6s^2$ in common but with variable occupation of the
(A) 6p levels
(B) 5p levels
(C) 4d levels
(D) 5d levels
(E) 4f levels

33. The lanthanide contraction refers to
(A) ionic radius of that series
(B) nuclear mass of that series
(C) valence electrons of the series
(D) the electronegativity
(E) the density of the series

34. If the K_{sp} for CaC_2O_4 is 2.6×10^{-9}, the concentration of oxalate ion needed to form a precipitate in a solution containing 0.02 moles per liter of calcium ions is
(A) 1.0×10^{-9}
(B) 1.3×10^{-7}
(C) 2.2×10^{-5}
(D) 5.2×10^{-11}
(E) 2.2×10^{-7}

35. A series circuit with a capacitive reactance of 20 ohms, an inductive reactance of 50 ohms, and a resistance of 40 ohms has an overall impedence, in ohms, of
(A) 10
(B) 50
(C) 70
(D) 110
(C) 70
(E) 30

36. When a strong beam of light is passed through smoke, the beam is partly scattered and becomes visible. This phenomenon is known as the
(A) Compton effert
(B) Zeeman effect
(C) Zernicke effect
(D) Tyndall effect
(E) Stark effect

37. The benzidine rearrangement is often used for
(A) aliphatic acids
(B) aromatic acids
(C) alcohols
(D) ketones
(E) diazo compounds

38. Mild oxidation with H_2O_2, converts azo compounds into
(A) azoxy compounds
(B) amines
(C) hydrazo compounds
(D) ketones
(E) diazonium salts

39. $\alpha.\beta$-Unsaturated carbonyl compounds undergo a ring closure reaction with conjugated dienes. This is known as the
(A) Hoffman reaction
(B) Sandmayer reaction
(C) Diels-Alder reaction
(D) Claison reaction
(E) Perkin reaction

40. A γ or δ-hydroxy acid loses water by esterification to yield a cyclic ester known as a
(A) epoxide
(B) lactam
(C) meso compound
(D) indole
(E) lactone

41. The weakest base among the following is
(A) ammonia
(B) methyl amine
(C) dimethyl amine
(D) pyridine
(E) pyrrole

42. The Skraup synthesis is a useful method for preparing substituted
(A) quinolines
(B) pyridine
(C) thiophene
(D) phenanthrene
(E) furan

43. The simplest of the five-membered heterocyclic nitrogen compound is
(A) pyridine
(B) pyrrole
(C) purine
(D) quinoline
(E) carbazole

44. Terminal residue analysis is the identifying of the amino acid residues at the ends of the peptide chain. A very successful reagent for the N-terminal residue is
(A) HCl
(B) carbobenzoxy chloride
(C) H_2SO_4
(D) DNFB
(E) NaOH

45. The keto-enol tautomer equilibrium exists in liquids. The percent enol form in pure liquid of acetone is about
(A) 80%
(B) 70%
(C) 50%
(D) 1.0%
(E) 2.5×10^{-4}%

46. The percent enol form in pure liquid of acetoacetaldehyde is about
(A) 98%
(B) 10%
(C) 1.0%
(D) 0.1%
(E) 10^{-3}%

Questions 47-50 are based on the following paragraphs:

An experimental investigation of the structure of chemical species seeks first of all to learn how the nuclei of the atoms in the molecule or radical are arranged in space. This information consists of the bond distances and bond angles in the structure. When the electron distributions are required, the idea is to use the nuclei themselves as probes to reveal the electron density which surrounds them. Nuclei are not unfeeling point charges. They have definite characters of their own which make them sensitive to the electrical environment. The study of effects caused by the interaction of nuclei with their surroundings forms the foundations of the magnetic resonance.

The significant properties of the nuclei are their magnetic moments and their electric quadrupole moments. Hydrogen atom has nuclear spin ½ and carbon 13 also has nuclear spin ½. An electron-spin resonance spectrum of a free radical containing a single hydrogen consists of two lines of equal intensity separated by K gauss. When the hydrogen is replaced by deuterium (nuclear spin 1), the spectrum is changed into one with three equally spaced lines of equal intensity with a spacing between adjacent lines of M gauss.

47. The magnetic moment of the proton is 2.79 u in nuclear magnetic units. What is the NMR frequency at 10 kG magnetic field?
(A) 1 kc
(B) 100 kc
(C) 1.5 mc
(D) 12 mc
(E) 42.6 mc

48. The magnetic moment of deuterium is 0.86 u in nuclear magnetic units. The ratio of K/M is about
(A) 2
(B) ½
(C) 6.5
(D) 13
(E) 1

49. For a radical containing two equivalent hydrogen atoms with a splitting K = 4 gauss, the total splitting should be
(A) 4 gauss
(B) 2 gauss
(C) 1 gauss
(D) 8 gauss
(E) 16 gauss

50. The intensity ratio of the radical containing three equivalent hydrogen atoms is
(A) 1 : 1 : 1
(B) 1 : 1 : 1 : 1
(C) 1 : 1 : 1 : 1 : 1
(D) 1 : 2 : 2 : 1
(E) 1 : 3 : 3 : 1

51 Nitrogen has nuclear spin of 1. The nuclear magnetic resonance of nitrogen has

(A) 1 line
(B) 2 lines
(C) 3 lines
(D) 4 lines
(E) 5 lines

52. The electron spin resonance of Cu^{++} has four lines. It follows that the nuclear spin of Cu is
(A) 1/2
(B) 1
(C) 3/2
(D) 2
(E) 4

53. The energy for a rigid rotator with quantum number J is
(A) $BJ(J+1)$
(B) $BJ+1$
(C) BJ^2
(D) $B \times J$
(E) $BJ-1$

54. The chemical formula of pyruvic acid is
(A) OHCCOOH
(B) $CH_3COCOOH$
(C) CH_3COCH_2COOH
(D) $CH_3COCOCH_3$
(E) OHCCHO

55. The Claisen condensation is often used in preparing
(A) β-hydroxyl ester
(B) δ-hydroxyl ester
(C) γ-hydroxyl ester
(D) γ-keto ester
(E) β-keto ester

56. Aldehydes and ketones react with α-bromo esters and metallic zinc to yield
(A) δ-keto esters
(B) β-keto alcohols
(C) β-hydroxyl esters
(D) δ-hydroxyl esters
(E) γ-keto acids

57. Glyceraldehyde has one of the following properties:
(A) one asymmetric carbon atom
(B) two asymmetric carbon atoms
(C) a meso compound
(D) four carbon atoms
(E) one hydroxyl group

In questions 58-60, make use of the following information:

The following lines are observed in the spectrum of a diatomic molecule:

118, 135, 152, 169, 186, 202, cm^{-1}

58. The rotation constant B for this molecule is
(A) 118 cm^{-1}
(B) 202 cm^{-1}
(C) 110 cm^{-1}
(D) 17 cm^{-1}
(E) 8.5 cm^{-1}

59. The energy in wavenumber of the level with $J = 10$ is
(A) 170
(B) 1700
(C) 850
(D) 935
(E) 1100

60. The quantum numbers involved in the transition which give the line at 169 cm^{-1} are
(A) 9 and 10
(B) 10 and 11
(C) 6 and 7
(D) 7 and 8
(E) 8 and 9

61. For a reversible cycle, the entropy change is
(A) always positive
(B) always negative
(C) always zero
(D) dependent on the temperature
(E) dependent on the pressure

62. The d orbitals will be split under trigonal bipyramidal ligand field into
(A) two levels
(B) three levels
(C) four levels
(D) five levels
(E) six levels

63. The shape of molecules and ions formed by non-transitional elements are determined mainly by

(A) the number of electron pairs around the central atom and the repulsions between them
(B) ionic radius
(C) heat of hydration
(D) heat of combustion
(E) paramagnetic or diamagnetic susceptibilities

64. Under the influence of dilute base or dilute acid, two molecules of an aldehyde may combine to form a(n)
(A) acid
(B) alcohol
(C) δ-hydroxyaldehyde
(D) β-hydroxyaldehyde
(E) β-hydroxyketone

65. Two moles of acetone under the influence of sodium hydroxide will yield
(A) 4-methyl-2-pentanone
(B) 4-hydroxy-2-pentanol
(C) 4-methyl-2-pentanoic acid
(D) 4-hydroxy-2-pentanal
(E) 4-hydroxy-4-methyl-2-pentanone

66. Acid anhydrides add to aromatic aldehydes in the presence of bases to yield
(A) α,β-unsaturated acids
(B) esters
(C) β,γ-unsaturated acids
(D) alcohols
(E) γ,β-unsaturated alcohols

67. Ba^{++} ions were added to a solution and a white precipitate was formed; this precipitate dissolved in HCl. Of the following, the correct inference that can be drawn from this information is that
(A) the solution contained SO_4^{-2} ions
(B) the solution contained $C_2O_4^{-2}$ ions
(C) the solution contained $CO_3^{=}$ions
(D) the solution contained $S^{=}$ ions
(E) the solution contained $SO_3^{=}$ions

68. Which one of the following pairs of ions *cannot* be separated by H_2S in an 0.3N acid solution?
(A) Al^{++}, Hg^{++}
(B) Bi^{+++}, Pb^{++}
(C) Ni^{++}, Cd^{++}
(D) Zn^{++}, Cu^{++}
(E) Ni^{++} ,Cu^{++}

69. Which one of the following represents the number of isomeric hexanes?
(A) 3
(B) 4
(C) 5
(D) 7
(E) 6

70. Which one of the following reagent solutions can be used to separate HgS and CuS?
(A) acetamide
(B) NH_4OH
(C) $(NH_4)_2S$
(D) $SnCl_2$
(E) HNO_3

71. A ketone *cannot* be made by which one of the following means?
(A) oxidation of a secondary alcohol
(B) dehydrogenation of a secondary alcohol
(C) heating volatile acids with MnO_2 at 300°
(D) hydrolysis of a cyanide
(E) reaction of acid chloride with organo-cadmium compounds

72. Which one of the following is the number of carbon atoms in 1 molecule of 2,2, dimethyl 4 ethyl hexane?
(A) 6
(B) 8
(C) 10
(D) 12
(E) 9

73. The stability of the cycloalkanes, as shown by the temperature at which the rings are broken by catalytic hydrogenation, is *least* for which of the following?
(A) cyclopropane
(B) cyclobutane
(C) cyclopentane
(D) cyclohexane
(E) cycloheptane

74. Which one of the following is the organic solvent that presents the greatest potential fire hazard?
(A) ethanol
(B) diethyl ether
(C) carbon tetrachloride
(D) kerosene
(E) acetic acid

75. In the reaction H • + • H →H:H
(A) energy is absorbed
(B) energy of released
(C) there is no change in energy
(D) the energy absorbed exceeds the input of energy
(E) the reaction is of first order

76. Layers of carbon atoms in graphite are held together by
(A) coordinate covalent bonds
(B) covalent bonds
(C) double bonds
(D) free electrons
(E) van der Waals' forces

77. The reaction of carboxylic esters with Grignard reagents is an excellent method for preparing
(A) aldehydes
(B) alkanes
(C) primary alcohols
(D) secondary alcohols
(E) tertiary alcohols

78. Which one is the most acidic in the following?
(A) RH
(B) NH_3
(C) C_2H_2
(D) ROH
(E) HOH

79. Which one is the most basic in the following?
(A) $RCOO^-$
(B) OH^-
(C) NH_2^-
(D) R^-
(E) RO^-

80. The Williamson synthesis is applied to
(A) ethers
(B) alkanes
(C) ketones
(D) alcohols
(E) phenols

81. The dipole moment of chlorobenzene is 1.73 D. We predict the dipole moment of p-dichlorobenzene should be
(A) 3.46 D
(B) 3.30 D
(C) 1.73 D
(D) 1.00 D
(E) 0.00 D

82. Which is the most active toward alcoholic silver nitrate?
(A) RCl
(B) RBr
(C) RI
(D) R_2SO_4
(E) RNO_2

83. The composition of compound A is 40% X and 60% Y. The composition of compound B is 25% X and 75% Y. According to the Law of Multiple Proportions the ratio of the weight of element Y in compounds A and B is which one of the following:
(A) 4:5
(B) 2:3
(C) 1:2
(D) 2:1
(E) 3:4

84. Of the following, the prediction having the greatest probability of correctness is that the compound formed between an alkali metal and a halogen would
(A) have a low melting point
(B) be insoluble in water
(C) conduct electricity in the solid state
(D) conduct electricity when molten
(E) have a low heat of fusion

85. Of the following, which one is a correct statement?
(A) The ionic radius of a metal is the same as its atomic radius
(B) The ionic radius of a metal is greater than its atomic radius
(C) The atomic radius of a non-metal is the same as its ionic radius
(D) The atomic radius of a non-metal is more than its ionic radius
(E) The ionic radius of a metal is less than its atomic radius

86. A mole of electrons is the same as a(n)
(A) ampere-second
(B) coulomb
(C) faraday
(D) unit-charge
(E) curie

87. When 2-bromooctane of specific rotation -34.6° is converted into the alcohol under low pH value where first-order kinetics are followed, there is obtained 2-octanol of specific rotation + 3.6°. The conversion could be explained by

(A) free radical mechanism
(B) salt effect
(C) carbonium mechanism
(D) carbanion mechanism
(E) chain reaction

88. In the S_N2 reaction mechanism, which one of the following is the most reactive?
(A) C_6H_6
(B) CH_3X
(C) C_2H_5X
(D) R_2CHX
(E) R_3CX

89. In the S_N1 reaction, the alkyl halide's reactivity is mainly dependent on how stable a carbonium ion it can form. We expect the most reactive to be
(A) CH_3X
(B) C_2H_5X
(C) R_2CHX
(D) R_3CX
(E) benzyl halide

90. Of the following, the statement that is *least* true of the first transition series of metals Sc-Zn, atomic numbers 21-30, is that
(A) they have unfilled 3d orbitals
(B) they form colored ions
(C) they possess characteristic metallic properties
(D) they have approximately the same atomic radii
(E) their oxides form strongly basic solutions in water

91. Pauling's electronegativity values for elements are useful in predicting
(A) coordination numbers
(B) dipole moments
(C) polarity of molecules
(D) position in the E.M.F. series
(E) the microwave spectrum

92. The directional character of covalent bonds of the sp^3 hybrid orbital types is
(A) planar
(B) square
(C) tetrahedral
(D) triangular
(E) octahedral

93. The structure of the ammonia molecule is probably
(A) planar
(B) linear
(C) pyramidal
(D) square
(E) tetrahedral

94. When more than an equimolecular amount of Ag^+ is added to a solution of $Cr(H_2O)_4Cl_3$, only 1/3 of the chloride is precipitated. This generally occurs because
(A) insufficient Ag^+ was added
(B) the temperature was too high
(C) inadequate mixing of the solution has been done
(D) two chloride atoms were held in a stable complex
(E) the reaction has not been completed

95. A confirmatory test frequently used for the nitrate ion involves the formation of which one of the following?
(A) a white precipitate
(B) an odorless gas
(C) a brown ring
(D) a purple layer
(E) a yellow layer

96. The removal of electrons from atoms is best described quantitatively in terms of
(A) bond energy
(B) electron affinity
(C) electronegativity
(D) ionization potential
(E) valence bond

97. The degree of ionic character in a chemical bond is best determined from its
(A) boiling point
(B) degree of ionization in a suitable solvent
(C) rotational spectrum
(D) melting point
(E) dipole moment

98. Hydrogen gas may be dried most readily in the laboratory by passing it through a tube containing which one of the following?
(A) $CaCO_3$
(B) $Ca_3(PO_4)_2$
(C) $CaCl_2$
(D) $Ca(OH)_2$
(5) $MgCl_2$

99. Which one of the following is a compound most likely to have a dipole moment?
(A) CS_2
(B) H_2S
(C) SO_3
(D) $SnCl_4$
(E) CCl_4

100. Compared with the alkaline earth metals the alkali metals exhibit
(A) greater hardness
(B) higher melting points
(C) smaller ionic radii
(D) lower ionization energies
(E) higher boiling points

101. Of the following devices, the one that is NOT a particle accelerator (atom smasher) is the
(A) cyclotron
(B) synchrotron
(C) linear accelerator
(D) thiatron
(E) bevatron

102. The ability of an ion to polarize or deform another ion with which it comes in contact will be greatest if it has
(A) high ionic charge and large radius
(B) high ionic charge and small radius
(C) low ionic charge and large radius
(D) low ionic charge and small radius
(E) neutral charge and large radius

103. Of the following, the ion that is *least* likely to form a complex with ammonia is
(A) Cu^{++}
(B) Mg^{++}
(C) Ni^{++}
(D) Ag^{+}
(E) Na^{+}

104. The reaction $C_{12}H_{26} \rightarrow C_6H_{12} + C_6H_{14}$ represents which one of the following?
(A) substitution
(B) synthesis
(C) cracking
(D) polymerization
(E) addition

105. Of the following, the compound with the lowest boiling point is
(A) ethyl chloride
(B) propyl chloride
(C) butly chloride
(D) amyl chloride
(E) methyl chloride

106. The Law of Conservation of Energy as applied to chemical reactions is implicit in the statement of a principle attributed to which one of the following scientists?
(A) Carnot
(B) Hess
(C) Le Chatelier
(D) Ostwald
(E) Fourier

107. In the reaction $A_{2(g)} + 2B_{2(g)} \rightleftarrows 2AB_{2(g)} +$ Heat, the equilibrium can be shifted to the left by
(A) decreasing the pressure and decreasing the temperature
(B) increasing the pressure and increasing the temperature
(C) decreasing the pressure and increasing the temperature
(D) increasing the pressure and decreasing the temperature
(E) adding more A_2 gas

108. The polarograph is an instrument used in the study of which one of the following?
(A) chemical composition
(B) chromatography
(C) dipole moments
(D) optical activity
(E) phosphorescence

109. When a liquid boils, there is, at the boiling point, an increase in
(A) entropy
(B) heat of vaporization
(C) free energy
(D) vapor pressure
(E) potential energy

110. Of the following, the gas having a diffusion rate three times as rapid as that of steam is (At. Wgts: C-12, H-1; O-16; He-4)
(A) helium
(B) hydrogen
(C) carbon dioxide
(D) methane
(E) carbon monoxide

111. A magnet will cause the greatest deflection of a beam of
(A) gamma rays
(B) neutrons
(C) electrons
(D) positrons
(E) alpha particles

112. Methyl alcohol and air passing through a heated tube containing a mixture of iron powder and molybdenum oxide forms

(A) carbon monoxide
(B) ethanol
(C) carbon dioxide
(D) formaldehyde
(E) acetaldehyde

113. The uncancelled spin of an unpaired electron in the atom of silver explains its
(A) paramagnetism
(B) ferromagnetism
(C) diamagnetism
(D) electrical conductivity
(E) antiferromagnetism

114. When iodine reacts with H_2S producing free sulfur, the reaction shows that
(A) sulfur is a stronger oxidizing agent than iodine
(B) sulfur has the same molecular structure as iodine
(C) H_2S is an oxidizing agent
(D) S^{-2} can be reduced to free sulfur
(E) iodine may be regarded as a stronger oxidizing agent than sulfur

115. Molecules of nitrogen tetroxide, N_2O_4, are
(A) yellow
(B) brown
(C) green
(D) colorless
(E) paramagnetic

116. It has been experimentally determined that in a molecule of water the bond angle between the two hydrogen atoms which are attached to a single oxygen atom is closest to which one of the following?
(A) 45 degrees
(B) 90 degrees
(C) 105 degrees
(D) 180 degrees
(E) 109 degrees

117. Glucose and fructose differ structurally in that glucose is a (an)
(A) aldehyde and fructose is an ether
(B) ketone and fructose is an aldehyde
(C) aldehyde and fructose is a ketone
(D) ketone and fructose is an ether
(E) amide and fructose is an acid

118. Diffusion occurs most rapidly in which one of the following?
(A) solids
(B) liquids
(C) gases
(D) gels
(E) colloidal particles

119. When titrating a weak base with a strong acid, the most suitable of the following indicators to use is
(A) phenolphthalein
(B) methyl orange
(C) brom thymol blue
(D) litmus
(E) p-nitrophenol

120. Heavy water made from $_1H^3$ and $_8O^{18}$ has a molecular weight of
(A) 18
(B) 20
(C) 22
(D) 24
(E) 26

121. If the solubility product of $BaSO_4$ is $1.5x10^{-9}$, its solubility in water is
(A) $1.5x10^{-9}$ moles per liter
(B) $3.9x10^{-5}$ moles per liter
(C) $7.5x10^{-5}$ moles per liter
(D) less than in dilute sulfuric acid
(E) $1.5x10^{-5}$ moles per liter

122. According to the orientation rules in organic chemistry, ortho-para directing groups are generally
(A) positive atoms or groups
(B) unsaturated groups
(C) molecules which are deactivated
(D) groups which decrease the electron density around the m position
(E) negative atoms or groups

123. Considering energy levels, the most probable electronic configuration for element No. 28 would be which one of the following?
(A) 2, 8, 18
(B) 2, 8, 10, 8
(C) 2, 8, 8, 8, 2
(D) 2, 8, 16, 2
(E) 2, 8, 9, 9

124. From the second law of thermodynamics, at at constant T and P, when only PV work is permitted, the condition of equilibrium is that the Gibbs' free energy is
(A) a constant
(B) increasing

124.
(C) decreasing
(D) a maximum
(E) a minimum

125. In an irreversible work cycle, the entropy is
(A) increased
(B) decreased
(C) a constant
(D) a minimum
(E) a maximum

126. At the triple point of a substance, the degree of freedom is
(A) four
(B) three
(C) two
(D) one
(E) zero

127. The coefficient of viscosity has the dimensions of
(A) $m^{-2}lt$
(B) $ml^{-1}t^{-1}$
(C) mlt^{-1}
(D) $m^{-1}lt$
(E) lt^{-1}

To answer Questions 128 and 129, use the following information:

	E°, volts
$H_2 = 2H^+ + 2e^-$	0.00
$Ag + I^- = AgI + e^-$	− 0.15

128. The E.M.F. of the cell
H_2 | HI soln. || AgI | Ag
is
(A) + 0.75 volts
(B) − 0.15 volts
(C) + 0.15 volts
(D) indefinite
(E) − 0.30 volts

129. The E.M.F. of the cell
H_2 | HI(0.01M) || AgI | Ag | AgI || HI(0.001M) || H_2 is approximately
(A) 2x0.0591
(B) − 0.0591
(C) + 0.591
(D) 0.0296
(E) − 0.1082

130. In the mass spectrometer, the basic method is called direction focusing. The method brings one of the following properties to a sharp focus.
(A) the same q of the ions
(B) the same M of the ions
(C) the same velocity of the ions
(D) the same isotope of an element
(E) the same q/M of the ions

131. The Planck radiation distribution law could be applied to evaluate
(A) the temperature at the surface of the sun
(B) the E.M.F. of the electric cell
(C) the average velocity of a molecule in the gas
(D) the efficiency of the heat engine
(E) the degree of freedom in some phase diagram

132. The triplet state of a molecule means the molecule has
(A) an unpaired electron
(B) been in the vibrational excited state
(C) been in the rotational excited state
(D) two paired electrons in the electronic excited state
(E) two spin-parallel electrons in the electronic excited state

133. A solution is made by dissolving 1.69 g NaCl in 870 g H_2O. Its molality is
(A) 1.00
(B) 10.0
(C) $1.0x10^{-6}$
(D) $1.50x10^{-5}$
(E) $3.3x10^{-2}$

134. At 24°C, the Henry's law constant for neon in water is $9.14x10^{7}$. If the pressure of the neon gas above the water is 724 Torr, it would dissolve in 10000g H_2O about
(A) $6.6x10^{-2}$g
(B) $9.14x10^{-7}$g
(C) 1.00 g
(D) $1.56x10^{-5}$g
(E) 10.0 g

135. The solubility product of Ag_2S which is brown in color is 10^{-12}. The K_{sp} for $Al(OH)_3$ is 5×10^{-33}. When a dilute solution of K_2S is added to a beaker containing AgC1, the precipitate changes in color from white to brown. The saturated solution formed when solid $Mg(OH)_3$ is shaken with water is less basic

than the saturated solution formed when $Al(OH)_3$ is shaken with water. The water solution in equilibrium with solid Ag_3PO_4 has 4 times the concentration of silver ion as the water solution in equilibrium with AgCl. On the basis of these facts, list the following substances in order of their decreasing solubility in water: Ag_2S, $Al(OH)_3$, AgCl, $Mg(OH)_3$ and Ag_3PO_4.

(A) AgCl, Ag_2S, Ag_3PO_4, $Al(OH)_3$, $Mg(OH)_3$
(B) Ag_2S, AgCl, Ag_3PO_4, $Mg(OH)_3$, $Al(OH)_3$
(C) Ag_3PO_4, AgCl, Ag_2S, $Al(OH)_3$, $Mg(OH)_3$
(D) AgCl, Ag_2S, $Al(OH)_3$, $Mg(OH)_3$, Ag_3PO_4
(E) Ag_2S, AgCl, Ag_3PO_4, $Al(OH)_3$, $Mg(OH)_3$

136. In polagraphy, calculations can be made from graphs of

(A) current vs. density
(B) current vs. volume
(C) current vs. voltage
(D) voltage vs. density
(E) voltage vs. volume

137. What is the maximum concentration of calcium ions that can be present in a liter of solution containing 3.0 moles of F^- ions? ($K_{sp} = 3.95 \times 10^{-11}$).

(A) 4.39×10^{-11}
(B) 1.09×10^{-12}
(C) 1.09×10^{-11}
(D) 4.39×10^{-12}
(E) none of the above.

138. Of the following sets of hydroxides, which are amphoteric?

(A) $Co(OH)_2$, $Zn(OH)_2$, $Al(OH)_3$
(B) $Al(OH)_3$, $Ni(OH)_2$
(C) $Al(OH)_3$, $Zn(OH)_2$
(D) $Ni(OH)_2$, $Co(OH)_2$
(E) $Co(OH)_2$, $Ni(OH)_2$, $Zn(OH)_2$

139. In a laboratory, a student performed a flame test with a green flame resulting. What element did he probably have?

(A) sodium
(B) potassium
(C) calcium
(D) barium
(E) tin

Given the following ions: Fe^{+++}, Ni^{++}, Pb^{++}, Cu^{++}, Hg^{++}, Cd^{++}.
Answer questions 140 and 141 on this basis.

140. What is the least number of reagents needed to separate these ions into groups?

(A) 1
(B) 2
(C) 3
(D) 4
(E) 5

141. Using H_2S as a reagent, a yellow ppt. was obtained. The cation was

(A) Cd^{++}
(B) Pb^{++}
(C) Cu^{++}
(D) Ni^{++}
(E) Fe^{+++}

142. In choosing an indicator, which of the following factors need not be considered?

(A) the pH at the equivalent point
(B) the pH range of the indicator
(C) the direction of titration
(D) the color of the indicator
(E) the equivalent weight of the indicator

143. Electrophoresis is a technique used for
(A) pyrolysing organic compounds with an electric current
(B) degradation of a compound by passing a current through a solution of it
(C) separation of a mixture of charged particles by the application of an electrical potential
(D) condensation of an aerosol with an electric spark
(E) deactivation of a thermally excited molecule by electrical discharge

144. Which of the following is used for the location of amino acids on a paper chromatograph

(A) phenetole

(B) hydrazine
(C) semicarbazine hydrochloride
(D) piperylene
(E) ninhydrin

145. What is the product of the reaction

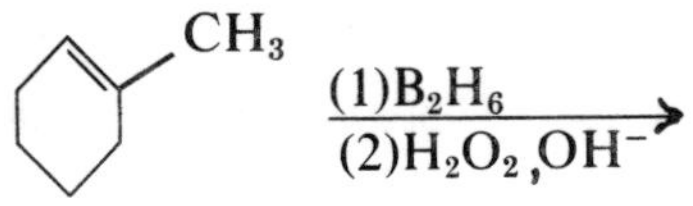

1-methylcyclohexene (CH_3) $\xrightarrow[(2)H_2O_2,OH^-]{(1)B_2H_6}$

(A) 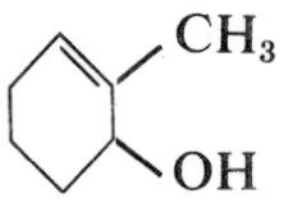 CH_3, OH
(B) 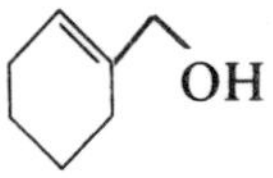 OH
(C) 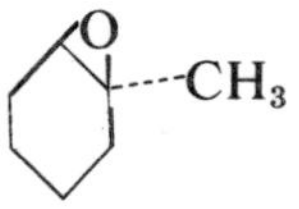 O, CH_3
(D) 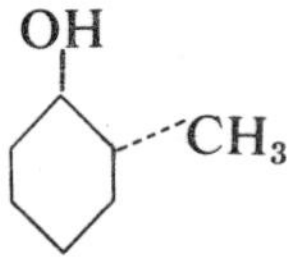 OH, CH_3
(E) 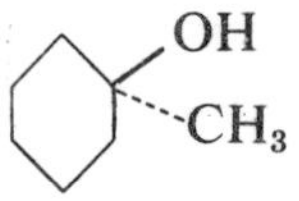 OH, CH_3

146. Allylic bromination of olefins is usually carried out with

(A) phenylmagnesium bromide
(B) pyridine perbromide
(C) α, α-dibromosuccinic acid
(D) N-bromosuccinimide
(E) α-bromotoluene

147. 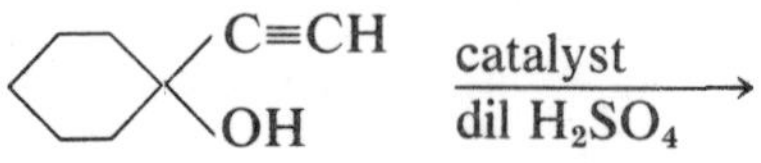 1-ethynylcyclohexanol ($C{\equiv}CH$, OH) $\xrightarrow[\text{dil } H_2SO_4]{\text{catalyst}}$

cyclohexanol bearing $\overset{O}{\overset{\|}{C}}$–CH, OH

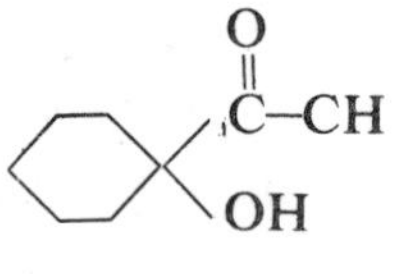

The catalyst for this reaction is

(A) Al_2O_3
(B) CuO
(C) HgO
(D) MnO_2
(E) OsO_4

148. For $CH_3{-}CH_2{-}CO{-}OAg + Br_2 \longrightarrow$ Product

The product is

(A) $CH_3{-}\underset{Br}{CH}{-}\overset{O}{\overset{\|}{C}}{-}OAg$
(B) $CH_3{-}CH_2{-}\overset{O}{\overset{\|}{C}}{-}Br$
(C) $CH_3{-}CH_2{-}CBr_2{-}OAg$
(D) $CH_3{-}CH_2{-}CH_2Br$
(E)  cyclopropane with Br, Br

149. DNA molecules contain nitrogenous bases linked to other constituents of the molecule. Which of the following is not found in DNA?

(A) guanidine
(B) thymine
(C) adenine
(D) guanine
(E) cytosine

150. In the Dumas method for determining the nigrogen content of an organic compound, the nitrogen is determined in the form of

(A) sodium cyanide
(B) gaseous ammonia
(C) cuprous cyanide
(D) gaseous nitrogen
(E) ammonium sulfate

END OF ADVANCED TEST (5) IN CHEMISTRY

ANSWER KEY TO ADVANCED TEST 5 IN CHEMISTRY

In order to help pinpoint your weaknesses, the specific area of each question is indicated in parentheses after the answer. Refer to textbooks and other study material wherever you have an incorrect answer.

Area Code

ORGANIC CHEMISTRY = O
INORGANIC CHEMISTRY = I
ANALYTICAL CHEMISTRY = A
PHYSICAL CHEMISTRY = P

1. D(P)
2. E(P)
3. C(P)
4. C(P)
5. D(P)
6. B(P)
7. A(O)
8. E(O)
9. D(O)
10. E(O)
11. A(O)
12. A(O)
13. A(O)
14. E(O)
15. B(O)
16. D(O)
17. E(P)
18. A(P)
19. E(P)
20. D(P)
21. E(P)
22. B(P)
23. A(P)
24. B(P)
25. E(O)
26. A(O)
27. C(I)
28. E(I)
29. D(I)
30. C(I)
31. D(I)
32. E(I)
33. A(I)
34 B(A)
35. B(P)
36. D(P)
37. E(O)
38. A(O)
39. C(O)
40. E(O)
41. E(O)
42. A(O)
43. B(O)
44. D(O)
45. E(O)
46. A(O)
47. E(P)
48. C(P)
49. D(P)
50. E(P)
51. C(P)
52. C(P)
53. A(P)
54. B(O)
55. E(O)
56. C(O)
57. A(O)
58. E(P)
59. D(P)
60. A(P)
61. C(P)
62. B(I)
63. A(I)
64. D(O)
65. E(O)
66. A(O)
67. E(I)
68. B(I)
69. C(O)
70. E(I)
71. D(O)
72. C(O)
73. A(O)
74. B(O)
75. B(P)
76. E(P)
77. E(O)
78. E(I)
79. D(I)
80. A(O)
81. E(O)
82. C(O)
83. C(I)
84. D(I)
85. E(P)
86. C(I)
87. C(O)
88. B(O)
89. E(O)
90. E(I)
91. C(P)
92. C(I)
93. C(I)
94. D(I)
95. C(I)
96. D(P)
97. E(P)
98. C(I)
99. B(P)
100. D(I)
101. D(P)
102. B(P)
103. E(I)
104. C(O)
105. E(O)
106. B(P)
107. C(P)
108. A(A)
109. A(P)
110. B(P)
111. C(P)
112. D(O)
113. A(P)
114. E(I)
115. B(I)
116. C(I)
117. C(O)
118. C(P)
119. B(A)
120. D(I)
121. B(I)
122. E(O)
123. D(I)
124. E(P)
125. A(P)
126. E(P)
127. B(P)
128. C(P)
129. B(P)
130. E(P)
131. A(P)
132. E(P)
133. E(I)
134. A(P)
135. A(A)
136. C(A)
137. D(A)
138. C(A)
139. D(A)
140. B(A)
141. A(A)
142. E(A)
143. C(O)
144. E(O)
145. D(O)
146. D(O)
147. C(O)
148. D(O)
149. A(O)
150. D(O)

Explanatory Answers for Advanced Test 5

1. **(D)** In Bohr units, the ratio of magnetic moment to angular momentum is equal to the g factor. For an electron, the magnetic moment is one Bohr magneton and the spin angular momentum is ½. Therefore the g factor is equal to 2.

2. **(E)** The only difference between the electron or Bohr magneton and the nuclear magneton is that m, the mass of the electron, is replaced by M, the proton mass.

3. **(C)** A free radical has one unpaired electron and a net spin angular momentum of ½ and a g factor of 2.

4. **(C)** In electron spin resonance, an external magnetic field is applied which is strong enough to uncouple the orbital and spin angular momentums and hence is an example of the Paschen-Back effect.

5. **(D)** The free radical peak will be split into four lines by interaction of the electron magnetic moment with the magnetic moments of the three equivalent hydrogen nuclei.

6. **(B)** The orbital angular momentum is zero in an s orbital and the spin angular momentum of the electron is ½.

7. **(A)** Terpenes, found in the essential oils of plants, have carbon skeletons of isoprene units joined in the regular head-to-tail fashion.

8. **(E)** One mole of solute in 1000g of camphor lowers the freezing point by 39.7°. Such a large cryoscopic constant makes molecular weight determinations convenient.

9. **(D)** In general, the greater the molecular weight or the larger the molecule, the greater the surface area and hence the greater the intermolecular forces which means a higher melting point. Thus the xylenes are expected to have a higher melting point than methane or butane. *p*-Xylene has the highest melting point because it exhibits a greater symmetry and hence fits into a crystal lattice more easily resulting in a more stable lattice.

10. **(E)** Compounds derived by replacing one or more of the methyl hydrogens in toluene, $C_6H_5CH_3$ are called benzyl if one methyl hydrogen is replaced, benzal if two are replaced, and benzo if all three are replaced.

11. **(A)** Dehydration proceeds with a carbonium ion mechanism and occurs more readily for those compounds which form the more stable carbonium ion. Therefore, the tertiary alcohol will dehydrate more readily than the other alcohols listed.

12. **(A)** In the Lucas test, alcohols are mixed with hydrochloric acid in the presence of zinc chloride and the type of alcohol is determined by the rate of formation of the alkyl chloride. Primary alcohols do not react with hydrochloric acid.

13. **(A)** The iodoform test consists of treating alcohol with sodium hypoiodite. Only those alcohols with the structure

$$\begin{array}{c} \text{H} \\ | \\ \text{R}-\text{C}-\text{CH}_3 \\ | \\ \text{OH} \end{array}$$

will give a positive test which is the formation of the yellow precipitate of iodoform, CHI_3.

14. **(E)** α-halogenation of aliphatic acids occurs with the use of phosphorus as the catalyst and is called the Hell-Volhard-Zelinsky reaction.

15. **(B)** Esterification of acids proceeds by the following reaction involving an alcohol:

$$RCOOH + R'OH \overset{H^+}{\rightleftharpoons} RCOOR' + H_2O$$

16. **(D)** The Haworth synthesis of naphthalene derivatives starts with benzenes and succinic anhydride and proceeds through stages of ring closure and aromatization using such familiar reactions as Friedel-Crafts acylation and Clemmensen reduction.

17. **(E)** The free energy change for a reaction is merely equal to the difference between the free energies of formation of the products and the reactants. Recalling that the standard free energies of formation of elemental forms are zero, the result for the equation indicated is

$$+(-94.3)+0-(-54.6)-(-32.8)=-6.9 \text{ kcal}$$

18. **(A)** The standard free energy change for a reaction is a measure of the deviation from equilibrium and is often called the driving force of the reaction. If the free energy change is zero, the system is in equilibrium. If the free energy change is negative the reaction can proceed spontaneously and net work can be abstracted from the system.

19. **(E)** See Explanation 18.

20. **(D)** As explained in 17, the free energy change for the reaction is

$$+(+36.0)+2(0)-(-4.1)=+40.1 \text{ kcal}$$

21. **(E)** The entropy change for the reaction

$$H_2(g)+\tfrac{1}{2}\,O_2(g)\rightarrow H_2O(g)$$

is $+(45.1)-(31.2)-\tfrac{1}{2}(49.1)$
$=-10.6$ cal/mole-deg.

22. **(B)** Using the equation

$$\Delta F=\Delta H-T\Delta S$$

and the result of 21, the enthalpy of formation of H_2O is found to be

$$-54.6+298(-10.6\cdot 10^{-3})=-57.8 \text{ kcal/mole}$$

23. **(A)** By convention, S_0, the entropy at absolute zero is taken to be zero for all crystalline elements. Since only entropy differences are examined in chemical problems, the actual value of the constant S_0 is of no significance because it cancels out in all calculations.

24. **(B)** Hydrogen atoms in crystal structures are difficult to locate by x-ray or electron diffraction because scattering of hydrogen is small compared to that of heavier nuclei. But the hydrogen nucleus is a strong scatterer of neutrons and may be studied by neutron diffraction.

25. **(E)** The structure of acrylic acid is

$$CH_2{=}CH-COOH$$

26. **(A)** Addition of HBr to

$$H_2C{=}CH-\overset{\displaystyle CH_3}{\underset{\displaystyle CH_3}{C}}-CH_3$$

proceeds with the formation of a secondary carbonium ion, but a 1,2 shift of a methyl group results in a more stable tertiary carbonium ion so that this shift is expected to occur.

27. **(C)** The dissociation of ClF_3 into ClF_2^+ and $ClF_4^=$ is less likely because Cl is too small for four partially charged fluorine atoms to crowd around.

28. **(E)** ClO_3F has a tetrahedral structure with the chlorine atom as the central atom.

29. **(D)** Chlorine and nitrogen have electronegativities closest to hydrogen so that there will be the least charge separation in compounds (C) and (D), but (D) will be the least polar of the two because the negative charge must be shared among four rather than three oxygen atoms and each Cl-O bond will be less polar.

30. **(C)** The structure of the isocyanate ion is

$$[C{=}N{=}O]^-$$

31. **(D)** The pseudohalogens which are a small class of singly negatively charged groups (as isocyanate in 30) exhibiting many similarities to halide ions, react with hydrogen to form acids which are much weaker than the halogen acids.

32. **(E)** The order of electron orbitals after 5p is 6s, 4f, 5d. After barium, in which the 6s level is filled, lanthanum adds a 5d electron. The succeeding 14 elements, the lanthanides, add 4f electrons until this shell is filled with lutetium. After lutetium, the rest of the 5d electrons are added.

33. **(A)** In going across the lanthanide series, the atomic radii decrease from 1.06A for lanthanum to .85A for lutetium.

34. **(B)** The solubility product for the reaction
$$CaC_2O_4 \rightleftharpoons Ca^{++} + C_2O_4^{--}$$
is given by
$$Ksp = [Ca^{++}]\,[C_2O_4^{--}] = 2.6 \cdot 10^{-9}$$
If the concentration of calcium ions is .02 m/l, then $1.3 \cdot 10^{-7}$ m/l of oxalate ion is needed before a precipitate will begin to form.

35. **(B)** The impedance, Z, of the circuit is given by
$$Z = [R^2 + (\omega L - \frac{1}{\omega C})^2]^{1/2}$$
Where R is the resistance, ω L is the inductive reactance, and $\frac{1}{\omega C}$ is the capacitive re-

reactance.

36. **(D)** The Tyndall effect is observed when light is scattered by small particles and it is frequently used to detect the presence of suspended particles in solution.

37. **(E)** The benzidine rearrangement is a conversion of a diazo compound, Ar-NH-NH-Ar′, to a biphenyl compound, NH_2-Ar-Ar′-NH_2.

38. **(A)** Upon oxidation with H_2O_2, azo compounds, Ar-N=N-Ar′, are converted to azoxy compounds, Ar-N$\overset{\to O}{=}$N-Ar′.

39. **(C)** The Diels-Alder reaction is represented below

40. **(E)** The reaction of a γ-hydroxy acid to form a γ-lactone is shown below

$$\underset{\displaystyle OH}{RCHCH_2CH_2COOH} \underset{OH^-}{\overset{H^+}{\rightleftharpoons}} \text{(γ-lactone: } H_2C\text{–}C(=O)\text{–O–CHR–}H_2C\text{)}$$

Similarly a δ-hydroxy acid forms a δ-lactone (six-membered ring).

41. **(E)** Pyrrole is the weakest base because the lone pair of electrons on the nitrogen atom is involved in the π electron cloud and cannot easily be shared with acids. This is not true of pyridine.

42. **(A)** The simplest example of the Skraup synthesis, the preparation of quinoline, is illustrated by the reaction

C_6H_5-NH_2 + CH_2OH–CHOH–CH_2OH + $C_6H_5NO_2$

(*aniline*) (*glycerol*)

$\xrightarrow[\text{heat}]{H_2SO_4,\ FeSO_4}$ quinoline + $C_6H_5NH_2 + H_2O$

(*quinoline*)

43. **(B)** The structure of pyrrole is

It is the only five-membered ring of the compounds listed.

44. **(D)** DNFB, 2,4-dinitrofluorobenzene, attacks the free amino group at the end of the peptide and yields a dinitrophenyl acid which can be separated and identified.

45. **(E)** Keto-enol tautomerism of this type usually favors the structure in which the hydrogen atom is bonded to the carbon rather than to a more electronegative atom.

46. **(A)** In dicarbonyl compounds such as aceto-acetaldehyde, the enol form may be stabilized by formation of an intramolecular hydrogen bond between the enolic hydrogen and the second carbonyl group.

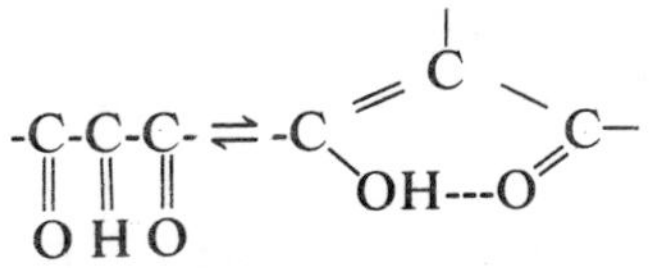

```
                      |
                      C
                  //     \
-C-C-C- ⇌ -C              C-
 ||  |  ||      \        //
 O  H  O         OH---O
```

Keto form   Enol form

47. **(E)** The potential energy of the proton in a magnetic field H_o is given by

$$U_m = uH_o = -m_n g_n B_n H_o$$

Since the nuclear spin may be aligned either parallel or antiparallel to the magnetic field, u may equal $+2{\cdot}79B_n$ or $-2{\cdot}79B_n$ where B_n is the nuclear magneton ($5.05{\cdot}10^{-24}$ erg gauss^{-1}). Therefore the energy spacing between the two levels is

$$\Delta E_k = (2{\cdot}79B_nH_o) - (-2{\cdot}79B_nH_o)$$
$$= 2(2{\cdot}79)(5.05{\cdot}10^{-24}) - (104)$$
$$= 28.2{\cdot}10^{-20} \text{ erg}$$

and the NMR frequency is

$$\gamma = \Delta E_k/h = \frac{28{\cdot}2{\cdot}10^{-20}}{6.6{\cdot}10^{-27}} = 42.6 \text{ mc}$$

48. **(C)** For the dueteron, μ is equal to +0.86, 0 and −0.86 for m_n equal to +1, 0 and −1 respectively.

$$\Delta E_m = (0.86B_nH_o) - (0) = 0.86B_nH_o$$
$$\frac{\Delta E_k}{\Delta E_m} = \frac{2(2.79)B_nH_o}{0.86\,B_nH_o} = 6.5$$

49. **(D)** The spectrum for a radical with two equivalent hydrogen atoms will consist of three peaks equally spaced and with intensities in the ratio of 1:2:1. Hence total splitting will be 8 gauss.

50. **(E)** For the three proton system, m_n may take on the values +3/2, +1/2, −1/2 and −3/2) There are three possible combinations of orientations of proton spins which yield $m_n = +½$ and $m_n = -½$. Therefore, the ratio of intensities will be 1:3:3:1.

51. **(C)** A nucleus of spin I has 2I +1 possible orientations of the nuclear spin in an external magnetic field.

52. **(C)** Here, it is given that 2I +1 is equal to 4. It follows that I = 3/2.

53. **(A)** The allowed energy levels for a rigid rotor are

$$E_r = \frac{h^2J(J+1)}{8\pi^2I} = BJ(J+1)$$

where B is called the rotational constant.

54. **(B)** Pyruvic acid is an α-keto acid and only **(B)** of the compounds listed fits this description.

55. **(E)** The Claisen condensation for preparing β-keto esters is illustrated below for the specific case of the preparation of ethyl acetoacetate:

$$2CH_3COOC_2H_5 + Na^{+-}OC_2H_5 \xrightarrow{C_2H_5OH}$$

$$CH_3COCH_2COOC_2H^-{}_5Na^+ + C_2H_5OH$$

$$\downarrow H^+$$

$$CH_3COCH_2COOC_2H_5$$

(ethyl acetoacetate)

56. **(C)** This is the Reformatsky reaction and the general reaction is shown below

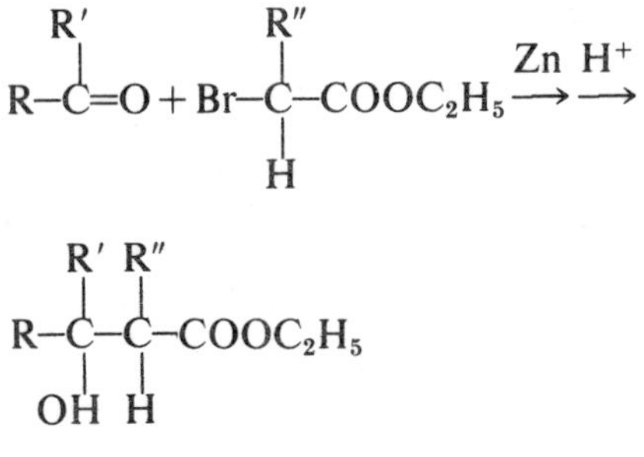

```
   R'         R''
   |          |               Zn  H+
R—C=O + Br—C—COOC2H5 ——→ ——→
              |
              H

   R' R''
   |  |
R—C—C—COOC2H5
   |  |
   OH H
```

57. **(A)** The structure of glyceraldehyde is shown below with the asymmetric carbon atom indicated by (*).

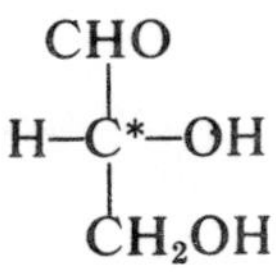

```
   CHO
   |
H—C*—OH
   |
   CH2OH
```

58. **(E)** The rotational energy levels are (see Explanation 53)

$$E = BJ(J+1)$$

Transitions between these levels are subject to the selection rule. $\Delta J = \pm 1$. Therefore the energy for a transition between adjacent rotational levels is

$$\Delta E = BJ(J+1) - B(J-1)(J) = 2JB$$

Consider two adjacent lines from the spectrum

$$\Delta E = 118\ cm^{-1} = 2JB$$

$$\Delta E' = 135\ cm^{-1} = 2J'B = 2(J+1)B$$

$$\Delta E' - \Delta E = 17\ cm^{-1} = 2B$$

$$B = 8.5\ cm^{-1}$$

59. **(D)** $E = BJ(J+1) = 8.5(10)(11) = 935\ cm^{-1}$

60. **(A)** $\Delta E = 2JB = 169\ cm^{-1}$

$$J = 169/2(8.5) = 10$$

$$J-1 = 9$$

61. **(C)** The entropy is a state function and the entropy of a given state is a certain value independent of how that state was reached. In completing a reversible cycle, the final state is identical to the initial state and the entropy change is zero.

62. **(B)** In a trigonal bipyramidal field (D_{3h} symmetry), the five d orbitals will split into a non-degenerate A_2'' level, a two-fold degenerate E' level and a two-fold E'' level.

63. **(A)** Adjacent bonds and lone election pairs will repel each other and spread out as much as possible in order to form a more stable molecule.

64. **(D)** The reaction described is the aldol condensation and is illustrated by the general reaction.

$$>C{=}O + -\underset{H}{\overset{|}{C}}-\overset{|}{C}{=}O \xrightarrow[\text{or base}]{\text{acid}} -\underset{HO}{\overset{|}{C}}-\overset{|}{\underset{|}{C}}-\overset{|}{C}{=}O$$

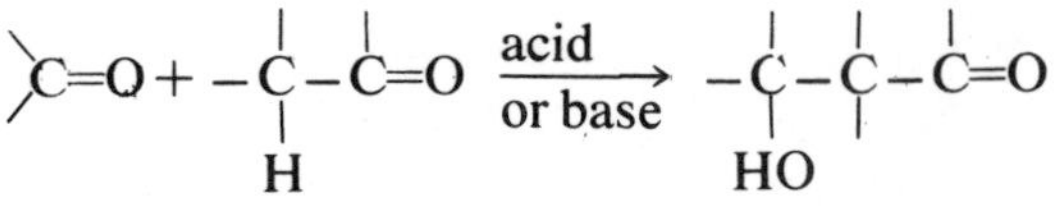

65. **(E)** This is another example of the aldol condensation, this time between two ketone molecules.

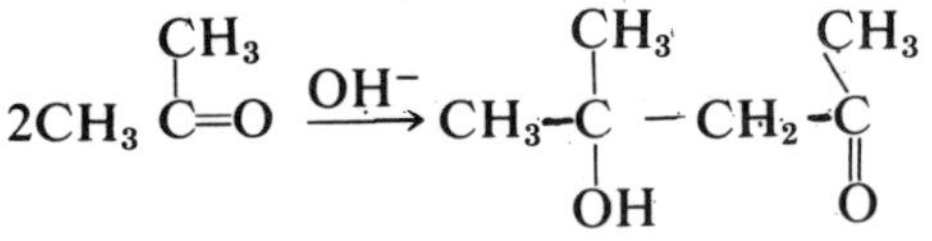

$$2CH_3\overset{CH_3}{\overset{|}{C}}{=}O \xrightarrow{OH^-} CH_3-\underset{OH}{\overset{CH_3}{\overset{|}{\underset{|}{C}}}}-CH_2-\underset{O}{\overset{CH_3}{\overset{\backslash}{\underset{\|}{C}}}}$$

66. **(A)** This reaction is called the Perkin condensation and, as shown by the general reaction, yields an additional acid derived from the anhydride

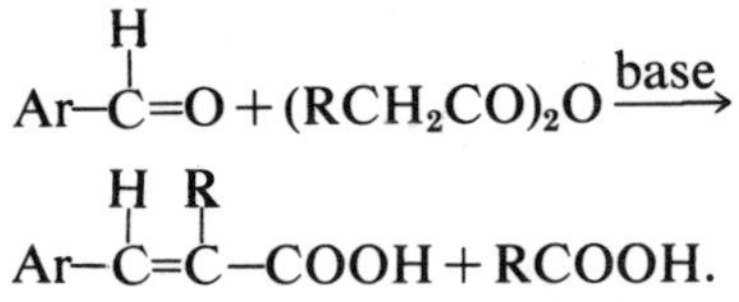

$$Ar-\overset{H}{\overset{|}{C}}{=}O + (RCH_2CO)_2O \xrightarrow{\text{base}}$$

$$Ar-\overset{H}{\overset{|}{C}}{=}\overset{R}{\overset{|}{C}}-COOH + RCOOH.$$

67. **(E)** Among the suggested answers, SO_4^{--}, CO_3^{--} and SO_3^{--} would give a white precipitate with Ba^{++}

However, on acidification with HC1, the SO_4^{--} precipitate would remain undissolved, the CO_3^{--} precipitate would evolve CO_2, and the SO_3^{--} precipitate would dissolve.

68. **(B)** Both Pb^{++} and Bi^{+++} belong in group II of the analytical table, and both sulfides are precipitated by the addition of H_2S in 0.3 N HCl to a solution of their salts.

69. **(C)** There are five different structural isomers of hexane:

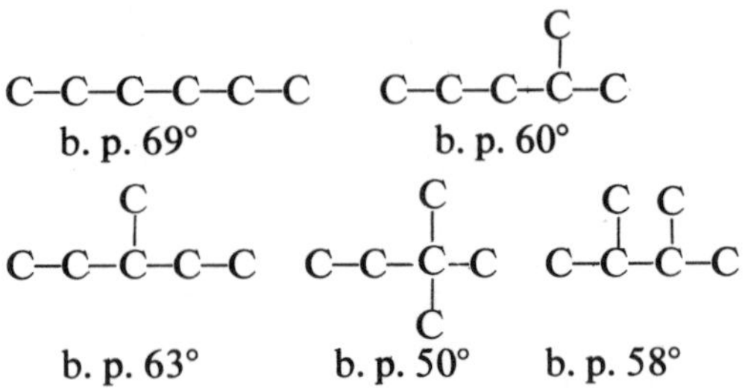

C–C–C–C–C–C (b. p. 69°)

C–C–C–C(C)–C (b. p. 60°)

C–C–C(C)–C–C (b. p. 63°)

C–C–C(C)(C)–C (b. p. 50°)

C–C(C)–C(C)–C (b. p. 58°)

70. **(E)** When a mixture containing CuS and HgS is treated with a few drops of 6M HNO_3, the CuS is dissolved as $Cu(NO_3)_2$, whereas

the HgS remains as a black precipitate, or is converted to a white precipitate of 2HgS, $Hg(NO_3)_2$,which may be colored yellow by traces of elemental sulfur.

71. **(D)** The hydrolysis of a cyanide leads to the production of a carboxylic acid:

$$R\text{–}CN + 2H_2O \xrightarrow{H^+} R\text{–}COOH + NH_3$$

72. **(C)** The following is the structure of 2, 2-dimethyl-4-ethylhexane:

```
    C
    |
C–C–C–C–C–C
    |     |
    C     C
          |
          C
```

73. **(A)** Because they are more strained than the other cycloalkanes, cyclopropane bonds are more easily broken by hydrogenation than are those of the other cyclic alkanes.

74. **(B)** Diethyl ether presents the greatest potential fire hazard. Being the most volatile, it can spread the fire more easily than the others. Also, it can be very readily oxidized to the highly explosive diethyl peroxide.

75. **(B)** The bond energy of the hydrogen molecule, or the energy that has to be supplied to break the molecule into its constituent atoms, is equal to the energy released when two atoms of hydrogen combine to form a molecule.

76. **(E)** By sp^2 hybridization, carbon, in the form of graphite, exists in flat aromatic layers, in which each carbon atom has a coordination number of 3. These layers are loosely held together by forces of the van der Waals type.

77. **(E)** Carboxylic esters react with two moles of Grignard reagents to form tertiary alcohols:

$$R\text{–}CO\text{—}OR' + R''MgX \rightarrow R\text{–}CO\text{–}R'' + XMg\text{–}OR'$$

$$R\text{–}CO\text{–}R'' + R''MgX \rightarrow R\text{–}C(R'')_2\text{–}OMgX$$

$$R\text{–}C(R'')_2\text{–}OMgX + H^+ \rightarrow R\text{–}C(R'')_2\text{–}OH + MgX^+$$

78. **(E)** Alkali acetylides can usually be hydrolized by water to give acetylenes and alkali hydroxides, showing that the equilibrium, $H-C\equiv C-Na + H_2O \rightleftharpoons H-C\equiv C-H +$ NaOH lies to the right. In effect, water is more acidic than acetylene. One could also come to the same conclusion by reasoning that, because oxygen is more electronegative than nitrogen and carbon, a hydrogen atom bound to oxygen should more readily form a proton than one bound to either carbon or nitrogen.

79. **(D)** The strongest base would, on protonation, yield the weakest acid. Among R-COOH, H_2O, NH_3, RH, and ROH, the weakest acid is obviously RH, since a hydrogen bound to carbon would be less easily lost as a proton than one bound to the more electronegative nitrogen and oxygen. Thus, RH is the weakest acid, and R^- is the strongest base.

80. **(A)** In the Williamson synthesis, an alkyl halide is allowed to react with a sodium alkoxide or phenoxide to yield either a symmetrical or an unsymmetrical ether:

$$R-X + NaOR \rightarrow R\text{–}O\text{–}R + NaX$$

$$R\text{–}X + NaOAr \rightarrow R\text{–}O\text{–}Ar + NaX$$

81. **(E)** p-Dichlorobenzene, Cl–C_6H_4–Cl, is a systemmetrical molecule, and is not expected to have a dipole moment.

82. **(C)** The reaction of alkyl halides with alcoholic silver nitrate can be looked upon as an electrophilic bimolecular displacement of the alkyl group on the halide by the positively charged silver ion:

$$R-I + Ag^+ \rightarrow R\ldots \overset{+}{I}\ldots Ag \rightarrow R^+ + AgI$$

Therefore, the halide which is largest and most easily polarizable would give the greatest ease of reaction.

83. **(C)** The Law of Multiple Proportions states that when two elements form more than one compound, the weights of one element combined with an arbitrarily fixed weight of the other element are in ratios of simple whole numbers.

In compound A, 3 parts by weight of Y combine with 2 parts by weight of X.

In compound B, 3 parts by weight of Y combine with 1 part by weight of X; or 6 parts of Y to 2 parts of X.

Therefore, the ratio of Y in A to that in B is 1 to 2.

84. **(D)** Because of the electronic configurations of the alkali metals and the halogens, compounds between the two classes of elements would be expected to be ionic. Thus, the particles would be held together by strong electrostatic forces. Such salts should, therefore, have high melting points, and the energy required to break down the ordered crystal lattices should be reflected in their large heats of fusion. A solvent like water, with high dielectric constant, would solvate the resulting ions, and the salts are expected to be soluble in water. The nature of the ionic lattice is such that there should be no free electrons that can conduct electricity in the solid state. However, in the molten state, the resulting stable ions would lead to good conduction of electricity.

85. **(E)** The ionization of a metal involves the removal of electrons from the outermost valence orbital. The resulting ion, left now with inner filled orbitals, has a smaller radius than the atomic radius of the metal.

86. **(C)** The faraday is the quantity of electricity required to cause the chemical alteration of 1 gram equivalent of matter at each electrode.

If one considers the reaction, $Ag^+ + e^- \rightarrow Ag$, then one mole of silver would be deposited by 1 mole of electrons, or 1 faraday.

87. **(C)** First-order kinetics in the solvolytic reaction can be visualized according to the following scheme:

$$\text{H}-\underset{\text{C}_6\text{H}_{13}}{\overset{\text{CH}_3}{\text{C}}}-\text{Br} \underset{}{\overset{\text{slow}}{\rightleftharpoons}} \text{(H)(CH}_3\text{)}\overset{+}{\text{C}}\text{(C}_6\text{H}_{13}\text{)} + \text{Br}^-$$

$$\text{(H)(CH}_3\text{)}\overset{+}{\text{C}}\text{(C}_6\text{H}_{13}\text{)} \xrightarrow{\text{fast } H_2O} \text{H}-\underset{\text{C}_6\text{H}_{13}}{\overset{\text{CH}_3}{\text{C}}}-\text{OH} + \text{H}^+$$

The slow step in this scheme is the formation of the carbonium ion which reacts in a fast step to yield the alcohol. Since the carbonium ion is flat and accessible to attack from both sides, the resulting alcohol would be completely racemic. However, there seems to be a slight net inversion in configuration. This is explained by the postulation that the departing bromide renders its side of the flat carbonium ion slightly less accessible to attack than the other side.

88. **(B)** The path of an S_N2 reaction is:

$$\text{R}_1-\underset{\text{R}_3}{\overset{\text{R}_2}{\text{C}}}-\text{X} + \text{Y}^- \rightarrow {}^{\delta-}\text{Y}\text{----}\underset{\text{R}_3}{\overset{\text{R}_1\ \text{R}_2}{\text{C}}}\text{----X}^{\delta-} \rightarrow \text{Y}-\underset{\text{R}_3}{\overset{\text{R}_1}{\text{C}}}-\text{R}_2 + \text{X}^-$$

Since the transition state is more crowded than the starting material, bulky groups would tend to retard the reaction—an effect referred to as steric hindrance.

89. **(E)** Among the factors that contribute to carbonium ion stability are (a) the possibility of resonance, and (b) the relief of steric strain.

Thus, a tertiary carbonium ion is more stable than a secondary carbonium ion, which is more stable than a primary carbonium ion. However, the resonance stabilization resulting from conjugation with a phenyl ring far outweighs the contributions from two additional alkyl groups, so that a benzyl cation is more stable than a tertiary cation with three alkyl substituents.

90. **(E)** Although the oxides of the first transition series of metals are basic, they are generally insoluble in water, and do not form strongly basic aqueous solutions. The group of metals whose oxides give strongly basic solutions are the alkali metals.

91. **(C)** Electronegativity is a measure of an element's electron affinity. Thus a scale of electronegativities would indicate the relative attraction which two atoms exert on the electron pair of a bond between them. This would allow prediction of the direction of polarization in the bond.

92. **(C)** sp^3 hybridization in carbon involves a mixing of the 2s orbital with the 2p orbitals to form four equivalent orbitals. Since the electron pairs in each orbital repel one another, the most stable configuration of the four equivalent orbitals is the one in which they are as far as possible from one another. The only way to satisfy this requirement and still preserve the equivalence of the orbitals is to place them in a tetrahedral orientation.

93. **(C)** The hybridization involved in the nitrogen of ammonia is similar to that of carbon in methane—sp^3. Three of the four sp^3 orbitals each contains one electron which is used to form a bond with hydrogen. The fourth orbital contains an unshared electron pair. Thus, looking only at the atoms, the nitrogen occupies the apex of a triangular pyramid. Actually, for ammonia, there is rapid inversion of the pyramid at ordinary temperatures:

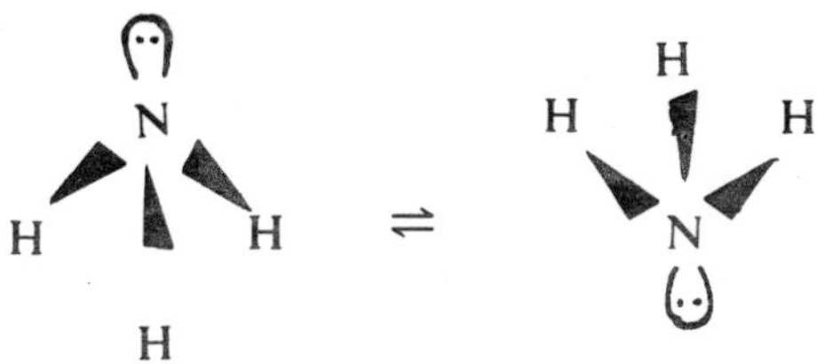

94. **(D)** In $Cr(H_2O)_4Cl_3$, the central chromium atom is coordinated to six ligands—four molecules of water and two chloride ions—arranged in an octahedral configuration around the metal ion. The third chloride ion is not involved in this coordination and is available in the solution to be precipitated with Ag^+ ions.

95. **(C)** The brown ring test is a good confirmatory evidence for the nitrate ion. It involves mixing the material with excess concentrated sulfuric acid, cooling, and then pouring ferrous sulfate solution carefully down the side of the test tube so as to form a layer on the surface of the sulfuric acid. A brown ring at the junction of the liquids indicates the presence of nitrate ion. This ring is due to the formation of the double compound, $FeSO_4$. NO.

96. **(D)** Because elements differ in their nuclear charges, and the shielding by inner orbitals of the outermost orbital, the ease of removal of an electron from the outermost orbital varies from one element to another. This ease of removal is measured in terms of the ionization potential, which is defined as the amount of work required to move an electron from the atom to an infinite distance. This is a measure of the attractive force between the nucleus and the outermost electron. On the other hand, the electronegativity of an atom is a measure of the attractive force between the atom and an incoming electron.

97. **(E)** The existence of a dipole between two chemically bonded atoms suggests an unequal sharing of the electron pair in the bond. This unequal sharing is what is meant by the ionic character of the bond, and is thus measurable in terms of the dipole moment.

98. **(C)** Among the compounds mentioned $CaCl_2$ is the only one that is used as a drying agent. It is easily hydrolyzed by water to give slaked lime and hydrochloric acid. Other useful drying agents are P_2O_5, Na_2SO_4, and $MgSO_4$.

99. **(B)** A linear symmetrical molecule like CS_2 cannot have a dipole moment. Also, the tetrahedral symmetry of CCl_4 and $SnCl_4$ precludes their possession of dipole moments. SO_3 is planar, with O-S-O bond angles of 120°. Like water, H_2S is non-linear, and has a dipole with the negative end directed towards the sulfur.

100. **(D)** In the alkali and alkaline earth metals, the outermost valence orbital is an s orbital. However, each alkaline earth metal has one more proton in its nucleus than the corresponding alkali metal. Since the nuclear charge is greater for the alkaline earths, the amount of work required to remove an electron from the valence orbital is larger for the alkaline earths than it is for the alkali metals. That is, the ionization potentials of the alkali metals are lower than those of the corresponding alkaline earth metals.

101. **(D)** A cyclotron is a magnetic resonance particle accelerator. "Bevatron" is the colloquial name for the 6 Bev proton synchrotron

at the University of California, Berkeley. There is a two-mile linear accelerator at Stanford University. There is currently no particle accelerator called a "thiatron."

102. **(B)** The ability of an ion to polarize another ion would depend on how strong an electric field that ion can set up at the position of the other ion. All else being equal, the field set up by an electric charge is directly proportional to the magnitude of the charge. Also, since the polarizing effects caused by a nucleus are opposed to those due to the orbital electrons, the effect of the nucleus would be most felt if the electrons were held close to the nucleus, rather than away from it where their opposing effect would be larger. That is to say, polarizing ability would be larger for smaller ionic radii.

103. **(E)** Ammonia complexes of metals involve the donation of the unshared electron pair on nitrogen to low-lying empty orbitals on the metal. The strongly electropositive sodium atom has no such low-lying orbitals in its ionic state. Therefore, the ion has very little affinity for extra electrons, and would not form an ammonia complex.

104. **(C)** The process whereby large hydrocarbons are broken up into smaller ones mainly by the action of heat is known as pyrolysis or cracking. It is widely used in the petroleum industry.

105. **(E)** Within any homologous series, boiling points and melting points increase with increasing molecular weight. Methyl chloride, the smallest member of the series, would have the lowest boiling point.

106. **(B)** Hess's Law states that the amount of heat evolved during the formation of a given substance is the same whether the compound is formed directly all at once or slowly in a series of intermediate stages. If the heat of formation were dependent on route, then it would be possible to contravene the law of conservation of energy and create energy by coupling two different routes in a cyclic process.

107. **(C)** The reaction as written shows that three volumes of reactants yield two volumes of product. That is, in going from left to right, there is a decrease in volume. Also, since heat evolution accompanies the forward reaction, the reverse reaction would be accelerated by heating. Thus, the reaction would be driven from right to left if the temperature is raised and the pressure is decreased to accommodate an increase in volume.

108. **(A)** Different ions in solution require different potentials to undergo oxidation or reduction. The polarograph is an instrument used to determine the redox potentials of ions in solution, and is so used in the study of the chemical composition of substances.

109. **(A)** By definition, the boiling point of a liquid is the temperature at which its vapor pressure is equal to the surrounding pressure. Therefore at constant ambient pressure, the vapor pressure of a liquid remains constant at its boiling point. Also, the heat of vaporization of a liquid depends only on temperature, and remains constant at the boiling point. By definition also, $\Delta S = \Delta H/T$, where ΔH is the heat of vaporization, and T is the boiling point in degrees Kelvin. Since both ΔH and T are positive, it can be concluded that the entropy rises when a liquid boils. However, $F = H - TS$. Therefore, at constant T, $\Delta F = \Delta H = T\Delta S = \Delta H - T\Delta H/T = 0$; and the free energy remains constant when a liquid boils.

110. **(B)** Graham's Law of gaseous diffusion states that the rate of diffusion at constant temperature and pressure is inversely proportional to the square root of the molecular weight.

Therefore, if steam diffuses at the rate of x liter/min., then a gas that diffuses three times as fast as steam has a molecular weight given by the following relationship:

$$x = k/\sqrt{18}$$

$$3x = k/\sqrt{M}$$

And $$\sqrt{M} = k/3x = k/3(k/\sqrt{18})$$

$$= \sqrt{18}/3$$

Therefore, $M = [\sqrt{18}/3]^2 = 18/9 = 2.$ and the gas is Hydrogen.

111. **(C)** The deflection suffered by a particle in a magnetic field is proportional to the magnetic moment of the particle. Since, with subatomic particles, this latter property is inversely related to mass, the electron has a much higher moment than the proton, neutron, or alpha particle. Gamma rays, being electromagnetic, do not possess magnetic moments.

112. **(D)** A mixture of iron and molybdenum oxide causes the dehydrogenation of alcohols. Such dehydrogenation of methanol leads to the production of formaldehyde:

$$H_3C{-}OH \rightarrow H_2C{=}O + H_2$$

113. **(A)** A spinning electrical charge creates a magnetic field around itself. The presence of this unbalanced spin in the silver atom causes the resulting magnetic field to interact strongly with an external magnetic field with the electron assuming the more stable orientation within this external field. This is known as a paramagnetic interaction.

114. **(E)** The reaction between iodine and hydrogen sulfide is:

$$I_2 + H_2S = 2HI + S.$$

Thus, the iodine is reduced by H_2S, or the iodine acts as an oxidizing agent. Since the reverse reaction – the oxidation of HI by sulfur – does not occur to any appreciable extent, it can be concluded that iodine is a stronger oxidizing agent than sulfur.

115. **(B)** The brown gas produced when concentrated nitric acid reacts with heavy metals such as copper or zinc is N_2O_4, which results from the dimerization of NO_2.

116. **(C)** The H–O–H bond angle in water has been observed to be about 105°. Two explanations are commonly advanced for this observation. On the one hand, it is claimed that the oxygen undergoes sp^3 hybridization to give four equivalent tetrahedrally oriented orbitals. But because a non-bonding electron pair is more diffuse than the electron pair in a bond, the non-bonding pairs crowd the bonding pairs from the tetrahedral angle of 109.5° to the observed 105°.

On the other hand, it is claimed that there is no hybridization on oxygen, that p orbitals are used to bond to hydrogen, and that dipole-dipole interaction between the O–H bonds causes an expansion from the expected 90° to the observed 105°.

117. **(C)** Glucose can react with Benedict's and Fehling's solutions because it is a reducing sugar or aldohexose. Fructose does not react with these solutions because it is a ketohexose.

118. **(C)** Diffusion is a kinetic phenomenon. In solids and liquids, the forces binding molecules together are large, and the motion of individual molecules is hindered by the interaction with other nearby molecules. These forces are much smaller in gases, and the individual molecules are better able to move about. Gases, therefore, diffuse faster than liquids or solids.

119. **(B)** The salt formed from a strong acid and a weak base would form an acidic aqueous solution. Therefore, its neutralization pH would be lower than 7. An indicator that changes its characteristics at a pH range lower than 7 is, therefore, required for the titration. Such an indicator is methyl orange, which changes its color within the pH range 3.1 to 4.4.

120. **(D)** The molecular weight of a substance is the sum of the weights of its constituent atoms. Heavy water containing two ${}_1H^3$ and one ${}_8O^{18}$ would have a molecular weight of $3 + 3 + 18 = 24$.

121. **(B)** The solubility product of $BaSO_4$ is defined as:

$$K_{sp} = [Ba^{++}]\,[SO_4^{--}]$$

If $K_{sp} = 1.5 \times 10^{-9} = 15 \times 10^{-10}$, then
solubility $= \sqrt{K_{sp}}$
$= 3.9 \times 10^{-5}$

122. **(E)** Ortho-para directing groups in nucleophilic aromatic substitution are those which can push electrons by means of resonance into the ortho and para positions of the aromatic ring:

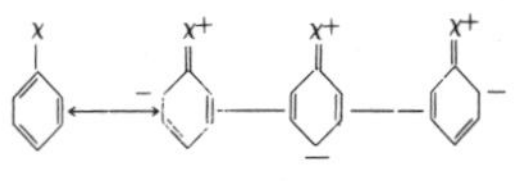

This can happen only if these groups are electron-rich or "negative."

123. **(D)** The aufbau principle states that orbitals are filled in the order of increasing energy. The 3d and 4s orbitals are of comparable energy. However, when there are more than two electrons to share between these levels, the 4s is usually first filled. Thus atom #28 would have the configuration:
$1s^2/2s^2,2p^6/3s^2,3p^6,3d^8/4s^2$; or, in terms of shells, 2,8,16,2.

124. **(E)** A spontaneous process is always accompanied by a negative change in the Gibb's free energy. Since a system spontaneously proceeds to equilibrium, its free energy would continue to decrease until it reaches a minimum at equilibrium.

125. **(A)** A reversible work cycle yields the maximum work, and is accompanied by a net entropy change of zero.

With an irreversible work cycle, however, some work is always converted to useless heat, so that the entropy of the system always rises.

126. **(E)** The triple point of a substance is that temperature and pressure at which liquid, solid and vapor are at equilibrium. Gibb's phase rule shows it to be an invariant point—that is, it has no degrees of freedom.

127. **(B)** For a fluid, the force required to move a layer of area A with a relative velocity v past another layer a distance d away can be shown to be:

$$F = nAv/d$$

where n is the viscosity coefficient.

Therefore, $n = dF/Av$

In dimensional units, this reduces to:

$$1 \times mlt^{-2}/1^2 \times 1t^{-1} = ml^{-1}t^{-1}$$

128. **(C)** In the left half of the cell, hydrogen is converted to H^+, and the resultant emf of the process is zero. At the right, Ag^+ is converted to Ag, with a resultant emf of +0.15 volt. The emf of the whole cell is the sum of the emf's of the two halves, and is equal to +0.15 volt.

129. **(B)** The cell as written is an electrolyte cell without transference, and its emf is given by the expression:

$$E = -(RT/F)\ \ln (c_1/c_2)$$

Therefore, $E = -(RT/F)\ \ln 0.01/0.001$
$= -0.0591$ volts.

130. **(E)** In direction focusing, a particle of mass M carrying a charge q is first accelerated through an electrical potential V and then deflected by means of a magnetic field H over a circular path of radius r. Accordingly, the following is true for the particle:

$$\frac{M}{q} = \frac{H^2r^2}{2V}$$

By keeping r and V constant and varying H, different values of M/q are brought to a focus at the collector.

131. **(A)** According to the Planck radiation distribution law, the density of radiant energy in unit volume in the frequency range f to (f + df) is given by the expression:

$$p(f)df = \frac{hf}{e^{hf/kT} - 1} \cdot \frac{8\pi f^2 df}{c^3}$$

In this equation, h is Planck's constant, k is Boltzmann's constant, c is the velocity of light, and T is measured in degrees Kelvin. Since all these quantities but T can be measured independently, it is possible to calculate the surface temperatures of remote bodies like the sun from the equation.

132. **(E)** For a system that contains one or more unpaired electrons, quantum mechanical principles show that the spin eigenvector can assume the values $-S, -S+1,$ ————, $S-1, S$, where S is the total spin of the system. There are, therefore, $2S+1$ eigenvalues for each S state, and the value $(2S+1)$ is known as the multiplicity of the system. When there are two unpaired electrons in a system, $S = 1$, and $(2S+1) = 3$. Such a system has a multiplicity of 3, and is said to be a triplet.

133. **(E)** The molality of a solution is the number of gram atoms of solute in 1000g of solvent. 1.69g of solute in 870g of water is equivalent to $1.69 \times 1000/870$ g of solute in 1000g of water. The gram molecular weight of NaCl is 58.5g. Therefore, 58.5g of NaCl in 1000g of water is 1 molal, and the molality of the given solution is:

$$\frac{1.69 \times 1000}{58.5 \times 870} = 3.3 \times 10^{-2} \text{ molal}$$

134. **(A)** Henry's Law for ideal solutions states that the mass of gas dissolved by a given volume of liquid at a given temperature is proportional to the pressure of gas with which it is in equilibrium.
If the Henry's law constant is 9.14×10^{-7} then 100g of water dissolve 9.14×10^{-7} g of neon at 1 Torr. Therefore, at 724 Torr, 10,000g of water would dissolve:

$$\frac{9.14 \times 10^{-7} \times 724 \times 10000}{1 \times 100} = 6.6 \times 10^{-2}\text{g}.$$

135. **(A)** Since the white precipitate of AgC1 changes to brown, we are allowed to assume that the new precipitate is Ag_2S. Thus Ag_2S is less soluable than AgC1. Even though the silver ion concentration for Ag_3PO_4 is four times that of AgCl, we must consider the K_{sp} of the substance.
Since the concentration of silver ion in AgCl must be greater than 10^{-6}, the K_{sp} for Ag_3PO_4 must be to the approximate order of 10^{-20}. Next we see that, since $Mg(OH)_3$ is less basic, it dissociates less and therefore has a smaller K_{sp}.

136. **(C)** Polagraphic graphs are current vs. voltage.

137. **(D)** The solubility product of CaF_2 is

$$K_{sp} = [Ca^{++}]\ [2\,F^-]^2 = 3.95 \times 10^{-11}$$

We can consider the total concentration of F^- to be 3 moles

$$[Ca^{++}] = \frac{3.95}{9.0} \times 10^{-11} = 4.39 \times 10^{-12}$$

138. **(C)** The hydroxides of aluminum, zinc, and chromium are amphoteric.

139. **(D)** Barium burns with a green flame.

140. **(B)** H_2S will separate the copper arsenic group (Cu^{++}, Cd^{++},Pb^{++}) from the rest. HC1 will separate the other two groups that are present.

141. **(A)** CdS is a yellow precipitate.

142. **(E)** All of these factors are important, depending upon the type of solution to be titrated.

143. **(C)** Electrically charged particles of different structures or sizes have different rates of migration under an applied electromotive force. The analytical technique which makes use of this property is known as electrophoresis.

144. **(E)** α-amino acids, and proteins or peptides which contain a free carboxylic acid group having an amino substituent, give a blue color when treated with a dilute solution of ninhydrin. One mole of carbon dioxide is produced for each mole of α-amino acid that reacts.

145. **(D)** Hydroboration of unsymmetrical cyclic ketones followed by oxidation with alkaline hydrogen peroxide leads to trans-2-alkyl cycloakanols. With 1-methyl-cyclohexene, therefore, the product is trans-2-methyl-cyclohexanol.

146. **(D)** N-bromosuccinimide, a free-radical brominating reagent, reacts with alkenes to yield allylic bromides—the Wohl-Ziegler reaction.

147. **(C)** Hydroxylation of terminal alkynes to yield methyl ketones is usually carried out with mercuric oxide as catalyst.

148. **(D)** Siver salts of carboxylic acids react with bromine to give carbon dioxide and alkyl or aryl bromide (the Hunsdiecker reaction).

149. **(A)** The four nitrogenous bases found in DNA are the two purines, adenine and guanine; and the two pyrimidines, cytosine and thymine. Guanidine, $H_2N\text{-}C\text{-}NH_2$, though basic, is not found in DNA.

150. **(D)** In the Dumas method for the determination of nitrogen, the weighed sample is mixed with powdered copper oxide in a tube and burned to give carbon dioxide, water and nitrogen. The vapors are then passed over hot copper gauze to reduce any oxides of nitrogen, and finally into a nitrometer containing potassium hydroxide solution. Thus, the determination is done with gaseous nitrogen.

ANSWER SHEET TEST (6)

No.	A	B	C	D	E	No.	A	B	C	D	E	No.	A	B	C	D	E	No.	A	B	C	D	E	No.	A	B	C	D	E
1						31						61						91						121					
2						32						62						92						122					
3						33						63						93						123					
4						34						64						94						124					
5						35						65						95						125					
6						36						66						96						126					
7						37						67						97						127					
8						38						68						98						128					
9						39						69						99						129					
10						40						70						100						130					
11						41						71						101						131					
12						42						72						102						132					
13						43						73						103						133					
14						44						74						104						134					
15						45						75						105						135					
16						46						76						106						136					
17						47						77						107						137					
18						48						78						108						138					
19						49						79						109						139					
20						50						80						110						140					
21						51						81						111						141					
22						52						82						112						142					
23						53						83						113						143					
24						54						84						114						144					
25						55						85						115						145					
26						56						86						116						146					
27						57						87						117						147					
28						58						88						118						148					
29						59						89						119						149					
30						60						90						120						150					

Advanced Test in Chemistry

(Sample 6)

Time: 3 hours

Directions: Select from the lettered choices that choice which best completes the statement or answers the question. Indicate the letter of your choice on the answer sheet.

1. Mercury formis amalgams with all but which one of the following?
(A) Ni
(B) Al
(C) Fe
(D) Zn
(E) Na

2. A suspension containing insoluble substances ZnS, CuS, HgS, Ag_2S and FeS is treated with 2N HCl: On filtering, the filtrate contained appreciable amounts of which one of the following groups?
(A) zinc and mercury
(B) silver and iron
(C) copper and mercury
(D) zinc and iron
(E) silver and copper

3. The compounds thioacetamide has been introduced into analytical chemistry to replace
(A) hydrogen sulfide
(B) dimethylglyoxime
(C) ammonium carbonate
(D) ammonium oxalate
(E) ammonium hydroxide

4. A common confirmatory test for the magnesium ion a sky-blue precipitate obtained by using one of the following reagents?
(A) benzil dioxime
(B) p-nitrobenzene azo resorcinol
(C) cupferron
(D) dimethylglyoxime
(E) thyroxine

5. Of the following, the reagent which can separate Fe^{+++} from Al^{+++} ions is
(A) KCNS
(B) NH_4OH
(C) $(NH_4)_2CO_3$
(D) NaOH
(E) H_2S

6. An alkali salt of palmitic acid is known as which one of the following?
(A) an alkaloid
(B) an alcoholate
(C) an ester
(D) a soap
(E) an epoxide

7. Of the metals listed below, the metal with highest melting point is
(A) titanium
(B) chromium
(C) molybdenum
(D) tungsten
(E) magnesium

8. Organic compounds of the type $RCONH_2$ are classified as
(A) amines
(B) amides
(C) ketones
(D) nitriles
(E) nitrosoniums

9. Aluminum carbide hydrolyzes to form which one of the following?
(A) CH_4
(B) C_2H_2
(C) CO_2
(D) CO
(E) C_2H_4

10. The congener of Gallium and Indium is which one of the following?
(A) Tb
(B) Th
(C) Tl
(D) Tm
(E) Ta

11. The number of carbon atoms in the cyclo-alkane of lowest molecular weight is
    (A) 3
    (B) 4
    (C) 5
    (D) 6
    (E) 7

12. Butyl alcohol, C_4H_9OH, is isomeric with
    (A) $C_3H_7COCH_3$
    (B) $C_2H_5COC_2H_5$
    (C) $CH_3COOC_2H_5$
    (D) $C_2H_5OC_2H_5$
    (E) $C_2H_5COOC_2H_5$

13. The structural formula for aspirin is
    (A) COOH
    O-C-CH_3
    ||
    O
    (B) COOH
    NH_2
    (C) NH_2
    SO-NH_2
    (D) 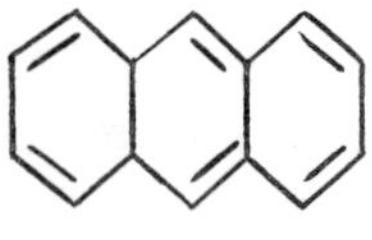
    (E) COOH
    O-C-CH_3
    ||
    O

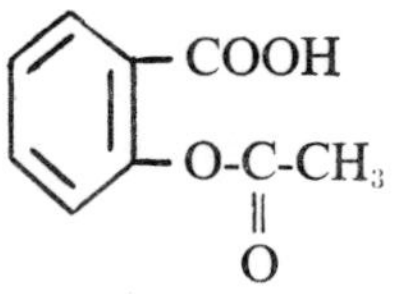

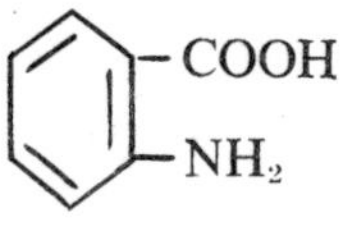

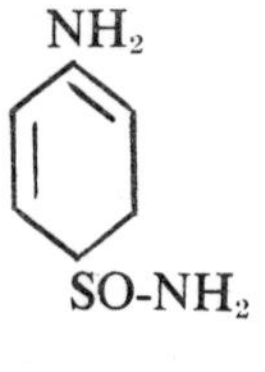

14. Which one of the following compounds is isomeric with urea?
    (A) ammonium cyanide
    (B) glycine
    (C) ammonium thiocyanate
    (D) thiourea
    (E) ammonium cyanate

15. The oxidation of secondary alcohols (general formula R_2CHOH) is used to prepare
    (A) aldehydes
    (B) ketones
    (C) hydrocarbons
    (D) esters
    (E) amides

16. Which one of the following statements is most in accord with the Pauli principle?
    (A) Four different quantum numbers are needed to describe each electron in an atom.
    (B) No more than one electron in an atom can have the same set of quantum numbers.
    (C) Eight electrons are needed to complete a shell.
    (D) Electrons must move in elliptical orbits.
    (E) Electrons have their own repulsion force.

17 The acid dissociation constants of H_2S and of HS^- are 10^{-7} and 10^{-13} respectively. The pH value in a 0.1 molar aqueous solution of H_2S is
    (A) 10^{-2}
    (B) 2
    (C) 3
    (D) 4
    (E) 5

18. Chlorination of a compound $C_{10}H_8$ produces two monochlorination compounds. How many dichloro products are there?
    (A) 3
    (B) 5
    (C) 7
    (D) 8
    (E) 9

19. The ionization potential of the He^+ ion compared to the ionization potential of the H atom (both species in the gaseous state) is
    (A) infinite
    (B) zero
    (C) same
    (D) greater
    (E) less

20. The molal constant-pressure heat capacity of gas at 298°K and 1 atom., in cal/deg-mole is about
(A) 2.98
(B) 4.97
(C) 11.75
(D) 8.90
(E) 6.85

21. From the collision theory of gas reactions, the collisions number of molecules is
(A) independent of the temperature
(B) linearly depend on the temperature
(C) proportional to the square root of the absolute temperature
(D) proportional to the cubic of the absolute temperature
(E) inversely proportional to the absolute temperature

22. Which molecule has the largest dipole moment?

(A) HCl
(B) H_2
(C) HI
(D) HBr
(E) HF

23. The moments of inertia of H_2S in gm-cm^2 are on the order of magnitude of

(A) 10^{-20}
(B) 10^{-30}
(C) 10^{-40}
(D) 10^{-50}
(E) 10^{-60}

24. The molarity of a solution of sodium chloride containing 100 gm of salt per 400 ml. of solution is about
(A) 1.71
(B) 0.25
(C) 4.27
(D) 58.50
(E) 0.50

25. At O°C and 1 atmosphere pressure, 49 ml. of oxygen and 23.5 ml of nitrogen will dissolve in 1 liter of water. The volume of air, in milliliters, under standard conditions that will dissolve in 1 liter of water is about
(A) 25.5
(B) 28.6
(C) 96.0
(D) 72.5
(E) 192.0

26. An element that has a specific heat of 0.113 cal/gm− C has an atomic weight of approximately
(A) 28
(B) 14
(C) 56
(D) 113
(E) 42

27. The principal product of the dehydration of 2-methyl pentanol-3 is which one of the following?

(A) 2-methyl pentene-1
(B) 2-methyl pentane
(C) 2 methyl-2 pentene
(D) 2 methyl-3 pentene
(E) methane

28. The relative unreactivity of the double bonds in the benzene ring has been explained by postulating which one of the following?
(A) optical isomerism
(B) ring contraction
(C) resonance
(D) hydrogen bonding
(E) hexagonal structure

29. The quantity 3.7×10^{10} disintegrations per second is known as which one of the following?
(A) Debye
(B) Rutherford
(C) Einstein
(D) Fermi
(E) Curie

30. In which one of the following groups do the elements show a complete transition from non-metallic to metallic character in both physical and chemical properties?
(A) III
(B) IV
(C) V
(D) VII
(E) I

31. Which one of the following orbital notations is used to represent

$^{39}_{19}K$?

(A) $ls^2\ 2s^2\ 2p^6\ 2d^{10}\ 2f^1$
(B) $Is^2\ 2s^2\ 2p^6\ 3s^9$
(C) $1s^2\ 2s^8\ 3s^9$
(D) $1s^2\ 2s^2\ 2p^6\ 3s^2\ 3p^6\ 4p^1$
(E) $1s^2 2s^2 2p^6 3s^2 3p^6 4s^1$

32. Of the following elements, the atom that contains the *least* number of neutrons is
(A) $^{235}_{92}U$
(B) $^{238}_{92}U$.
(C) $^{239}_{93}Np$
(D) $^{239}_{94}Pu$
(E) $^{240}_{93}Np$

33. Xenon, until recently thought to be inert, has been combined chemically with which one of the following?
(A) oxygen
(B) rubidium
(C) fluorine
(D) germanium
(E) chlorine

34. To which one of the following spectral ranges does a frequency of 10^{16} cycles/second belong?
(A) far infrared
(B) near infrared
(C) visible
(D) ultraviolet
(E) microwave

35. Which one of the following is a device to detect radioactive particles that incorporates a superheated liquid?
(A) spintharoscope
(B) cloud chamber
(C) bubble chamber
(D) scintillation counter
(E) spark chamber

36. K-capture refers to which one of the following?
(A) adsorption of potassium on palladium black
(B) reaction of potassium with other elements
(C) combination of a gamma ray and any K electron
(D) transfer of an electron to a K orbital
(E) combination of a nucleus with a K electron

37. The electron sub shell generally drawn as three mutually perpendicular double lobes is that known as
(A) p
(B) (z)g
(C) d
(D) f
(E) s

38. With which one of the following does hydrogen form ionic hydrides?
(A) most elements
(B) most of the active elements
(C) active metals
(D) active nonmetals
(E) non-active metals

39. If three liters of a solution of H_3PO_4 contain 294 grams of H_3PO_4, what is the normality of the solution?
Atomic weights: H = 1; O = 16, P = 31
(A) 0.1
(B) 1
(C) 3
(D) 9.8
(E) 5

40. If a concentrated solution of a certain salt has a vapor pressure that is lower than the partial pressure of water vapor in the air at the same temperature, the salt is likely to be
(A) deliquescent
(B) efflorescent
(C) effervescent
(D) unaffected by atmospheric components
(E) precipitated

41. In the following nuclear equation: the missing particle is a(n)

$$_{30}Zn^{68} + {}_{0}n^{1} \rightarrow {}_{28}Ni^{65} + ?$$

(A) neutron
(B) alpha particle
(C) beta particle
(D) positron
(E) electron

42. Of the following, the reagent commonly used to test for glucose is
(A) Lugol's solution
(B) Nessler's reagent
(C) tincture of iodine
(D) Van Slyke's reagent
(E) Benedict's solution

43. If 1 molal aqueous solutions of the following solutes are prepared and their boiling points are determined, the one with the highest boiling point would be
(A) $MgSO_4$
(B) $Al_2(SO_4)_3$
(C) K_2SO_4
(D) $C_6H_5SO_3H$
(E) $CaCl_2$

44. Of the following, the device that *cannot* detect radioactivity is a(n)
(A) spinthariscope
(B) electroscope
(C) ammeter
(D) photographic film
(E) cloud chamber

45. Of the following, which one is the property of K and Cl that determines the relative acidity of KOH and HOCl?
(A) electronegativity
(B) atomic radius
(C) oxidation potential
(D) melting point
(E) boiling point

46. Which one of the following represents the ratio of the rate of diffusion of oxygen to that of hydrogen?
(A) 1:1
(B) 1:2
(C) 1:8
(D) 1:4
(E) 1:3

47. Which one of the following is the freezing point of a solution of 30 gm of urea dissolved in 250 gm of water?
(A) – 0.52°C
(B) – 1.04°C
(C) – 1.86°C
(D) – 3.72°C
(E) – 0.01°C

48. A cylinder contains 0.3 mole of nitrogen, 0.1 mole of oxygen, and 0.1 mole of helium. If the total gas pressure equals 1 atmosphere, the partial pressure of oxygen, in mm. of Hg, is which one of the following?
(A) 304
(B) 380
(C) 456
(D) 760
(E) 152

49. Solutions of brown sugar can be decolorized best by passing them through which one of the following?
(A) coke
(B) carbon black
(C) animal charcoal
(D) graphite
(E) sodium chloride

50. Which one of the following is closest to the weight, in grams, of 1 liter of hydrogen (STP)?
(A) 0.01
(B) 0.1
(C) 1.0
(D) 22.4
(E) 273

51. Consider an electric dipole with a distance R between the ends. The force between the ends is inversely proportional to
(A) R
(B) R^2
(C) R^3
(D) R^4
(E) R^5

52. The magnitude of electric dipole is measured in the units of Debye, which is
(A) 10^{-10}esu–cm.
(B) 10^{-12}esu–cm.
(C) 10^{-14}esu–cm.
(D) 10^{-16}esu–cm.
(E) 10^{-18}esu–cm.

53. Potassium has body-centered cubic structure in solid metal. How many atoms are in a unit cell?
(A) 1
(B) 2
(C) 3
(D) 4
(E) 6

54. The magnetic moment is measured in the unit of Bohr magneton, which is about the order of
(A) 10^{-10} erg/gauss
(B) 10^{-16} erg/gauss
(C) 10^{-27} erg/gauss
(D) 10^{-5} erg/gauss
(E) 10^{-20} erg/gauss

55. Jahn-Teller effect is in the field of
(A) nuclear physics
(B) thermodynamics
(C) vibronic interaction
(D) kinetic theory of gas
(E) surface chemistry

56. If the probability, $P(E_i)$, of a system being in the ith state of energy E_i is $P(E_i)=\exp(-BE_i)/\sum_i \exp(-BE_i)$, the probability distribution is called
(A) Carnot
(B) Dirac
(C) Fermi
(D) Bose
(E) Boltzmann

57. The Beer's law is often used in
(A) opticochemical measurement
(B) thermochemistry
(C) radioactive dating
(D) electrochemistry
(E) polymer chemistry

58. Which of the following factors do *not* help determine the effectiveness of a bimolecular collision in bringing about a reaction?
(A) orientation of particles
(B) ease of energy dispersal
(C) quantum state
(D) activation energy
(E) inert material

59. From the kinetic theory of gases, the molecular dimension of Cl_2 could be roughly determined by gas viscosity measurement. Its value is about
(A) 10^{-5}cm
(B) 10^{-6}cm
(C) 10^{-7}cm
(D) 10^{-8}cm
(E) 10^{-9}cm

60. When the temperature increases, the surface tension of a film will usually be
(A) constant
(B) increased
(C) decreased
(D) changed indefinitely
(E) zero

61. The entropy of fusion of a monatomic solid is usually in the range of
(A) 10 to 20 cal/deg mole
(B) 20 to 30 cal/deg-mole
(C) 30 to 40 cal/deg-mole
(D) 40 to 50 cal/deg-mole
(E) 2.0 to 5.0 cal/deg-mole

To answer Questions 62 and 63, use the following information:

$$-\Delta F = RT \ln K$$

$$\frac{d(\ln K)}{dT} = \frac{\Delta H}{RT^2}$$

62. The standard free energy of liquid chlorine is 1146 cal/mole with respect to gaseous Cl_2. The saturated vapor pressure at 25°C will be
(A) 1 atm
(B) 2 atms
(C) 3 atms
(D) 0.5 atm
(E) 6.9 atms

63. The dissociation constant K of water at 1227°C is 1.90×10^{-11} and it is 3.90×10^{-19} at 727°C. The heat of the reaction $2H_2 + O_2 \rightarrow 2H_2O$ will be
(A) 5 kcal
(B) 10 kcal
(C) 50 kcal
(D) 110 kcal
(E) 1 kcal

64. Compound X has the formula C_8H_{10}. Nitration produces one mononitration product and three dinitration products. X could be
(A) ethylbenzene
(B) o-xylene
(C) p-xylene
(D) m-xylene
(E) octane

65. When solids are dissolved in water, the heat of solution depends on the relative magnitude of two energies which are
(A) dissociation and ionization energies
(B) lattice and vibrational energies
(C) dissociation and hydration energies
(D) lattice and ionization energies
(E) lattice and hydration energies

66. Acetylene has the point group
(A) C_{2h}
(B) C_{2v}
(C) $C_{\infty v}$
(D) $D_{\infty h}$
(E) D_{6h}

67. In the equilibrium reaction
$AX \rightleftharpoons A + X - y$ cal.
(1 vol.) (1 vol.) (1 vol.)
the equilibrium will be displaced toward the right by
(A) a decrease in temperature and pressure
(B) an increase in temperature and pressure
(C) an increase in temperature and a decrease in temperature
(D) an increase in pressure and a decrease in temperature
(E) an increase in volume

68. The empirical (simplest) formula of a compound containing 54.6% of carbon, 9.1% of hydrogen, and 36.6% of oxygen is
(A) C_3H_6O
(B) $C_4H_9O_2$
(C) $C_4H_8O_2$
(D) C_5H_9O
(E) C_2H_4O

69. At standard temperature and pressure, the density of CCl_4 vapor (At. Wgts:C = 12; Cl = 35.5) in grams/liter is
(A) 2.56
(B) 3.70
(C) 4.52
(D) 6.88
(E) 3.44

70. If the K_{sp} for CaC_2O_4 is $2.6x10^{-9}$, the concentration of oxalate ion needed to form a precipitate in a solution containing 0.02 moles per liter of calcium ions is
(A) $1.0x10^{-9}$
(B) $1.3x10^{-7}$
(C) $2.2x10^{-5}$
(D) $5.2x10^{-11}$
(E) $2.6x10^{-8}$

71. If a saturated solution of $La_2(C_2O_4)_3$ contains $1.1x10^{-6}$ moles/liter, the solubility product constant for this substance is
(A) $1.2x10^{-12}$
(B) $1.6x10^{-30}$
(C) $1.6x10^{-34}$
(D) $1.7x10^{-28}$
(E) $1.2x10^{-30}$

72. If 5.2 grams of non-volatile solute are dissolved in 125 grams of water and the boiling point of the solution was 100.78°C., the molecular weight of the solute is approximately
(A) 14
(B) 98
(C) 42
(D) 56
(E) 28

73. A catalyst employed in the Friedel-Crafts synthesis is
(A) sodium
(B) cuprous chloride
(C) zinc
(D) magnesium iodide
(E) aluminum chloride

74. Of the following, the only compound that does *not* contain a double or triple bond is
(A) H_2O
(B) HCN
(C) CO
(D) N_2
(E) C_2H_4

75. The maximum number of p-type orbitals possible in any sub-shell is
(A) 2
(B) 4
(C) 5
(D) 7
(E) 3

76. Of the following, the elements whose compounds are most often colored are the
(A) alkali metals
(B) alkaline earth metals
(C) halogens
(D) transition elements
(E) nitrogen series

77. The new international standard adopted for the determination of atomic weights is
(A) F^{19}
(B) O^{16}
(C) Ca^{40}
(D) H^1
(E) C^{12}

78. The theory postulating complete ionization of strong electrolytes was advanced by
(A) Arrhenius
(B) Ostwald
(C) Brönsted
(D) Debye and Huckel
(E) Lewis

79. Of the following, the element possessing the highest electro-negativity is
(A) lithium
(B) cesium
(C) oxygen
(D) astatine
(E)· fluorine

80. The Heisenberg principle postulates that
(A) the momentum and position of an electron cannot be known simultaneously
(B) two electrons may not occupy the same orbit
(C) for every proton there must exist an anti-proton
(D) every radioactive decay results in the production of isotopic lead
(E) the momentum and position of an electron can be known simultaneously

81. Van der Waal's forces between molecules increase with increasing
(A) temperature
(B) volume
(C) ionic radius
(D) ionization potential
(E) number of electrons

82. An atom containing an odd number of electrons is
(A) paramagnetic
(B) diamagnetic
(C) ferromagnetic
(D) hypermagnetic
(E) antiferromagnetic

83. The solid crystal NaCl belongs to the following structure:
(A) single cubic
(B) tetragonal
(C) monoclinic
(D) hexagonal
(E) triclinic

84. How many Bravais lattices can exist in nature?
(A) 7
(B) 17
(C) 32
(D) 5
(E) 14

85. In solids, Debye theory predicts that the heat capacity of a solid as a function of temperature should depend only on the characteristic temperature. Its value for various solids is in the range of
(A) 0.1 – 1.0
(B) 100 – 1000
(C) $10^3 - 10^4$
(D) $10^{-3} - 10^{-2}$
(E) $10^4 - 10^6$

86. The Born-Haber cycle is used in the field of
(A) heat engine
(B) refrigeration
(C) molecular determination
(D) solid state physics
(E) radiation chemistry

87. A device that measures the amount of incident radiation is called a (n)
(A) actinometer
(B) wave guide
(C) thermocouple
(D) refractometer
(E) polarograph

88. The energy (in eV) of a photon having a wavelength of 0.1A is
(A) 1ev
(B) 12.4 eV
(C) 124eV
(D) 0.12 eV
(E) $1.24\text{x}10^5$eV

89. One electron-volt (eV) is the energy obtained by an electron on passing a potential drop of 1 volt. It is equivalent to
(A) 1.60×10^{-9} erg
(B) 4.80×10^{-18} erg
(C) 1.60×10^{-12} erg
(D) 4.80×10^{-4} erg
(E) 6.62×10^{-27} erg

90. An electric current of 2,000 amp flows through a copper electrolyzer. In one hour we can obtain one of the following weights of copper:
(A) 10 g
(B) 50 g
(C) 100 g
(D) 500 g
(E) 2700 g

91. Silver is removed electrolytically from 200ml of a 0.1 N solution of silver nitrate by a current of 0.1 amp. How long will it take to remove half of the silver from the solution?
(A) 10 minutes
(B) 16 minutes
(C) 100 minutes
(D) 160 minutes
(E) 1000 minutes

92. Which one of the following compounds in the most acidic in the series?
(A) CH_3COOH
(B) CH_3CH_2OH
(C) $CH_2ClCOOH$
(D) $CHCl_2COOH$
(E) CCl_3COOH

93. 45 ml of lithium hydroxide were needed to completely neutralize 30 ml of 2M phosphoric acid. The molarity of the lithium hydroxide was
(A) 1.3
(B) 2.0
(C) 2.7
(D) 4.0
(E) 5.0

94. The formula for hydoxylamine hydrochloride is
(A) NH_2Cl
(B) $NH_4OH \cdot HCl$
(C) $NH_3OH^+ - Cl^-$
(D) $(NH_2Cl)\,OH$
(E) $NH_4OH \cdot HCl$

95. When 14 grams of phosphoric acid (Mol. Wgt =98) are dissolved in 250 grams of water, the resulting solution is
(A) 0.14 molar
(B) 0.19 normal
(C) 0.28 normal
(D) 0.57 molal
(E) 0.25 normal

96. If at standard temperature and pressure 25 liters of a gas weigh 50 grams, the molecular weight of the gas is closest to which one of the following?
(A) 22
(B) 34
(C) 45
(D) 56
(E) 90

97. The barium ion may be separated from strontium ions by employing
(A) Na_2CO_3 and HCl
(B) $K_4Fe(CN)_6$ and NH_4NO_3
(C) $(NH_4)_2CO_3$ and NH_4OH
(D) K_2CrO_4 and $HC_2H_3O_2$
(E) H_2S and HCl

98. The group reagent for the silver group in qualitative analysis is
(A) H_2S
(B) H_2S+NH_3
(C) $(NH_4)_2CO_3$
(D) HCl
(E) NaOH

99. Since lead has an atomic weight of 207.2 and a density of 11.4 g/c.c., its atomic volume is
(A) 1.13c.c.
(B) 9.1c.c.
(C) 18.2c.c.
(D) 36.4c.c.
(E) 1.82c.c.

100. A Tyndall effect would most likely be observed in which one of the following?
(A) solution
(B) precipitate
(C) sol
(D) solvent
(E) vapor

101. Assuming that n = principal quantum number, quantum mechanics postulates that the electron population of any energy level in an atom is limited to
(A) 2n
(B) n
(C) $2n^2+2$
(D) $2n^2-2$
(E) $2n^2$

102. The atom with atomic number 20 will most likely combine chemically with the atom whose atomic number is
(A) 14
(B) 10
(C) 11
(D) 21
(E) 16

103. As the atomic number of the elements in the second period of the periodic table increases, the ionization
(A) generally increases
(B) generally decreases
(C) first increases the decreases
(D) first decreases then increases
(E) keeps constant

104. The simplest crystalline symmetry for a solid is
(A) monoclinic
(B) rhombic
(C) tetragonal
(D) triclinic
(E) cubic

105. If a given substance can crystallize in two or more forms, it is called
(A) isotopic
(B) isomorphic
(C) isotropic
(D) polymorphic
(E) isotonic

106. The heat of crystallization is numerically equal to the heat of
(A) formation
(B) solution
(C) vaporization
(D) fusion
(E) sublimation

107. The inert gas with the lowest boiling point is
(A) helium
(B) radon
(C) xenon
(D) argon
(E) krypton

108. The formula for hydrazoic acid is
(A) HN_3
(B) H_3N
(C) HNO_2
(D) H_4N_2
(E) NH_2OH

109. In the reaction:
$2KMnO_4 + 16HCl \rightarrow 5Cl_2 + 2MnCl_2 + 2KCl + 8H_2O$
the reduction product is
(A) Cl_2
(B) HCl
(C) H_2O
(D) KCl
(E) $MnCl_2$

110. In the reaction:
$4P + 3KOH + 3H_2O \rightarrow 3KH_2PO_2 + PH_3$
(A) phosphorus is reduced only
(B) phosphorus is oxidized only
(C) phosphorus is neither oxidized nor reduced
(D) hydrogen has changed its valence state
(E) phosphorus is both oxidized and reduced

111. The transition element with the lowest atomic number is
(A) sodium
(B) actinum
(C) scandium
(D) lanthanum
(E) iron

112. Water at 100°C has a vapor pressure, expressed in mm. of Hg, equal to
(A) 100
(B) 0
(C) 760
(D) 1013
(E) 76

113. The conjugate base of H_3O^+ is
(A) H^+
(B) H_2O
(C) H_2O_2
(D) OH^-
(E) H

114. Of the following, the substance which has the highest boiling point is
(A) H_2Se
(B) H_2S
(C) H_2Te
(D) H_2O
(E) H_3N

115. The temperature of one liter of gas at constant pressure is changed from 0°C to 273°C. The new volume of gas, expressed in liters, is
(A) 1
(B) 0.5
(C) 2
(D) 2.5
(E) 3

116. In electrolysis, oxidation takes place at the
(A) anode
(B) cathode
(C) anode or cathode
(D) anode and cathode
(E) solution

117. The most basic species among the following is
(A) F^-
(B) OH^-
(C) NH^-_2
(D) CH^-_3
(E) H_2O

118. If an electron travels with a velocity of 1/100th the speed of light in the first Bohr orbit, its velocity (relative still to the speed of light) in the 5th Bohr orbit is
(A) 0.002
(B) 0.1
(C) 0.5
(D) 0.7
(E) 0.25

119. Which one of the following is a chemical name for the compound $(C_6H_5)_2AsCl$?
(A) phenyldichlorarsine
(B) diethyl chlorarsine
(C) ethyl dichlorarsine
(D) chloro-diphenyl
(E) diphenyl chlorarsine

120. From the vibration spectrum of HC1, we know the vibration frequency of $f=8.65x10^{13}$ sec^{-1}. The force constant of a harmonic oscillator with this frequency would be
(A) 4.0×10^2 dynes/cm
(B) 4.80×10^5 dynes/cm
(C) 4.80 dynes/cm
(D) 48 dynes/cm
(E) 4.80×10^{10} dynes/m

121. Microwave spectroscopy has a wavelength in or about the range from
(A) 10^{-8}cm to 10^{-6}cm
(B) 10^{-6}cm to 10^{-4}cm
(C) 1 mm to 1 cm
(D) 1 meter to 10 meter
(E) 10 meter to 10^3 meter

122. The radioactive decay process is an example of
(A) classical mechanic effect
(B) quantum tunnel effect
(C) Soret effect
(D) Pauli exclusion principle
(E) thermodynamic effect

123. The free radicals are very easily detected by which one of the following instruments?
(A) nuclear spin spectrometer
(B) coulometer
(C) calorimeter
(D) ion-exchange column
(E) electron spin spectrometer

124. The molecule ethane has a hinder rotation barrier which is about
(A) 0.5 Kcal/mole
(B) 1.0 Kcal/mole
(C) 1.5 Kcal/mole
(D) 3.0 Kcal/mole
(E) 10.0 Kcal/mole

125. The partition function is used in the field of
(A) Electrochemistry
(B) Statistical Mechanics
(C) Nuclear reaction
(D) Phase rule
(E) Photochemistry

126. The Miller indices are often used in the area of
(A) single crystal
(B) polymer
(C) solution
(D) surface chemistry
(E) molecular spectrum

Questions 127 and 128 make use of the following information:

Heat of fusion for ice at O°C=1436 cal/mole
H_2O (liquid) $C_P = 18$ cal/mole-deg
H_2O (solid) $C_P = 8.6$ cal/mole-deg
$dS=C_p/TdT$

127. The change in entropy (S) during the solidification of 1 mole of water at O°C is
(A) zero
(B) −10 cal/mole-deg
(C) −18 cal/mole-deg
(D) −9.4 cal/mole-deg
(E) +5.26 cal/mole-deg

128. The change in entropy during the solidification of 1 mole of super-cooled water at $-20°$ C is
(A) zero
(B) 18 cal/mole-deg
(C) +5.26 cal/mole-deg
(D) +6.00 cal/mole-deg
(E) −8.6 cal/mole-deg

129. Proteins play an important role in biochemistry. They usually consist of——— different amino acids.
(A) twenty-six
(B) fifteen
(C) ten
(D) three
(E) eight

130. An unknown oxidizing agent contains the element Y in the +5 state. If it takes 26.98ml of 0.1326N Na_2SO_3 to reduce $7.16x10^{-4}$ mole of $YO(OH)_2^+$ to a lower state, the final oxidation state of Y is

(A) −2
(B) −1
(C) zero
(D) +1
(E) +2

131. A 3.7818 g. sample of copper (50%) is dissolved in HNO_3 and diluted to 250 ml. If 25 ml of that solution required 50 ml. of thiosufate solution for titration of the liberated iodine, what is the copper titer of the thiosulfate solution?

(A) 3.78×10^{-2}
(B) 1.9×10^{-3}
(C) 3.78×10^{-3}
(D) 1.9×10^{-2}
(E) 3.78×10^{-4}

132. What is the normality of a 50% solution of acetic acid whose density is 1.00 g/ml?

(A) 10.0
(B) 5.0
(C) 6.23
(D) 8.47
(E) none of the above

133. In order to isolate the members of the arsenic subgroup, it is necessary to boil the group solution with H_2O_2 prior to precipitation with H_2S. The reason for this is

(A) to convert all the arsenite, H_3ArO_3, to arsenate, H_3ArO_4
(B) the insolubility of SnS in $(NH_4)_2S$
(C) the oxidation of arsenic to higher oxidation state so that it may react with $(NH_4)_2S$ to form complexes
(D) to regulate the acidic medium of the H_2S solution to insure ppt. of the correct cations
(E) the reduction of group members to lower oxidation states

134. Which statement is not true in regard to the properties of acid-base indicators?

(A) They are colored materials.
(B) They are weak acids and bases.
(C) The magnitude of their ionization constant determines the pH at which a color change will occur.
(D) In using an indicator, a large quantity should be used in order to clearly perceive the color change.
(E) Temperature is a factor in their titrations.

135. The Paneth-Fajans-Hahn law states when two or more types of ions are available for adsorption onto the surface of a colloid,

(A) the ion in greater concentration will be preferentially adsorbed
(B) a multicharged ion will be adsorbed more readily
(C) the ion with the ionic size as lattice ion will be adsorbed preferentially
(D) the ion which forms a compound with the lowest solubility with one of the lattice ions will be adsorbed preferentially
(E) the ion which has the lowest ionization potential will be adsorbed preferentially

136. The most significant factor in determining both the selectivity and overall extent of counter-ion adsorption is

(A) ionic concentration of the mother liquor
(B) ionic size factor
(C) Paneth-Fajans-Hahn law
(D) ionic charge
(E) temperature

137. Contamination of a ppt. due to post-precipitation,

(A) decreases with time
(B) decreases at higher temperature
(C) occurs only when contaminant is added after ppt. forms
(D) can be controlled by adjusting the pH of the solution prior to precipitation
(E) can be controlled by varying the concentration of the ppt. reagent

138. Two electrodes are immersed in a solution of $CdSO_4$ Possible factors determining whether concentration polarization will occur at the cathode are

I. rate of reaction of the cadmium at the electrode if no concentration polarization existed
II. rate at which Cd^{++} can move into the vicinity of the electrode from the bulk of the solution
III. temperature

The factor or factors which bring about concentration polarization is (are)
(A) I only
(B) II only
(C) III only
(D) I and II only
(E) I and III only

139. In titrating an acid, 20ml of a 0.01N NaOH solution were used to determine the equivalence point. The total volume at the equivalence point was 50ml. Which of the following indicators could be used to determine the equivalence point? (pH ranges are in the brackets.)

(A) picric acid (0.1-0.8)
(B) 2,6-dinitrophenol (2.0-4.0)
(C) congo red (3.0-5.0)
(D) methyl orange (3.2-4.4)
(E) bromocresol blue (3.8-5.4)

140. Represented below are successive steps in the ionization of phosphoric acid.
$H_3PO_4 \rightleftharpoons H^+ + H_2Po_4^-$ $K_1 = 7.52 \times 10^{-3}$
$H_2PO_4 \rightleftharpoons H^+ + HPo_4^{-2}$ $K_2 = 6.22 \times 10^{-8}$
$HPO_4 \rightleftharpoons H^+ + PO_4^{-3}$ $K_3 = 4.79 \times 10^{-13}$
A titration is carried out using NaOH. It is possible to measure the pK_2 of phosphoric acid by experimentally determining the pH's of the equivalence points of the first and second ionization. However the pK_1 cannot be so determined. The reason is that

(A) the concentration of $H_2PO_4^{-2}$ and H_3PO_4 can never be equal due to the large dissociation constant for the former
(B) it is impossible to measure the pK_1 because of the inaccuracy of measuring the pH of the first equivalence pt. due to the dissociation of $H_2PO_4^{-2}$
(C) the pH value equal to the pK_1 occurs at such a low pH that the addition of even small amounts of strong base will overshoot this point
(D) since one of the products in the titration is water, which is present in such large quantities, the K_1 cannot be measured
(E) NaOH is not a weak base

141. The IUPAC name for

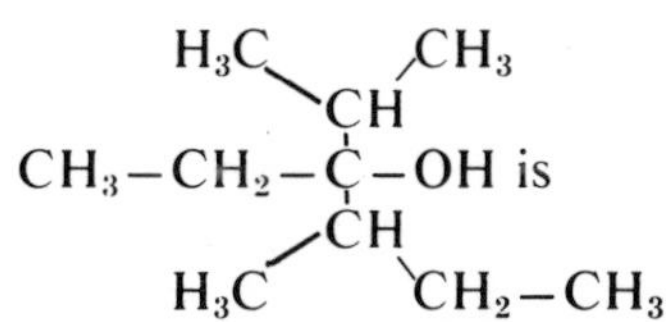

(A) i-propyl-sec-butylpropanol
(B) 2, 4-dimethyl -3-ethyl-3-hexanol
(C) 3, 5-dimethyl-5-ethyl-4-hexanol
(D) ethyl-i-propyl-sec-buthylcarbinol
(E) 3-i-propyl-4-methyl-3-hexanol

142. Lindlar catalyst is used for

(A) the nitration of aromatic hydrocarbons
(B) the partial reduction of benzene to 1, 4-cyclohexadiene
(C) the partial reduction of alkynes to cis olefins
(D) the dehydration of secondary alcohols
(E) the hydration of terminal alkynes to aldehydes

143. Which of the following is a monosaccharide?

(A) sucrose
(B) galactose
(C) maltose
(D) lactose
(E) cellobiose

144. Acetophenone may be converted to ethylbenzene with

(A) $H_2 + Pt$
(B) $Na + C_2H_5OH$
(C) $Li + NH_3$
(D) $Li\,AlH_4$
(E) $Zn(Hg) + HCl$

145. The infrared spectrum of a compound, C_3H_6O, shows significant peaks only in the 3,600 cm^{-1} and 1020cm^{-1} regions. Its structure is

(A) $CH_2{=}CH\text{-}CH_2OH$
(B) $CH_2{=}CH\text{-}O\text{-}CH_3$
(C) $CH_3\text{-}\overset{O}{\overset{\|}{C}}\text{-}CH_3$
(D) 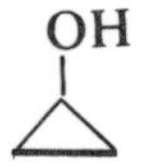 OH
(E) 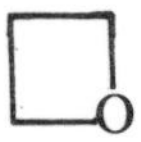 O

146. The NMR spectrum of a compound, C_3H_6O, shows a three-proton triplet (J = 7 cps) at 1.05 ppm, a two-proton quadruplet (J = 7 cps) at 2.3 ppm and a one-proton singlet at 9.77 ppm downfield from TMS. Its structure is

(A) 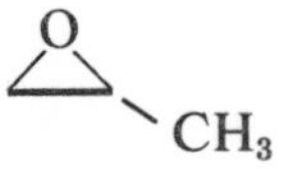 O CH_3
(B)  OH
(C) $CH_3\text{-}O\text{-}CH{=}CH_2$
(D) $CH_2{=}CH\text{-}CH_2\text{-}OH$
(E) $CH_3\text{-}CH_2\text{-}CO\text{-}H$

147. If the rate of solvolysis of methyl benzoate in a given solvent is known, and the appropriate reaction and substituent constants are known, the rate of solvolysis of methyl-p-nitrobenzoate can be calculated by the

(A) Hammond equation
(B) Kekule equation
(C) Woodward equation
(D) Hammett equation
(E) Fieser equation

148. Chromic acid oxidation of phenanthrene yields phenanthraquinone. In terms of molecular orbital theory, the most stable structure for the product is

(A) 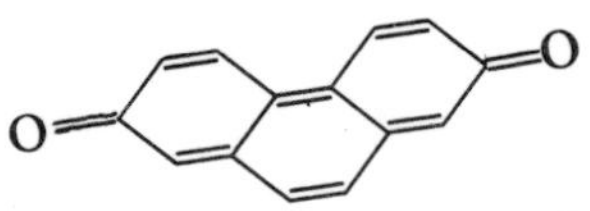 O O

(B)
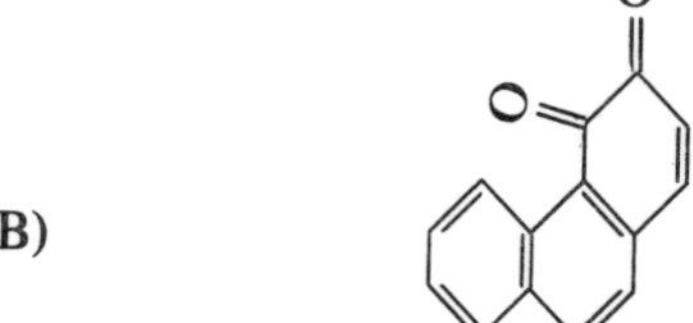

(C)
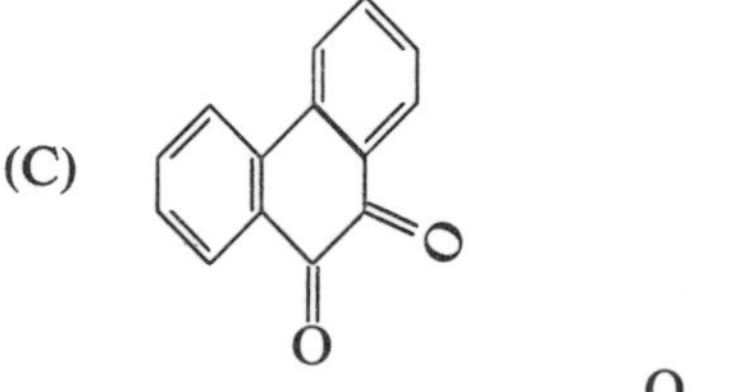

(D)
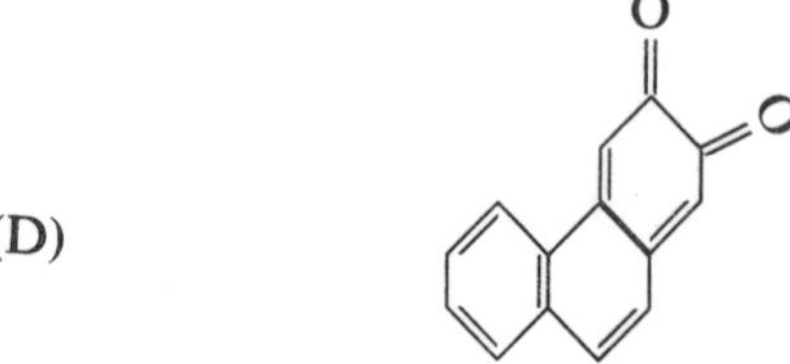

(E)
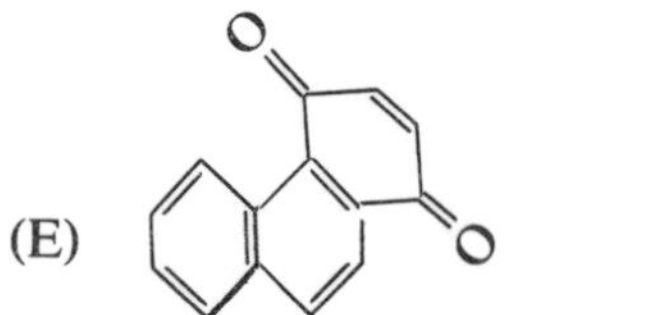

149. Consider the following series of reactions:

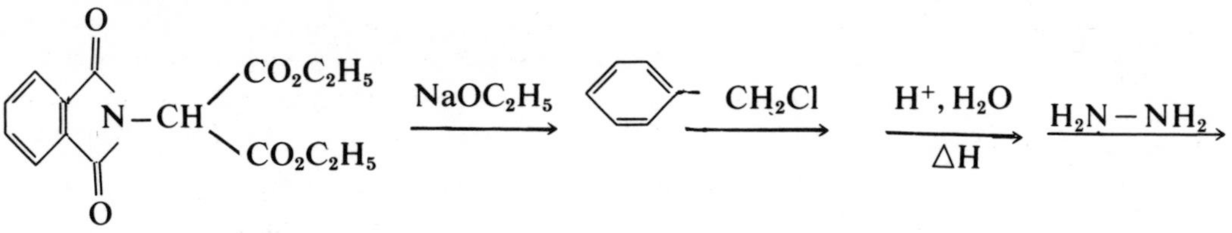

$$\text{Phthalimido-}CH(CO_2C_2H_5)_2 \xrightarrow{NaOC_2H_5} \xrightarrow{C_6H_5-CH_2Cl} \xrightarrow[\Delta H]{H^+, H_2O} \xrightarrow{H_2N-NH_2}$$

The final product is:

(A) 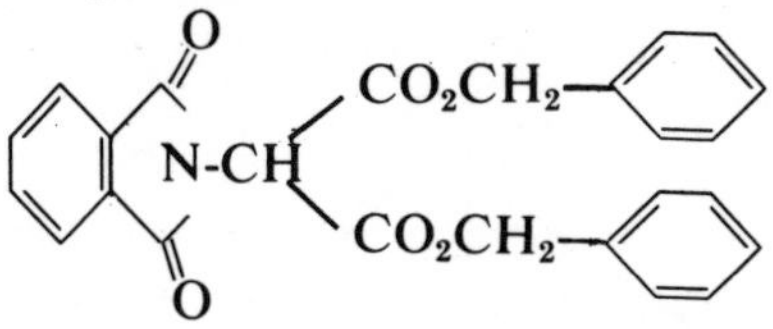 Phthalimido-N-CH$(CO_2CH_2-C_6H_5)_2$

(B) 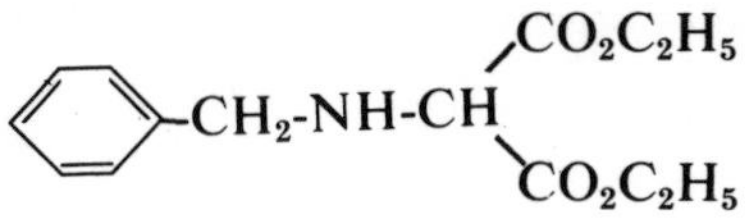 C_6H_5-CH_2-NH-CH$(CO_2C_2H_5)_2$

(C) $(C_6H_5-CH_2)_2N-CH_2-C(OH)=N-NH_2$

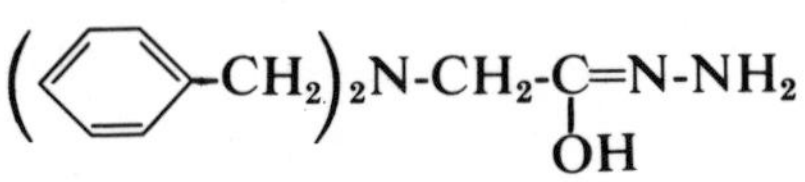

(D) 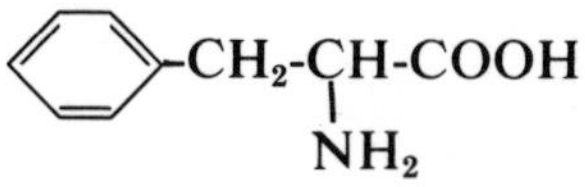 C_6H_5-CH_2-CH(NH_2)-COOH

(E) 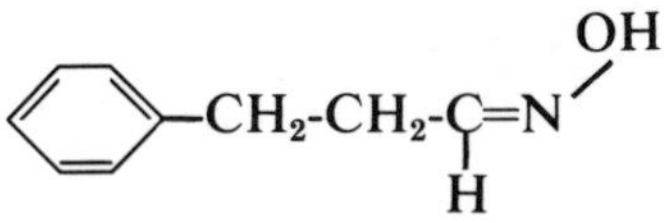 C_6H_5-CH_2-CH_2-CH=N-OH

150. In 1900, Gomberg reported the synthesis and identification of the first organic free radical, which was

(A) $(CH_3)_3C\cdot$

(B) $H_3C\cdot$

(C)  $C_6H_5\cdot$

(D) 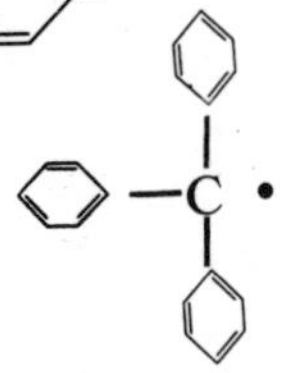 $(C_6H_5)_3C\cdot$

(E) 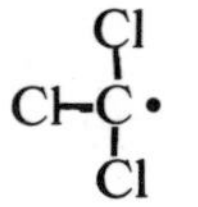 $Cl_3C\cdot$

END OF ADVANCED TEST (6) IN CHEMISTRY

ANSWER KEY TO ADVANCED TEST 6 IN CHEMISTRY

In order to help pinpoint your weaknesses, the specific area of each question is indicated in parentheses after the answer. Refer to textbooks and other study material wherever you have an incorrect answer.

Area Code

ORGANIC CHEMISTRY = O
INORGANIC CHEMISTRY = I
ANALYTICAL CHEMISTRY = A
PHYSICAL CHEMISTRY = P

1. C(I)
2. C(I)
3. A(I)
4. B(I)
5. D(I)
6. D(O)
7. D(I)
8. B(O)
9. A(I)
10. C(I)
11. A(O)
12. D(O)
13. A(O)
14. E(O)
15. B(O)
16. B(P)
17. D(I)
18. E(O)
19. D(P)
20. B(P)
21. C(P)
22. E(P)
23. C(P)
24. C(I)
25. B(P)
26. C(I)
27. C(O)
28. C(O)
29. E(P)
30. C(I)
31. E(I)
32. A(P)
33. C(I)
34. D(P)
35. C(P)
36. E(P)
37. A(P)
38. C(I)
39. C(I)
40. A(I)
41. B(P)
42. E(O)
43. B(I)
44. C(P)
45. A(P)
46. D(P)
47. D(I)
48. E(I)
49. B(O)
50. B(I)
51. B(P)
52. E(P)
53. B(P)
54. E(P)
55. C(I)
56. E(P)
57. A(A)
58. E(P)
59. D(P)
60. C(P)
61. E(P)
62. E(P)
63. D(P)
64. C(O)
65. E(P)
66. D(P)
67. C(P)
68. B(I)
69. D(I)
70. B(I)
71. D(I)
72. E(I)
73. E(O)
74. A(I)
75. E(I)
76. D(I)
77. E(I)
78. D(I)
79. E(I)
80. A(P)
81. B(P)
82. A(P)
83. A(P)
84. E(P)
85. B(P)
86. D(P)
87. A(P)
88. E(P)
89. C(P)
90. E(I)
91. D(I)
92. E(O)
93. D(A)
94. C(I)
95. D(I)
96. C(I)
97. D(I)
98. D(I)
99. C(I)
100. C(P)
101. E(P)
102. E(I)
103. A(I)
104. E(P)
105. D(P)
106. D(P)
107. A(I)
108. A(I)
109. E(I)
110. E(I)
111. C(I)
112. C(I)
113. B(I)
114. D(I)
115. C(P)
116. A(P)
117. D(I)
118. A(P)
119. E(O)
120. B(P)
121. C(P)
122. B(P)
123. E(P)
124. D(O)
125. B(P.
126. A(P)
127. E(P)
128. D(P)
129. A(O)
130. C(I)
131. C(A)
132. D(A)
133. B(A)
134. D(A)
135. D(A)
136. A(A)
137. D(A)
138. D(A)
139. C(A)
140. A(A)
141. B(O)
142. C(O)
143. B(O)
144. E(O)
145. D(O)
146. E(O)
147. D(O)
148. C(O)
149. D(O)
150. D(O)

Explanatory Answers for Advanced Test 6

1. **(C)** Iron and platinum are the only metals that do not form amalgams with mercury.

2. **(C)** The sulfide ion concentration in 2N HCl is greatly reduced because of the formation of H_2S. Therefore, only the very insoluble sulfides, in this case CuS and Hg_2S, which require very low sulfide concentrations to maintain the precipitate, are not soluble in 2N HCl.

3. **(A)** Thioacetamide $CH_3{-}\overset{S}{\overset{\|}{C}}{-}NH_2$ is often used as a source of H_2S.

$$CH_3{-}\overset{S}{\overset{\|}{C}}{-}NH_2 + H_3O^+ + H_2O \rightarrow CH_3{-}\overset{O}{\overset{\|}{C}}{-}OH +$$

$$NH_4^+ + H_2S$$

4. **(B)** The solution thought to contain the Mg^{+2} ion is heated to dryness with NaOH to eliminate any NH_3 present. HCl is added, then a small amount of p-nitrobenzene azo resorcinol (sometimes called S. and O. reagent), and the solution is made basic with NaOH. If the Mg^{+2} ion is present, $Mg(OH)_2$ will precipitate out with the dye absorbed to give a blue-colored lake.

5. **(D)** $Fe(OH)_3$ is not soluble in strong NaOH solution while $A1(OH)_3$ is amphoteric and dissolves in excess NaOH.

6. **(D)** Alkali metal salts of fatty acids of 10 to 18 carbon atoms, of which palmitic acid $CH_3(CH_2)_{14}COOH$ is one, are known as soaps. This soap is $CH_3(CH_2)_{14}COONa$.

7. **(D)** The melting point of metals increases with atomic number going down any particular periodic table group. Tungsten (W) is the third and heaviest member of the transition series chromiun, molybdenum, and tungsten. Magnesium and titanium are much lighter metals with lower melting points. This high melting point is made use of in electric lights where tungsten filaments are used because they do not melt easily.

8. **(B)** Monoacyl derivatives $-\overset{O}{\overset{\|}{C}}-$ of ammonia and primary or secondary amines are called amides and have the general formula

$$R{-}\overset{O}{\overset{\|}{C}}{-}NH_2$$

9. **(A)** Al_4C_3 is a methanide ionic type carbide apparently containing the C^{-4} ion. Upon hydrolysis, it yields methane (CH_4).

$$Al_4C_3 + 12\ H_2O \rightarrow 4\ Al(OH)_3 + 3\ CH_4$$

10. **(C)** The congener (allied with or member of the same group) of gallium and indium is thallium (T1). They are all Group III metals.

11. **(A)** Cyclopropane, C_3H_6, is the lowest molecular weight cycloalkane and has a three-membered carbon ring.

12. **(D)** Isomers are compounds with the same molecular formula but differing in at least one chemical or physical property. In this case, the chemical structure of the isomers is different.

13. **(A)** Aspirin is ortho-acetylsalicylic acid.

14. **(E)** Urea, $CO(NH_2)_2$ is isomeric with ammonium cyanate, NH_4OCN. The molecular formula is the same but the chemical structure is different.

15. **(B)** Oxidation of secondary alcohols, R_2CHOH, will give ketones, $R_2C{=}O$ by removal of one hydrogen to convert the hydroxyl group to a carbonyl group.

16. **(B)** The Pauli exclusion principle states that no more than one electron in one atom may have the same four quantum numbers. Physically speaking, this excludes having two electrons on the same atom in the same place at the same time.

17. **(D)** For the equilibrium $H_2S \rightarrow H^+ + HS^-$

$$K_{ion} = \frac{[H^+][HS^-]}{[H_2S]} = 10^{-7}$$

Initially, $[H_2S] = 0.1M$
After equilibrium, $[H^+] = [HS^-] = X$ and $[H_2S] = 0.1 - X$

$$K = 10^{-7} = \frac{X^2}{0.1 - X}.$$

So, $[H^+] = X = 10^{-4}$ approx. Then, pH = 4
The H ion contribution from HS^- dissociation is negligible.

18. **(E)** $C_{10}H_8$ is naphthalene

and the two monochloro positions are 1(4, 5, or 8) and 2(3, 6, 0r 7. There are ten possible dichloro products whose positions are (1,2), (1,3), (1,4), (1,5), (1,6), (1,7), (1,8), (2,3), (2,6), and (2,7).

19. **(D)** The ionization potential of He^+ is greater than that for the H atom because the He nucleus has a +2 charge, and hence more tightly binds the lone electron than the +1 charge on the H nucleus.

20. **(B)** From the kinetic theory of gases, the kinetic energy for a gas $E = 3/2RT$. For a change in kinetic energy due to a temperature change, $\Delta E = 3/2R\Delta T$. The heat capacity at constant volume is the heat required to raise the temperature one degree, so $C_v = 3/2R$. The heat capacity at constrant pressure $C_p = C_v + R$
$C_p = 3/2R + R = 5/2R = 5/2(1.98) = 4.97$ cal/deg-mole

21. **(C)** The collision number is proportional to the velocity of the molecule, v. The kinetic energy $E = \frac{1}{2}mv^2 = f(v)$. Thus, the collision number is proportional to the square root of the absolute temperature.

22. **(E)** Since F is the most electronegative element, it will most strongly attract the electron on the H atom and H–F will be the most ionic of the compounds listed. Therefore, it will have the largest dipole moment. H_2,' being symmetrical, has no dipole moment.

23. **(C)** The moment of inertia of a molecule is $I = \sum_i m_i r_i^2$ where m_i is the mass of the ith atom and r_i is the distance of the *i*th atom from the center of gravity. The atomic masses are H, about 10^{-24} gms. and S, about 32×10^{-24} gms. The distances involved are on the order of 1 or 2 angstroms or about 10^{-8} cm. So, I is on the order of magnitude of 10^{-40} gm.–cm^2.

24. **(C)** 100 gms. of NaCl (molecular weight 23 + 35.5) equal 1.71 moles. So, the solution has 1.71 moles of NaCl per 400 ml of solution or 4.27 moles of NaCl per 1000 ml of solution. Molarity is defined as moles of solute per 1000 ml of solution.

25. **(B)** Air contains about 20% oxygen and 80% nitrogen. Using Henry's law, the amount of a gas that dissolves in a liquid is proportional to the partial pressure of the gas above the liquid. In this case, since we are working with constant pressure, partial volumes are used. If 49 ml of pure oxygen dissolves in 1 liter of water, then for the 0.2 mole fraction of oxygen, 0.2 × 49 ml or 9.8 ml will dissolve. For nitrogen, 0.8 × 23.5 or 18.8 ml of nitrogen will dissolve. So, the total volume of gas dissolving is 28.6 ml.

26. **(C)** Using the Petit-Dulong formula, the specific heat, C, of an element times its approximate atomic weight equals 6.3. If C = 0.113, the approximate atomic weight is 6.3/0.113 = 56 g./mole.

27. **(C)** The double bond preferentially forms at the 2 position because the 2-methyl group is slightly electron withdrawing, thus making the hydrogen attached to the 2 carbon atom more easily removed.

28. **(C)** Resonance theory explains the relative unreactivity of the benzene double bond by making the resonant hybrids of several different electronic structures more stable than any single structure by an amount of energy called the resonance energy. Many different electronic resonant forms can be written for benzene.

29. **(E)** The curie is the standard measure of radioactivity and was named after the Curies who did nuch of the original work in radioactivity.

30. **(C)** The lightest Group V member is nitrogen which is completely non-metallic. The heaviest Group V member is bismuth which is a true metal. Thus the transition from non-metal to metal takes place within the group. Group I contains only metals (Li to Fr). The lightest members of Groups III and IV (B and C) are semimetals. The heaviest member of Group VII (I) has mainly non-metallic properties.

31. **(E)** ${}_{19}K^{39}$ has 19 electrons and the ground state electronic configuration is $1s^2\ 2s^2\ 2p^6\ 3s^2\ 3p^6\ 4s^1$. For the same shell, s orbital, containing 2 electrons, is filled before the p orbital holding 6 electrons. The 2d and 2f orbitals are filled after the 4s orbital.

32. **(A)** The number of neutrons in a nucleus is equal to the atomic weight (right superscript) minus the atomic number (left subscript). ${}_{92}U^{235}$ has 235-92 equals 143 neutrons.

33. **(C)** Several xenon fluorides have recently been prepared including XeF_2, XeF_4, and XeF_6.

34. **(D)** The frequency range of the infrared spectrum is 10^{11} to $4x10^{14}$ cps. The visible spectrum range is $4x10^{14}$ to $7.5x10^{14}$ cps. The ultraviolet spectrum range is $7.5x10^{14}$ to $3x10^{18}$ cps.

35. **(C)** As radioactive particles pass through a chamber containing superheated liquid, bubbles form along the path. These bubble tracks are photographed to give a record of their trail.

36. **(E)** K capture is the capture of an electron in the K shell (1s electron) by the nucleus which makes the nucleus unstable and results in the emission of radioactive rays.

37. **(A)** There are three p orbitals, p_x, p_y, and p_z, which are double lobes pointed along the x, y, and z directions respectively.

38. **(C)** Hydrogen is much more electronegative than the "active" metals, alkali and some alkaline earth metals, and hydrides of these metals are ionic with the H^- ion present.

39. **(C)** 294 gms. of H_3PO_4 (molecular weight = 98 gms./mole) in 3 liters of solutions is a 1.0 molar solution. 1 mole of H_3PO_4 contains 3 equivalents, so the 1.0 M solution is 3 normal.

40. **(A)** A deliquescent salt is a salt that hydrolyzes strongly in solution and consequently, in concentrated solution, there are significantly fewer molecules of water available to become vapor.

41. **(B)** The complete reaction is

$${}_{30}Zn^{68} + {}_0n^1 \rightarrow {}_{28}Ni^{65} + {}_2He^4$$

The alpha particle is a helium nucleus.

42. **(E)** Benedict's solution is prepared from cupric sulfate, sodium carbonate, and sodium citrate. Glucose reduces the cupric ion to red cuprous oxide, whose presence is a positive test for glucose.

43. **(B)** The solution with the highest boiling point would contain the most solute particles. $Al_2(SO_4)_3$ dissociates into 5 particles, 2 Al + 3 SO_4^{-2} ions, the most particles formed by any of the electrolytes on the list.

44. **(C)** An ammeter measures the flow of electric current and is not able to detect directly radioactivity.

45. **(A)** Cl is more electronegative than H and when HOCl is hydrolyzed in solution, the H-O bond, which is weaker than the O-Cl

bond, is broken giving H ions. K is less electronegative than H and when KOH is hydrolyzed, the K-O bond, which is weaker than the O-H bond, is broken giving OH^- ion.

46. **(D)** According to Graham's law of diffusion, where R is the rate of diffusion and m is the mass,

$$R(D_2)/R(H_2) = m^{1/2}(H_2)/m^{1/2}(D_2) = (2)^{1/2}/(32)^{1/2} = 1/4$$

47. **(D)** 30 gms. of urea $CO(NH_2)_2$ (molecular weight = 60) is ½ mole. ½ mole in 250 gms. of water is equivalent to 2 moles per 1000 gms. of water. The freezing point lowering constant for water is −1.86°C per mole of solute per 1000 gms. of water. Therefore, for 30 gms. of urea in 250 gms. of water, the freezing point is −3.72°C.

48. **(E)** The partial pressure of oxygen in the cylinder is equal to the mole fraction of oxygen times the total gas pressure or 0.1 mole of O_2/0.5 moles gas x 1 atm. equals 0.2 atms. Since 1 atm. is 760 mm. Hg, 0.2 atms. equals 152 mm. Hg pressure.

49. **(B)** Carbon black has the greatest surface area and adsorptivity of all the materials listed and is the best decolorizer.

50. **(B)** Using the ideal gas law, PV = nRT and the relation that n = number of moles = W (weight)/MW(molecular weight),

$$W = PVMW/RT$$
$$= \frac{(1\text{ atm})\,(1\text{ liter})\,(2\text{ gms./mole})}{(0.082\text{ liter-atm/mole° K})\,(273°K)}$$
$$W = 0.1\text{ gms.}$$

51. **(B)** Coulomb's law states that the force between two charges is inversely proportional to the square of the distance between them.

52. **(E)** The electronic charge is on the order of 10^{-10} esu and molecular distances are on the order of a few angstroms or 10^{-8} cm. The magnitude of the dipoles (charge x distance) is about 10^{-18} esu-cm which is defined as 1 Debye unit.

53. **(B)** The unit cell is defined as the smallest reproducible structure of the crystal. For potassium, the unit cell contains the body-centered K atom and 1/8 of each corner K atom.

54. **(E)** The Bohr magneton $B_m = eh/4\pi m_e c$ where e(= $5x10^{-10}$esu) is the electronic charge, h(= $6x10^{-27}$erg–sec) is Planck's constant, m_e(= 10^{-27}gms.) is the electronic mass, and c(= $3x10^{10}$cm/sec) is the velocity of light.

$$B_m = (5x10^{-10})(6x10^{-27})/4\pi(10^{-27})(3x10^{10})$$
$$= 10^{-20}\text{ approx.}$$

55. **(C)** The Jahn-Teller effect is the separation of the degenerate electronic states in a given symmetry so as to remove the degeneracy. Changing the symmetry changes the vibrations of the molecules, and consequently separates degenerate electronic states.

56. **(E)** The Boltzmann distribution is used in Statistical Thermodynamics and is valid when E_j is only an infinitesimal part of the total energy of the system and the energy of the other parts of the system are independent of E_j.

57. **(A)** Beer's law is used in opticochemical measurements and states that $\ln I_o/I = abc$, where I_o is the intensity of radiation before going through the sample, I is the intensity of the transmitted radiation, a is a constant called the molar absorptivity, b is the cell length, and c is the concentration in appropriate units of the component that absorbs the incident radiation.

58. **(E)** Orientation effects are important in that the reacting groups must be close to each other. If the reaction involves changes in the electronic quantum state, the reaction will be much slower. The activation energy is the energy needed to bring the reacting groups close enough to form a bond. In ho-

monuclear molecules, dispersal of excess energy given off by a collision is hindered by the lack of additional vibrational degrees of freedom. Inert material does not take part in collisions that lead to reactions.

59. **(D)** Regardless of the technique used in the determination, the dimensions of small molecules are on the order of several angstroms or 10^{-8} cm.

60. **(C)** The surface tension of a film decreases with a temperature increase. This results from increased molecular motion which reduces the ordering due to the intermolecular attractions.

61. **(E)** The entropy of fusion of a monatomic solid $S_f = \Delta H_f/T_f$ where ΔH_f is the heat of fusion and T_f is the fusion temperature. For monatomic solids, normal values range from 2 to 5 cal./mole–deg.

62. **(E)** For the process $Cl_{2(g)} \rightarrow Cl_{2(1)}$, the equilibrium constant $K = P_{Cl2(g)}$. At 298°K, with $F = -1146$ cal./mole $\ln K = -(1146)/2(298) = 2.0$ approx.
Therefore, $K = e^2 = 7$ atms. approx. The saturated vapor pressure $P_{Cl2(g)}$ is equal to about 7 atms.

63. **(D)** $d(\ln K)/dt = \Delta H/RT^2$, so $d(\ln K) = \Delta H dt/RT^2$

or $\ln K_2/K_1 = -(\Delta H/R)(1/T_2 - 1/T_1)$
$\ln(3.90 \times 10^{-19}/1.90 \times 10^{-11})$
$= \ln 2 \times 10^{-8} = 2.3 \log_{10} 2 \times 10^{-8}$
$2.3 \log_{10} 2 \times 10^{-8} = 2.3(-8) = -18.4$
$-18.4 = -\Delta H/2.00(1/1000 - 1/1500)$
$= -\Delta H/6000$
$\Delta H = 18.4(6000) = 110{,}000$ cal/mole
$= 110$ kcal/mole

64. **(C)** Ethylbenzene, o-xylene, and m-xylene would give 2 or more mononitration products. The formula for octane is C_8H_{18}. p-xylene gives one mononitration product and 3 dinitration products.

65. **(E)** The heat of solution depends on the relative magnitude of the lattice and hydration energies. The lattice energy is the amount of energy required to make gaseous ion from the crystal. The hydration energy is the energy liberated in separating water molecules and attracting them to the gaseous ions.

66. **(D)** Linear molecules all have a C_∞ axis along the molecular axis and fall in the point groups $C_{\infty v}$ or $D_{\infty h}$. Linear molecules with a center of symmetry fall in the $D_{\infty h}$ point group.

67. **(C)** The reaction is endothermic and leads to an increase in volume. Thus it would be driven towards the right by increasing the temperature (providing more heat), and by lowering the pressure to accommodate the increase in volume.

68. **(B)** The empirical formula is found by dividing the proportion of each constituent by the atomic weight of that constituent, and adjusting the ratios to the lowest common multiples:

Carbon = 54.6/12 = 4.5
Hydrogen = 9.1/1 = 9.1
Oxygen = 36.6/16 = 2.3

These ratios are closest to $C_4H_9O_2$.

69. **(D)** At standard conditions, 1 mole of gas occupies 22.4 liters. Therefore, at STP, 154g of $CC1_4$ occupy 22.4 liters.
Therefore, weight per liter of CCl_4 is 154/22.4 = 6.88 liters.

70. **(B)** K_{sp} for CaC_2O_4 is $[Ca^{++}]\ [C_2O_4^{-2}] = 2.6 \times 10^{-9}$. If $[Ca^{++}] = 2 \times 10^{-2}$, then concentration of oxalate needed to start precipitation is $K_{sp}/[Ca^{++}] = 2.6 \times 10^{-9}/2 \times 10^{-2} = 1.3 \times 10^{-7}$

71. **(D)** For $La_2(C_2O_4)_3$, K_{sp} is $[La^{+++}]^2 [C_2O_4^{--}]^3$. A solution containing 1.1×10^{-6} moles/liter of $La_2(C_2O_4)_3$ contains 2.2×10^{-6} moles of La^{+++}; and 3.3×10^{-6} moles of $C_2O_4^{--}$.
Therefore, the solubility product is:
$(2.2 \times 10^{-6})^2 \times (3.3 \times 10^{-6})^3 = 1.74 \times 10^{-28}$.

72. **(E)** The boiling point elevation is related to the molality by the equation:

$$\Delta T_b = K_b\left(\frac{1000w_2}{w_1M_2}\right)$$

where ΔT_b is the boiling point elevation, K_b is the ebullioscopic constant for the solvent, w_2 is the weight in grams of solute with molecular weight, M_2, dissolved in w_1 grams of solvent.

From the above,

$$M_1 = K_b\left(\frac{1000w_2K_b}{w_1 \times \Delta T_b}\right)$$

For water, $K_b = 0.51°$

Therefore, M_2 is $\dfrac{1000 \times 5.2 \times 0.51}{125 \times 0.78} = 28g.$

73. **(E)** The Friedel-Crafts reaction is the alkylation of an aromatic compound by means of an alkyl halide with aluminum halide as catalyst:

$R{-}X + AlX_3 \rightarrow R^+ + AlX_4^-$

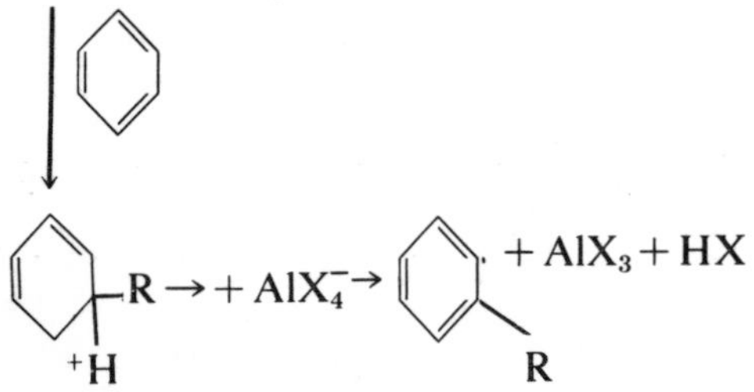

$$\text{(benzene)} \downarrow$$

$$\text{(ring)}{-}R \rightarrow + AlX_4^- \rightarrow \text{(ring)} + AlX_3 + HX$$

^+H R

74. **(A)** The presence of multiple bonds in a molecule shows that the molecule is unsaturated. The compounds are represented by the following valence-bond structures:

H–O–H H-C≡N C=O N≡N (H)(H)C=C(H)(H)

Examination of the above structures shows that water is the only one without multiple bonds.

75. **(E)** Quantum mechanical principles show that any orbital with an angular momentum quantum number, L, can be oriented within a field in a total of (2L+1) directions. All p-type orbitals have angular momentum quantum numbers of 1, and can yield a total of 3 orbitals with magnetic quantum numbers: 1, 0, and −1.

76. **(D)** Transition metals have relatively low-lying empty d and f orbitals, which, on ligand bonding, can be split into different energy levels. This splitting is usually of such a magnitude that electronic transitions between the levels are associated with energies in the visible range of the electromagnetic spectrum. This explains why many compounds of the transitions elements are colored.

77. **(E)** Early atomic weights were based on the Hydrogen atom as a standard. Later, O^{16} was adopted as the standard of measurement. In 1961, the International Union of Pure and Applied Chemistry adopted C^{12} as the latest international standard for atomic weights.

78. **(D)** Debye and Hückel first gave a complete mathematical treatment of interionic attractions in the explanation of deviations from Arrhenius' predictions for strong electrolytes.

79. **(E)** Along any Period in the Periodic Table, electronegativity increases from left to right; i.e., with increase in atomic number. Along any Group, electronegativity increases from bottom to top; i.e., with decrease in atomic number. Thus, fluorine is the most electronegative element in the Table.

80. **(A)** The principle of uncertainty is named after Heisenberg, its discoverer, and states that a simultaneous measurement of the velocity and position of a body or particle will be subject to errors whose product can be no smaller than h, Planck's constant. That is, $\delta v \cdot \delta p \geqslant h$

81. **(B)** Van der Waals forces are weak, short-range intermolecular and interatomic forces. The polarizabilities and permanent dipole moments of the particles are important contributors to these forces. For many particles, polarizability is directly proportional to the volume of the particle.

82. **(A)** An electron, because of its intrinsic spin, has an associated magnetic moment. In atoms and molecules, the moment of any electron can be neutralized by pairing it with another electron of opposite spin. For an odd

number of electrons, however, this device will always leave at least one electron unpaired, resulting in an atom or molecule with a permanent magnetic moment. Such atoms or molecules are said to be paramagnetic.

83. **(A)** Sodium chloride has a face-centered cubic crystal structure. Each unit cell contains four molecules in which each atom of sodium has six equidistant chlorine atoms as nearest neighbors, and vice versa. Since these nearest neighbors are at the corners of a regular octahedron, the association is usually said to involve an octahedral coordination.

84. **(E)** Bravias showed in 1848 that all possible three-dimensional lattices could be assigned to one of only 14 classes: triclinic, simple monoclinic, side-centered monoclinic, simple orthorhombic, end-centered orthorhombic, face-centered orthorhombic, body-centered orthorhombic, hexagonal, rhombohedral, simple tetragonal, body-centered tetragonal, simple cubic, body-centered cubic, and face-centered cubic.

85. **(B)** The characteristic temperature from the Debye theory for the specific heats of crystals is given as $\Theta_D = h\nu_m/k$, where Θ_D is the characteristic temperature, h is Planck's constant, k is Boltzmann's constant, and ν_m is the maximum vibrational frequency of the crystal. As determined from neutron-scattering experiments, the value of ν_m is such that Θ_D lies in the range 100-1000 for most substances.

86. **(D)** The Born-Haber cycle provides a method in solid-state physics for calculating crystal energies from thermochemical data. For example, for NaCl crystals:

$$\begin{array}{ccccc} Na^+(g) & + & Cl^-(g) & \xrightarrow{-E_c} & NaCl(c) \\ -e \uparrow I & & +e \uparrow -A & & \downarrow -\Delta H_f \\ Na(g) & + & Cl(g) & \xleftarrow{\lambda s + \frac{1}{2}D_o} & Na(c) + \frac{1}{2}Cl_2(g) \end{array}$$

where E_c is the crystal energy; ΔH_f is the standard heat of formation of NaCl(c); λ_s is the heat of sublimation of Na(c); D_o is the energy of dissociation of $Cl_2(g)$ into atoms; I is the ionization potential of Na; and A is the electron affinity of Cl.

87. **(A)** An actinometer measures the intensity of photochemically active radiation by determining the fluorescence of a screen or the extent of a chemical reaction initiated by the incident radiation.

88. **(E)** Energy can be calculated from the relationship, $E = h\nu$, where Planck's constant has the value, $h = 6.624 \times 10^{-27}$ erg. sec. Since the velocity of light is 3×10^{10} cm/sec, a wave with a wavelength of 0.1×10^{-8} cm has a frequency of 3×10^{19}/sec. Therefore, $E = 6.624 \times 10^{-27} \times 3 \times 10^{19}$ ergs.
But 1 eV $= 1.6 \times 10^{-12}$ erg.
Therefore, in electron volts,

$$E = \frac{6.624 \times 10^{-27} \times 3 \times 10^{19}}{1.6 \times 10^{-12}} \text{ eV}$$

$$= 1.24 \times 10^5 \text{ eV}.$$

89. **(C)** The kinetic energy acquired by an electron of charge 4.8×10^{-10} statcoulombs falling through a potential of 1 volt (or 1/300 electrostatic volt) is

$$4.8 \times 10^{-10} \times 1/300 = 1.6 \times 10^{-12} \text{ ergs}.$$

90. **(E)** 1 coulomb is the quantity of electricity obtained by the flow of 1 ampere for 1 second. 96,500 coulombs are required to deposit 1 gram equivalent weight of matter during electrolysis. For copper, the gram equivalent weight is half the atomic weight, or 36.7g
2,000 amp flowing for 1 hr
$= 2000 \times 3600 = 7{,}200{,}000$ coul.
Therefore, weight of copper deposited is:

$$\frac{36.7 \times 7{,}200{,}000}{96{,}500} = 2{,}700\text{g of copper.}$$

91. **(B)** A 0.1N solution of $AgNO_3$ contains 0.1 moles of Ag^+ in 1000ml of solution.
200ml of this solution would contain 0.02 moles of Ag^+.
1 ampere requires 96,500 seconds to deposit 1 mole of Ag^+ from solution.
Therefore, to deposit 0.01 moles of Ag^+ from solution using 0.1 ampere, one needs:

$$96{,}500 \times \frac{1}{0.1} \times 0.01 \text{ sec.}$$

$$= 9{,}650 \text{ sec.}$$
$$= 16.83 \text{ min.}$$

92. (E) In general, carboxylic acids are more acidic than aliphatic alcohols. Among the four acetic acids, the one with the greatest number of chlorine substituents is expected to be the most acidic. This is due to the fact that chlorine, being strongly electronegative, causes an inductive pull of electrons from the carboxyl group, rendering the latter more liable to part with a proton.

93. (D) The equation for the complete neutralization of phosphoric acid by LiOH is:

$$H_3PO_4 + 3LiOH \rightarrow Li_3PO_4 + 3H_2O$$

Thus, 1 mole of phosphoric acid requires 3 moles of LiOH for complete neutralization. Therefore,

$$M_bV_b = 3M_aV_a$$

(where M_a and V_a are, respectively, the molarity and volume of the acid.)

$$45M_b = (3)\cdot(30)\cdot(2)$$

$$M_b = 4.0$$

94. (C) The structure of Hydroxylamine is

```
H
|
H-N-OH, and its hydrochloride is:
```

```
     H
     |
[H-N-OH]+ Cl-
     |
     H
```

95. (D) Concentration which is measured in terms of the number of moles of solute per 1000 g. of solvent is known as molality. 14 g. of phosphoric acid in 250g. of water is equivalent to 56g. in 1000g. of water.

This is the equivalent of 56/98 moles of acid in 1000g of water, or 0.57 molal.

96. (C) At STP 1 mole of a gas occupies 22.4 liters. Therefore, the number of moles in 25 liters is 25/22.4 moles. If 25/22.4 moles of the gas weigh 50g, then 1 mole would weigh [(50)(22.4)]/25 = 45g.

97. (D) Barium can be separated from calcium and strontium by means of its chromate which is much less soluble than calcium and strontium chromates. The efficiency of separation is increased by controlling the concentration of chromate ion with a mixture of ammonium acetate and acetic acid.

98. (D) The silver group (or Group I in the analytical Tables) consists of Ag^+, Hg^+, and Pb^{++}. These ions are characterized by the insolubility of their chlorides in aqueous solution, and the reagent for the group is HCl.

99. (C) By definition, the atomic volume of an element is the volume occupied by 1 gram atom of the element. 1 gram atom of lead weighs 207.2g. If 11.4g of Pb occupy 1cc., then 207.2g of Pb would occupy 207.2/11.4 = 18.2cc.

100. (C) The Tyndall effect is the scattering of light by the comparatively large particles encountered in a colloidal solution.

101. (E) The application of quantum mechanical principles shows that the various electronic shells can contain the following maximum number of electrons:

Shell K = 2	where n = 1.
Shell L = 8	n = 2.
Shell M = 18	n = 3.
Shell N = 32	n = 4.

Examination of this series shows that the maximum number of electrons for any shell with quantum number n is $2n^2$.

102. (E) The electronic configuration of atom #20 is: $1s^22s^22p^63s^23p^64s^2$. By giving up the two outermost electrons the element would acquire the closed stable configuration of Argon. Therefore, it would most likely combine with an element that needs these two electrons to close its outermost shell. Answer E is such an element. With the configuration $1s^22s^22p^63s^23p^4$, this element would also acquire Argon's configuration on gaining two electrons.

103. (A) As the atomic number increases along any period, the nuclear charge increases and makes it progressively more more difficult to remove an electron from the outermost shell.

104. (E) The cubic lattice is regarded as simplest since one needs know only the length of a side of the unit cell to define the entire structure.

105. **(D)** Certain substances exist in two or more different crystalline forms. Such substances are said to be polymorphic. Some well-known examples are sulfur, silicon dioxide and calcium carbonate.

106. **(D)** The process of melting (or fusion) involves the breaking down of the forces that hold atoms or molecules into rigid crystalline frameworks.

107. **(A)** Barring special effects, boiling points decrease with decreasing atomic number along any group in the Periodic Table. Helium, atom #2, is the smallest of the inert gases, and has the lowest boiling point.

108. **(A)** Hydrazoic acid is the protonated form of the azide ion, N_3^-. H_3N is ammonia; HNO_2 is nitrous acid; H_4N_2 is hydrazine, and NH_2OH is hydroxylamine.

109. **(E)** In going from $KMnO_4$ to $MnCl_2$, the manganese changes its formal valence from +7 to +2. Thus, Mn has been reduced and the product of this reduction is $MnCl_2$.

110. **(E)** The phosphorus is converted to both KH_2PO_4 and PH_3. In the former product, phosphorus has a formal oxidation of +5, and in the latter product it has an oxidation of −3. Thus, the starting phosphorus has been both oxidized and reduced.

111. **(C)** Scandium, atom #21, is the first element in the first series of transition elements, a series to which Fe, atom #26, also belongs. Sodium, atom #11, is not a transition element.

112. **(C)** 100°C is the boiling point of water at standard atmospheric pressure, or 760 mm of Hg. By definition, the boiling point of any liquid is the temperature at which its vapor pressure is equal to atmospheric pressure.

113. **(B)** The conjugate base of a substance, A, is that substance which, on protonation, would yield A. In other words, it is the substance obtained by removing a proton from A.

$$H_3O^+ - H^+ \rightarrow H_2O.$$

114. **(D)** Due to its unique ability to form strong hydrogen bonds and create an extensive 3-dimensional ordering of its molecules, water has a much higher boiling point than would be extrapolated from analogous substances like H_2S and H_2Se.

115. **(C)** From Charles' Law, the volume of a given mass of gas is directly proportional to its Absolute Temperature.
Thus, $V_1/T_1 = V_2/T_2$; or, $V_2 = V_1T_2/T_1$.
Therefore, the volume at 273°C of 1 liter of gas at 0°C would be:

$$V_2 = (1)(546)/273 = 2 \text{ liters}.$$

116. **(A)** In electronic terms, oxidation is the removal of electrons. In an electrolytic cell, negatively charged ions move to the positively charged anode which removes electrons from the ions to give neutral species.

117. **(D)** The most basic species would hold most tightly on to a proton. Thus, protonation of a strong base yields a weak acid, and vice versa. Among HF, H_2O, NH_3, CH_4 and H_3O^+, CH_4 is the least acidic. This is due to the fact that carbon is not electronegative enough to polarize the C-H bond and produce a proton. Therefore, among the original alternatives, CH_3^- is the most basic species.

118. **(A)** By equating the electrostatic and centrifugal forces on the electron, and taking account of the quantization requirement, Bohr was able to show that the velocity of an electron in its orbit should be given by the expression:
$v = 2\pi e^2/nh$.
That is, $v \alpha 1/n$.
Therefore, if $v = c/100$ for $n = 1$, then for $n = 5$, $v = c/(5)(100) = 0.002$.

119. **(E)** The compound contains two phenyl groups, one arsenic atom, and one chlorine atom. Its name should, therefore, be diphenyl chlorarsine.

120. **(B)** For a harmonic oscillator, the frequency is related to the force constant, k, by the equation:
$\nu = \frac{1}{2\pi} \frac{[k]^{1/2}}{[\mu]^{1/2}}$, where μ is the reduced mass,

which, for HCl can be equated to the mass of the hydrogen atom. That is, $k = 4\pi^2\nu^2\mu$.

$$= (4)(3.14)^2(8.65)^2(10^{26})(1.66)(10^{-24})$$
$$= (4.8)(10^5) \text{ dynes/cm.}$$

121. **(C)** Microwave spectroscopy is used for the determination of transitions between rotational energy levels, which are about two orders of magnitude smaller than differences between vibrational energy levels. Since infrared radiation has wavelengths in the 1 to 15 micron region, microwave radiation should be in the wave length range of 1mm to 1cm.

122. **(B)** According to Heisenberg's uncertainty principle, there is a finite non-zero probability of finding an electron in the region of negative energy. Since de Broglie associates all bodies with waves, the former property is found also with other atomic particles, and is known as the tunnel effect. One of the best examples of this effect is the emission of a α particle in a radioactive disintegration. The random nature of this emission is a reflection of the fact that the position of the particle is subject to the laws of probability.

123. **(E)** Free radicals are characterized by their possession of unpaired electrons. Since electrons have an intrinsic spin, electron spin spectrometers provide a sensitive method of detecting unpaired electrons, or free radicals.

124. **(D)** Because of Van der Waal's forces, there is an energy difference between the staggered and the eclipsed conformations of ethane. This difference is known as torsional strain, and is attributed to greater interaction between vicinal substituents in the eclipsed conformation. The maximum torsional interaction for two eclipsed substituents is 1 kcal/mole. Ethane, in its eclipsed conformation, has three such pairs, and has a torsional strain of 3 kcal/mole. Torsional strain is also referred to as "Pitzer strain."

125. **(B)** A partition function is an expression giving the distribution of molecules or atoms into different energy states in a system. It is most often encountered in statistical treatments of atomic and molecular parameters.

126. **(A)** According to the Haüy Law, the intercepts of any crystal plane on the crystal axes may be expressed as rational fractional multiples of the crystal parameters. The Miller indices are the reciprocals of these fractions, reduced to integral proportions.

127. **(E)** The entropy change accompanying a change of state is given as:

$$\Delta S = \frac{\Delta H}{T} \cdot \text{ For the present case,}$$

$$\Delta S = 1436/273 = 5.4 \text{ cal/mole-deg}$$

128. **(D)** The entropy change for the solidification of water at $-20°C$ is the sum of the entropy change for solidification at 0°C and the entroopy change in cooling solid water from 0°C to $-20°C$. For the first process, $\Delta S = 5.4$ cal/deg. mole. For the second process, we use: $\delta S = (C_p/T)\delta T$.

Therefore,

$$\Delta S = \int_{T_1}^{T_2} (C_p/T)dT = -C_p \ln\frac{T_2}{T_1}$$

For this case, $\Delta S = 8.6 \ln 253/273 = 0.6$ cal/mole-deg. The total entropy change is $5.4 + 0.6 = 6.0$ cal/mole-deg.

129. **(A)** Hydrolysis of several different kinds of proteins has shown that they are built up from a total of 26 amino acids.

130. **(C)** 26.98ml of 0.1326N solution of Na_2SO_3 contains (26.98)(0.1326) milliequivalents of Na_2SO_3. By definition, the equivalent weight of Na_2SO_3 is that weight which would cause a one electron reduction of an oxidizing agent. If the amount of oxidizing agent used is 7.16×10^{-1} millimoles, then the # of electrons involved in the redox reaction is:

$$\frac{26.98 \times 0.1326}{7.16 \times 0.1} = 5 \text{ electrons.}$$

$Y^{+5} + 5e^- \rightarrow Y^0$, and the final oxidation state of Y is zero

131. **(C)** Since the sample contains 50% copper, the weight of copper is 1.89 g. This is dissolved in HNO_3 and diluted to 250 ml. So

we now have a solution which is 1.89 gm/250 ml strong. A 25ml sample is taken and titrates against 50 ml thiosulfate solution. The amount of copper in this portion is 0.189 gm. The titer is $0.189/50 = 3.78 \times 10^{-3}$

132. **(D)** Normality is moles per liter

$$\text{number moles} = \frac{PV}{MW}$$

where P = density
V = volume

$$\text{number moles} = \left[\frac{(1.0)(1000\ \text{ml})(.5)}{59}\right] = 8.47$$

$$N = 8.47$$

133. **(B)** The separation of the arsenic subgroup depends on the fact that the sulfides of arsenic, antimony and tin(IV) are soluble in $(NH_4)_2S$. However, SnS (II) is insoluble in $(NH_4)_2S$ and we must oxidize all the tin (II) to tin (IV).

134. **(D)** Large quantities of indicator will interfere with the titration by using up an appreciable amount of acid or base and introducing serious error in the determination of the correct concentration.

135. **(D)** Paneth-Fajans-Hahn's law states that, when two or more types of ions are available for adsorption, and when other factors are considered equal, an ion which forms a compound with the lowest solubility with one of the lattice ions will be adsorbed preferentially.

136. **(A)** The counter ions are farther from the lattice ions and, as a result, the probability of forming a compound with the latter is small. Because of the presence of solvent molecules, the ionic charge effect and size effect are small. Temperature has little effect. So, concentration is the most important factor.

137. **(D)** Post-precipitation increases both with time and higher temperatures. Also it occurs if the contaminant is added before or after precipitation. Introducing more reagent will increase the post-precipitation since more undesired compound will be formed. Using less reagent will result in lower yields of the desired compound.

138. **(D)** Concentration polarization occurs when ions are removed from the vicinity of the electrode quickly such that, if the Cd^{++} from the bulk of the solution cannot move in to replace them, no current flows. The rate Cd^{++} ions react before a potential is applied will also determine how fast the Cd^{++} are depleted.

139. **(C)** The H^+ is:
$meq_A = meq_B = N_B \times ml_B = .2$ meq.

$$[H^+] = \frac{0.2\ \text{meq}}{50\ \text{ml}} = 0.0004\ \text{eq/l}$$

$$pH = -\log(4 \times 10^{-4}) = 3.4$$

Congo red's range includes this pH value. Methyl orange just includes this value so it will not be as effective.

140. **(A)** To determine the pK_1 it is necessary that the concentration of H_3PO_4 and H_2PO_4 be equal at some point in the titration.

$$pH = pK_1 + \log\left(\frac{H_2PO_4^-}{H_3PO_4}\right)$$

However this is difficult since $H_2PO_4^-$ has a sufficiently large ionization constant such that the concentration of $H_2PO_4^-$ will be decreasing even as the concentration of H_3PO_4 does.

141. **(B)** The IUPAC system of naming requires that the compound adopt the name of the longest carbon chain, with substituents numbered so as to yield the smallest sum. With these criteria, the correct name for the compound is 2, 4-dimethyl-3-ethyl-3-hexanol.

142. **(C)** Ordinary palladium catalyst is strong enough to hydrogenate alkynes to alkanes. However, when it is "poisoned" with lead on calcium carbonate, it carries out only partial reductions of alkynes to give cis-olefins.

143. **(B)** Sucrose is a disaccharide of glucose and fructose; maltose consists of two glucose units; lactose of galactose and glucose; and cellobiose of two glucose monomers.

144. **(E)** Carbonyl groups may be reduced to methylene groups by the Clemmensen method which employs amalgamated zinc and hydrochloric acid.

145. **(D)** The spectrum shows that the compound lacks both a double bond and a carbonyl group. The $1020 cm^{-1}$ band suggests the presence of a cyclopropyl ring, and the $3600 cm^{-1}$ band suggests a secondary alcohol; leading, therefore, to cyclopropanol.

146. **(E)** A triplet spin-coupled to a quadruplet suggests the presence of an ethyl group in a molecule; leading automatically to propionaldehyde as the correct structure of the compound.

147. **(D)** L. P. Hammett discovered that certain reactions had rates which could be predicted on the basis of an equation,

$$\log(k/k_0) = \sigma\rho$$

where k is the rate of the proposed reaction, k_0 is the rate of a standard reaction, ρ is a reaction parameter and σ is a substituent parameter. The equation is named after its discoverer.

148. **(C)** The most stable structure is the one in which two conjugated benzene rings are left intact as in (C), since the resonance energy of biphenyl is more than that of naphthalene.

149. **(D)** The series constitutes the phthalimidomalonic ester synthesis of α-amino acids, and leads to the production of phenylalanine.

150. **(D)** Although Paneth had earlier demonstrated the possible existence of methyl radicals, Gomberg's synthesis of triphenylmethyl radicals was the first unequivocal synthesis of organic free radicals.

ANSWER SHEET

1	A	B	C	D	E	31	A	B	C	D	E	61	A	B	C	D	E	91	A	B	C	D	E	121	A	B	C	D	E
2	A	B	C	D	E	32	A	B	C	D	E	62	A	B	C	D	E	92	A	B	C	D	E	122	A	B	C	D	E
3	A	B	C	D	E	33	A	B	C	D	E	63	A	B	C	D	E	93	A	B	C	D	E	123	A	B	C	D	E
4	A	B	C	D	E	34	A	B	C	D	E	64	A	B	C	D	E	94	A	B	C	D	E	124	A	B	C	D	E
5	A	B	C	D	E	35	A	B	C	D	E	65	A	B	C	D	E	95	A	B	C	D	E	125	A	B	C	D	E
6	A	B	C	D	E	36	A	B	C	D	E	66	A	B	C	D	E	96	A	B	C	D	E	126	A	B	C	D	E
7	A	B	C	D	E	37	A	B	C	D	E	67	A	B	C	D	E	97	A	B	C	D	E	127	A	B	C	D	E
8	A	B	C	D	E	38	A	B	C	D	E	68	A	B	C	D	E	98	A	B	C	D	E	128	A	B	C	D	E
9	A	B	C	D	E	39	A	B	C	D	E	69	A	B	C	D	E	99	A	B	C	D	E	129	A	B	C	D	E
10	A	B	C	D	E	40	A	B	C	D	E	70	A	B	C	D	E	100	A	B	C	D	E	130	A	B	C	D	E
11	A	B	C	D	E	41	A	B	C	D	E	71	A	B	C	D	E	101	A	B	C	D	E	131	A	B	C	D	E
12	A	B	C	D	E	42	A	B	C	D	E	72	A	B	C	D	E	102	A	B	C	D	E	132	A	B	C	D	E
13	A	B	C	D	E	43	A	B	C	D	E	73	A	B	C	D	E	103	A	B	C	D	E	133	A	B	C	D	E
14	A	B	C	D	E	44	A	B	C	D	E	74	A	B	C	D	E	104	A	B	C	D	E	134	A	B	C	D	E
15	A	B	C	D	E	45	A	B	C	D	E	75	A	B	C	D	E	105	A	B	C	D	E	135	A	B	C	D	E
16	A	B	C	D	E	46	A	B	C	D	E	76	A	B	C	D	E	106	A	B	C	D	E	136	A	B	C	D	E
17	A	B	C	D	E	47	A	B	C	D	E	77	A	B	C	D	E	107	A	B	C	D	E	137	A	B	C	D	E
18	A	B	C	D	E	48	A	B	C	D	E	78	A	B	C	D	E	108	A	B	C	D	E	138	A	B	C	D	E
19	A	B	C	D	E	49	A	B	C	D	E	79	A	B	C	D	E	109	A	B	C	D	E	139	A	B	C	D	E
20	A	B	C	D	E	50	A	B	C	D	E	80	A	B	C	D	E	110	A	B	C	D	E	140	A	B	C	D	E
21	A	B	C	D	E	51	A	B	C	D	E	81	A	B	C	D	E	111	A	B	C	D	E	141	A	B	C	D	E
22	A	B	C	D	E	52	A	B	C	D	E	82	A	B	C	D	E	112	A	B	C	D	E	142	A	B	C	D	E
23	A	B	C	D	E	53	A	B	C	D	E	83	A	B	C	D	E	113	A	B	C	D	E	143	A	B	C	D	E
24	A	B	C	D	E	54	A	B	C	D	E	84	A	B	C	D	E	114	A	B	C	D	E	144	A	B	C	D	E
25	A	B	C	D	E	55	A	B	C	D	E	85	A	B	C	D	E	115	A	B	C	D	E	145	A	B	C	D	E
26	A	B	C	D	E	56	A	B	C	D	E	86	A	B	C	D	E	116	A	B	C	D	E	146	A	B	C	D	E
27	A	B	C	D	E	57	A	B	C	D	E	87	A	B	C	D	E	117	A	B	C	D	E	147	A	B	C	D	E
28	A	B	C	D	E	58	A	B	C	D	E	88	A	B	C	D	E	118	A	B	C	D	E	148	A	B	C	D	E
29	A	B	C	D	E	59	A	B	C	D	E	89	A	B	C	D	E	119	A	B	C	D	E	149	A	B	C	D	E
30	A	B	C	D	E	60	A	B	C	D	E	90	A	B	C	D	E	120	A	B	C	D	E	150	A	B	C	D	E

ANSWER SHEET

1 A B C D E
2 A B C D E
3 A B C D E
4 A B C D E
5 A B C D E
6 A B C D E
7 A B C D E
8 A B C D E
9 A B C D E
10 A B C D E
11 A B C D E
12 A B C D E
13 A B C D E
14 A B C D E
15 A B C D E
16 A B C D E
17 A B C D E
18 A B C D E
19 A B C D E
20 A B C D E
21 A B C D E
22 A B C D E
23 A B C D E
24 A B C D E
25 A B C D E
26 A B C D E
27 A B C D E
28 A B C D E
29 A B C D E
30 A B C D E
31 A B C D E
32 A B C D E
33 A B C D E
34 A B C D E
35 A B C D E
36 A B C D E
37 A B C D E
38 A B C D E
39 A B C D E
40 A B C D E
41 A B C D E
42 A B C D E
43 A B C D E
44 A B C D E
45 A B C D E
46 A B C D E
47 A B C D E
48 A B C D E
49 A B C D E
50 A B C D E
51 A B C D E
52 A B C D E
53 A B C D E
54 A B C D E
55 A B C D E
56 A B C D E
57 A B C D E
58 A B C D E
59 A B C D E
60 A B C D E
61 A B C D E
62 A B C D E
63 A B C D E
64 A B C D E
65 A B C D E
66 A B C D E
67 A B C D E
68 A B C D E
69 A B C D E
70 A B C D E
71 A B C D E
72 A B C D E
73 A B C D E
74 A B C D E
75 A B C D E
76 A B C D E
77 A B C D E
78 A B C D E
79 A B C D E
80 A B C D E
81 A B C D E
82 A B C D E
83 A B C D E
84 A B C D E
85 A B C D E
86 A B C D E
87 A B C D E
88 A B C D E
89 A B C D E
90 A B C D E
91 A B C D E
92 A B C D E
93 A B C D E
94 A B C D E
95 A B C D E
96 A B C D E
97 A B C D E
98 A B C D E
99 A B C D E
100 A B C D E
101 A B C D E
102 A B C D E
103 A B C D E
104 A B C D E
105 A B C D E
106 A B C D E
107 A B C D E
108 A B C D E
109 A B C D E
110 A B C D E
111 A B C D E
112 A B C D E
113 A B C D E
114 A B C D E
115 A B C D E
116 A B C D E
117 A B C D E
118 A B C D E
119 A B C D E
120 A B C D E
121 A B C D E
122 A B C D E
123 A B C D E
124 A B C D E
125 A B C D E
126 A B C D E
127 A B C D E
128 A B C D E
129 A B C D E
130 A B C D E
131 A B C D E
132 A B C D E
133 A B C D E
134 A B C D E
135 A B C D E
136 A B C D E
137 A B C D E
138 A B C D E
139 A B C D E
140 A B C D E
141 A B C D E
142 A B C D E
143 A B C D E
144 A B C D E
145 A B C D E
146 A B C D E
147 A B C D E
148 A B C D E
149 A B C D E
150 A B C D E

ANSWER SHEET

1	A	B	C	D	E	31	A	B	C	D	E	61	A	B	C	D	E	91	A	B	C	D	E	121	A	B	C	D	E
2	A	B	C	D	E	32	A	B	C	D	E	62	A	B	C	D	E	92	A	B	C	D	E	122	A	B	C	D	E
3	A	B	C	D	E	33	A	B	C	D	E	63	A	B	C	D	E	93	A	B	C	D	E	123	A	B	C	D	E
4	A	B	C	D	E	34	A	B	C	D	E	64	A	B	C	D	E	94	A	B	C	D	E	124	A	B	C	D	E
5	A	B	C	D	E	35	A	B	C	D	E	65	A	B	C	D	E	95	A	B	C	D	E	125	A	B	C	D	E
6	A	B	C	D	E	36	A	B	C	D	E	66	A	B	C	D	E	96	A	B	C	D	E	126	A	B	C	D	E
7	A	B	C	D	E	37	A	B	C	D	E	67	A	B	C	D	E	97	A	B	C	D	E	127	A	B	C	D	E
8	A	B	C	D	E	38	A	B	C	D	E	68	A	B	C	D	E	98	A	B	C	D	E	128	A	B	C	D	E
9	A	B	C	D	E	39	A	B	C	D	E	69	A	B	C	D	E	99	A	B	C	D	E	129	A	B	C	D	E
10	A	B	C	D	E	40	A	B	C	D	E	70	A	B	C	D	E	100	A	B	C	D	E	130	A	B	C	D	E
11	A	B	C	D	E	41	A	B	C	D	E	71	A	B	C	D	E	101	A	B	C	D	E	131	A	B	C	D	E
12	A	B	C	D	E	42	A	B	C	D	E	72	A	B	C	D	E	102	A	B	C	D	E	132	A	B	C	D	E
13	A	B	C	D	E	43	A	B	C	D	E	73	A	B	C	D	E	103	A	B	C	D	E	133	A	B	C	D	E
14	A	B	C	D	E	44	A	B	C	D	E	74	A	B	C	D	E	104	A	B	C	D	E	134	A	B	C	D	E
15	A	B	C	D	E	45	A	B	C	D	E	75	A	B	C	D	E	105	A	B	C	D	E	135	A	B	C	D	E
16	A	B	C	D	E	46	A	B	C	D	E	76	A	B	C	D	E	106	A	B	C	D	E	136	A	B	C	D	E
17	A	B	C	D	E	47	A	B	C	D	E	77	A	B	C	D	E	107	A	B	C	D	E	137	A	B	C	D	E
18	A	B	C	D	E	48	A	B	C	D	E	78	A	B	C	D	E	108	A	B	C	D	E	138	A	B	C	D	E
19	A	B	C	D	E	49	A	B	C	D	E	79	A	B	C	D	E	109	A	B	C	D	E	139	A	B	C	D	E
20	A	B	C	D	E	50	A	B	C	D	E	80	A	B	C	D	E	110	A	B	C	D	E	140	A	B	C	D	E
21	A	B	C	D	E	51	A	B	C	D	E	81	A	B	C	D	E	111	A	B	C	D	E	141	A	B	C	D	E
22	A	B	C	D	E	52	A	B	C	D	E	82	A	B	C	D	E	112	A	B	C	D	E	142	A	B	C	D	E
23	A	B	C	D	E	53	A	B	C	D	E	83	A	B	C	D	E	113	A	B	C	D	E	143	A	B	C	D	E
24	A	B	C	D	E	54	A	B	C	D	E	84	A	B	C	D	E	114	A	B	C	D	E	144	A	B	C	D	E
25	A	B	C	D	E	55	A	B	C	D	E	85	A	B	C	D	E	115	A	B	C	D	E	145	A	B	C	D	E
26	A	B	C	D	E	56	A	B	C	D	E	86	A	B	C	D	E	116	A	B	C	D	E	146	A	B	C	D	E
27	A	B	C	D	E	57	A	B	C	D	E	87	A	B	C	D	E	117	A	B	C	D	E	147	A	B	C	D	E
28	A	B	C	D	E	58	A	B	C	D	E	88	A	B	C	D	E	118	A	B	C	D	E	148	A	B	C	D	E
29	A	B	C	D	E	59	A	B	C	D	E	89	A	B	C	D	E	119	A	B	C	D	E	149	A	B	C	D	E
30	A	B	C	D	E	60	A	B	C	D	E	90	A	B	C	D	E	120	A	B	C	D	E	150	A	B	C	D	E

ANSWER SHEET

1 A B C D E	31 A B C D E	61 A B C D E	91 A B C D E	121 A B C D E
2 A B C D E	32 A B C D E	62 A B C D E	92 A B C D E	122 A B C D E
3 A B C D E	33 A B C D E	63 A B C D E	93 A B C D E	123 A B C D E
4 A B C D E	34 A B C D E	64 A B C D E	94 A B C D E	124 A B C D E
5 A B C D E	35 A B C D E	65 A B C D E	95 A B C D E	125 A B C D E
6 A B C D E	36 A B C D E	66 A B C D E	96 A B C D E	126 A B C D E
7 A B C D E	37 A B C D E	67 A B C D E	97 A B C D E	127 A B C D E
8 A B C D E	38 A B C D E	68 A B C D E	98 A B C D E	128 A B C D E
9 A B C D E	39 A B C D E	69 A B C D E	99 A B C D E	129 A B C D E
10 A B C D E	40 A B C D E	70 A B C D E	100 A B C D E	130 A B C D E
11 A B C D E	41 A B C D E	71 A B C D E	101 A B C D E	131 A B C D E
12 A B C D E	42 A B C D E	72 A B C D E	102 A B C D E	132 A B C D E
13 A B C D E	43 A B C D E	73 A B C D E	103 A B C D E	133 A B C D E
14 A B C D E	44 A B C D E	74 A B C D E	104 A B C D E	134 A B C D E
15 A B C D E	45 A B C D E	75 A B C D E	105 A B C D E	135 A B C D E
16 A B C D E	46 A B C D E	76 A B C D E	106 A B C D E	136 A B C D E
17 A B C D E	47 A B C D E	77 A B C D E	107 A B C D E	137 A B C D E
18 A B C D E	48 A B C D E	78 A B C D E	108 A B C D E	138 A B C D E
19 A B C D E	49 A B C D E	79 A B C D E	109 A B C D E	139 A B C D E
20 A B C D E	50 A B C D E	80 A B C D E	110 A B C D E	140 A B C D E
21 A B C D E	51 A B C D E	81 A B C D E	111 A B C D E	141 A B C D E
22 A B C D E	52 A B C D E	82 A B C D E	112 A B C D E	142 A B C D E
23 A B C D E	53 A B C D E	83 A B C D E	113 A B C D E	143 A B C D E
24 A B C D E	54 A B C D E	84 A B C D E	114 A B C D E	144 A B C D E
25 A B C D E	55 A B C D E	85 A B C D E	115 A B C D E	145 A B C D E
26 A B C D E	56 A B C D E	86 A B C D E	116 A B C D E	146 A B C D E
27 A B C D E	57 A B C D E	87 A B C D E	117 A B C D E	147 A B C D E
28 A B C D E	58 A B C D E	88 A B C D E	118 A B C D E	148 A B C D E
29 A B C D E	59 A B C D E	89 A B C D E	119 A B C D E	149 A B C D E
30 A B C D E	60 A B C D E	90 A B C D E	120 A B C D E	150 A B C D E

FOR FURTHER STUDY

ARCO BOOKS FOR MORE HELP

Now what? You've read and studied the whole book, and there's still time before you take the test. You're probably better prepared than most of your competitors, but you may feel insecure about one or more of the probable test subjects.

Perhaps you've discovered that you are weak in language, verbal ability or mathematics. Why flounder and fail when help is so easily available? Why not brush up in the privacy of your own home with one of these books?

And why not consider the other opportunities open to you? Look over the list and make plans for your future. Start studying for other tests *now*. You can then pick and choose your *ideal* position, instead of settling for the first *ordinary* job that comes along.

Each of the following books was created under the same expert editorial supervision that produced the excellent book you are now using. Though we only list titles and prices, you can be sure that each book performs a real service, and keeps you from fumbling and from failure. Whatever your goal. . . Civil Service, Trade License, Teaching, Professional License, Scholarships, Entrance to the School of your choice. . .you can achieve it through the proven Question and Answer Method.

S3709

CIVIL SERVICE AND TEST PREPARATION—GENERAL

Title	Order No.	Price
Able Seaman, Deckhand, Scowman	01376-1	5.00
Accountant—Auditor	00001-5	8.00
Addiction Specialist, Senior, Supervising, Principal	03351-7	8.00
Administrative Assistant—Principal Administrative Associate	00148-8	8.00
Air Traffic Controller, Morrison	04593-0	10.00
American Foreign Service Officer	04219-2	8.00
Apprentice, Mechanical Trades	00571-8	6.00
Assistant Accountant	00056-2	8.00
Assistant Civil Engineer	01228-5	8.00
Assistant Station Supervisor	03736-9	6.00
Associate and Administrative Accountant	03863-2	8.00
Attorney, Assistant—Trainee	01084-3	10.00
Auto Machinist	04379-2	8.00
Auto Mechanic, Autoserviceman	00514-9	8.00
Bank Examiner—Trainee and Assistant	01642-6	5.00
Battalion and Deputy Chief, F.D.	00515-7	6.00
Beginning Office Worker	00173-9	6.00
Beverage Control Investigator	00150-X	4.00
Bookkeeper—Account Clerk	00035-X	8.00
Bridge and Tunnel Officer—Special Officer	00780-X	5.00
Building Custodian	00013-9	8.00
Bus Maintainer—Bus Mechanic	00111-9	8.00
Bus Operator	01553-5	5.00
Buyer, Assistant Buyer, Purchase Inspector	01366-4	6.00
Captain, Fire Department	00121-6	10.00
Captain, Police Department	00184-4	10.00
Carpenter	00135-6	6.00
Case Worker	01528-4	8.00
Cashier, Housing Teller	00703-6	6.00
Cement Mason—Mason's Helper, Turner	03745-8	6.00
Chemist—Assistant Chemist	00116-X	5.00
City Planner	01364-8	6.00
Civil Engineer, Senior, Associate, & Administrative	00146-1	8.00
Civil Service Arithmetic and Vocabulary	00003-1	5.00
Civil Service Course, Gitlin	00702-8	5.00
Teacher's Manual for Civil Service Course, Gitlin	03838-1	2.00
Civil Service Handbook	00040-6	3.00
Claim Examiner—Law Investigator	00149-6	5.00
Clerk New York City	00045-7	4.00
Clerk—Steno Transcriber	00838-5	6.00
College Office Assistant	00181-X	5.00
Complete Guide to U.S. Civil Service Jobs	00537-8	3.00
Construction Foreman and Supervisor—Inspector	01085-1	8.00
Consumer Affairs Inspector	01356-7	6.00
Correction Captain—Deputy Warden	01358-3	8.00
Correction Officer	00186-0	8.00
Court Officer	00519-X	8.00
Criminal Law Handbook for Law Enforcement Officer, Salottolo	02399-6	12.00
Criminal Science Handbook, Salottolo	02407-0	5.00
Detective Investigator, Turner	03738-5	8.00
Dietitian	00083-X	8.00
Draftsman, Civil and Mechanical Engineering (All Grades)	01225-0	6.00
Electrical Engineer	00137-2	10.00
Electrical Inspector	03350-9	8.00
Electrician	00084-8	8.00
Electronic Equipment Maintainer	01836-4	8.00
Elevator Operator	00051-1	3.00
Employment Interviewer	00008-2	8.00
Employment Security Clerk	00700-1	6.00
Engineering Technician (All Grades)	01226-9	8.00
Exterminator Foreman—Foreman of Housing Exterminators	03740-7	6.00
File Clerk	04377-6	6.00

Title	Order No.
Fire Administration and Technology	00604
Firefighting Hydraulics, Bonadio	00572
Fireman, F.D.	0001
Food Service Supervisor—School Lunch Manager	0137
Foreman	00191
Foreman of Auto Mechanics	0136
Gardener, Assistant Gardener	0134
General Entrance Series	01961
General Test Practice for 101 U.S. Jobs	04421
Guard—Patrolman	00122
Homestudy Course for Civil Service Jobs	01587
Hospital Attendant	00012
Hospital Care Investigator Trainee (Social Case Worker I)	01674
Hospital Clerk	01718
Hospital Security Officer	03866
Housing Assistant	00054
Housing Caretaker	00504
Housing Inspector	00055
Housing Manager—Assistant Housing Manager	00813
Housing Patrolman	00192
How to Pass Employment Tests, Liebers	00715
Internal Revenue Agent	00093
Investigator—Inspector	01670
Junior Administrator Development Examination (JADE)	01643
Junior Federal Assistant	01729
Laboratory Aide	01121
Laborer—Federal, State and City Jobs	00566
Landscape Architect	01368
Laundry Worker	01834
Law and Court Stenographer	00783
Law Enforcement Positions	00500
Librarian	00060
Lieutenant, F.D.	00123
Lieutenant, P.D.	00190
Machinist—Machinist's Helper	01123
Mail Handler—U.S. Postal Service	00126
Maintainer's Helper, Group A and C—Transit Electrical Helper	00175
Maintenance Man	04349
Management and Administration Quizzer	01727
Management Analyst, Assistant-Associate	03864
Mathematics, Simplified and Self-Taught	00567
Mechanical Apprentice (Maintainer's Helper B)	00176
Mechanical Aptitude and Spatial Relations Tests	00539
Mechanical Engineer—Junior, Assistant & Senior Grades	03314
Messenger	00017
Mortuary Caretaker	01354
Motor Vehicle License Examiner	00018
Motor Vehicle Operator	00576
Motorman (Subways)	00061
Nurse	00143
Office Aide, Turner	04704
Office Assistant GS 2-4	04275
Office Machines Operator	00728
1540 Questions and Answers for Electricians	00754
1340 Questions and Answers for Firefighters, McGannon	00857
Painter	01772
Parking Enforcement Agent	00701
Patrol Inspector	04301
Peace Corps Placement Exams	01641
Personnel Examiner, Junior Personnel Examiner	00648
Plumber—Plumber's Helper	00517
Police Administration and Criminal Investigation	00565
Police Administrative Aide	02345

Title	Number	Price
e Officer—Patrolman P.D, Murray	00019-8	6.00
.e Science Advancement—Police Promotion Course	02636-7	15.00
ewoman	00062-7	6.00
Office Clerk-Carrier	00021-X	6.00
al Inspector	00194-1	5.00
al Promotion Foreman—Supervisor	00538-6	6.00
naster	01522-5	5.00
tice for Civil Service Promotion	00023-6	8.00
tice for Clerical, Typing and Stenographic Tests	04297-4	6.00
:ipal Clerk—Stenographer	01523-3	8.00
ation and Parole Officer	04203-6	8.00
essional and Administrative Career Examination (PACE)	03653-2	6.00
essional Careers Test	01543-8	6.00
essional Trainee—Administrative Aide	01183-1	5.00
ic Health Sanitarian	00985-3	8.00
oad Clerk	00067-8	4.00
oad Porter	00128-3	4.00
Estate Assessor—Appraiser—Manager	00563-7	8.00
lent Building Superintendent	00068-6	5.00
Car Inspector (T.A.)	03743-1	8.00
:ation Foreman (Foreman & Asst. Foreman)	01958-1	6.00
:ation Man	00025-2	4.00
ol Crossing Guard	00611-0	4.00
or Clerical Series	01173-4	6.00
r Clerk—Stenographer	01797-X	8.00
or File Clerk, Turner	00124-0	8.00
or and Supervising Parking Enforcement Agent	03737-7	6.00
or Typist	03870-5	6.00
eant, P.D.	00026-0	10.00
Clerk	03684-2	6.00
l Supervisor	04190-0	8.00
Attendant	00828-8	4.00
Positions: Senior Administrative Associate and Assistant	03490-4	6.00
Trooper	00078-3	8.00
stician—Statistical Clerk	00058-9	5.00
ographer—Typist (Practical Preparation)	00147-X	6.00
ographer—U.S. Government Positions GS 2-7	04388-1	6.00
ekeeper—Stockman (Senior Storekeeper)	01691-4	8.00
Structural Apprentice	00177-1	5.00
Structure Maintainer Trainee, Groups A to E, Turner	03683-4	6.00
Supervising Clerk (Income Maintenance)	02879-3	5.00
Supervising Clerk—Stenographer	04309-1	8.00
Supervision Course	01590-X	8.00
Surface Line Dispatcher	00140-2	6.00
Tabulating Machine Operator (IBM)	00781-8	4.00
Taking Tests and Scoring High, Honig	01347-8	4.00
Telephone Maintainer: New York City Transit Authority	03742-3	5.00
Telephone Operator	00033-3	8.00
Test Your Vocational Aptitude, Asta & Bernbach	03606-0	6.00
Towerman (Municipal Subway System)	00157-7	5.00
Trackman (Municipal Subways)	00075-9	5.00
Track Foreman: New York City Transit Authority	03739-3	6.00
Traffic Control Agent	03421-1	5.00
Train Dispatcher	00158-5	5.00
Transit Patrolman	00092-9	5.00
Transit Sergeant—Lieutenant	00161-5	4.00
Treasury Enforcement Agent	00131-3	8.00
U.S. Postal Service Motor Vehicle Operator	04426-8	8.00
U.S. Professional Mid-Level Positions Grades GS-9 Through GS-12	02036-9	6.00
U.S. Summer Jobs	02480-1	4.00
Ventilation and Drainage Maintainer: New York City Transit Authority	03741-5	6.00
Vocabulary Builder and Guide to Verbal Tests	00535-1	5.00
Vocabulary, Spelling and Grammar	00077-5	5.00
Welder	01374-5	8.00
X-Ray Technician (See Radiologic Technology Exam Review)	03833-0	8.00

MILITARY EXAMINATION SERIES

Title	Number	Price
Practice for Army Classification and Placement (ASVAB)	03845-4	6.00
Practice for the Armed Forces Tests	04362-8	6.00
Practice for Navy Placement Tests	04560-4	6.00
Practice for Air Force Placement Tests	04270-2	6.00
Practice for Officer Candidate Tests	01304-4	6.00
Tests for Women in the Armed Forces	03821-7	6.00
U.S. Service Academies	01544-6	6.00

HIGH SCHOOL AND COLLEGE PREPARATION

Title	Number	Price
ican College Testing Program Exams	04363-6	5.00
Arithmetic Q & A Review, Turner	02351-1	5.00
s Handbook of Job and Career Opportunities	04328-8	3.95
r Business English, Classen	04287-7	2.95
ornia High School Proficiency Examination	04412-8	4.95
olic High School Entrance Examination	00987-X	5.00
ollege Board's Examination, McDonough & Hansen	02623-5	5.00
ge By Mail, Jensen	02592-1	4.00
ge Entrance Tests, Turner	01858-5	5.00
Easy Way to Better Grades, Froe & Froe	03352-5	1.75
ents of Debate, Klopf & McCroskey	01901-8	5.00
clopedia of English, Zeiger	00655-X	3.95
sh Grammar: 1,000 Steps	02012-1	6.00
ish Grammar and Usage for Test-Takers, Turner	04014-9	6.00
Florida Literacy Test, Morrison	04669-4	4.95
English with Ease, revised edition, Beckoff	03911-6	5.00
e to Financial Aids for Students in Arts and Sciences r Graduate and Professional Study, Searles & Scott	02496-8	3.95
High School Entrance and Scholarship Tests, Turner	00666-8	5.00
High School Entrance Examinations—Special Public and Private High Schools	02143-8	5.00
How to Obtain Money for College, Lever	03932-9	5.00
How to Prepare Your College Application, Kussin & Kussin	01310-9	2.00
How to Use a Pocket Calculator, Mullish	04072-6	4.95
How to Write Reports, Papers, Theses, Articles, Riebel	02391-0	6.00
Letter-Perfect:The Accurate Secretary, Gilson	04038-6	6.00
Mastering General Mathematics, McDonough	03732-6	5.00
New York State Regents Scholarship	00400-2	5.00
Organization and Outlining, Peirce	02425-9	4.95
Preliminary Scholastic Aptitude Tests—National Merit Scholarship Qualifying Tests (PSAT-NMSQT)	00413-4	4.00
Practice for Scholastic Aptitude Tests	04303-2	1.50
Scholastic Aptitude Tests	04341-5	5.00
Scoring High on Reading Tests	00731-1	5.00
Triple Your Reading Speed, Cutler	02083-0	5.00
Typing for Everyone, Levine	02212-4 E	3.95

PROFESSIONAL CAREER EXAM SERIES

Action Guide for Executive Job Seekers and Employers, Uris .... ______ 01787-2 3.95
Air Traffic Controller, Morrison ...... ______ 04593-0 8.00
Automobile Mechanic Certification Tests, Sharp ...... ______ 03809-8 6.00
Bar Exams ...... ______ 01124-6 5.00
The C.P.A. Exam: Accounting by the "Parallel Point" Method, Lipscomb ...... ______ 02020-2 15.00
Certified General Automobile Mechanic, Turner ...... ______ 02900-5 6.00
Computer Programmer, Luftig ...... ______ 01232-3 8.00
Computers and Automation, Brown ...... ______ 01745-7 5.95
Computers and Data Processing Examinations: CDP/CCP/CLEP ...... ______ 04670-8 10.00
Dental Admission Test, Arco Editorial Board ...... ______ 04293-1 6.00
Graduate Management Admission Test ...... ______ 04360-1 6.00
Graduate Record Examination Aptitude Test ...... ______ 00824-5 5.00
Health Insurance Agent (Hospital, Accident, Health, Life) ...... ______ 02153-5 5.00
How a Computer System Works, Brown & Workman ...... ______ 03424-6 5.95
How to Become a Successful Model—Second Edition, Krem ...... ______ 04508-6 2.95
How to Get Into Medical and Dental School, revised edition, Shugar, Shugar & Bauman ...... ______ 04095-5 4.00
How to Make Money in Music, Harris & Farrar ...... ______ 04089-0 5.95
How to Remember Anything, Markoff, Dubin & Carcel ...... ______ 03929-9 5.00
The Installation and Servicing of Domestic Oil Burners, Mitchell & Mitchell ...... ______ 00437-1 10.00
Instrument Pilot Examination, Morrison ...... ______ 04592-2 9.95
Insurance Agent and Broker ...... ______ 02149-7 8.00
Law School Admission Test, Candrilli & Slawsky ...... ______ 03946-9 6.00
Life Insurance Agent, Snouffer ...... ______ 04306-7 8.00
Medical College Admission Test, Turner ...... ______ 04289-3 6.00
Miller Analogies Test—1400 Analogy Questions ...... ______ 01114-9 5.00
National Career Directory ...... ______ 04510-8 5.95
The 1978-79 Airline Guide to Stewardess and Steward Careers, Morton ...... ______ 04350-4 5.95
Notary Public ...... ______ 00180-1 6.00
Nursing School Entrance Examinations, Turner ...... ______ 01202-1 6.00
Oil Burner Installer ...... ______ 00096-1 8.00
The Official 1978-79 Guide to Airline Careers, Morton ...... ______ 03955-8 5.95
Playground and Recreation Director's Handbook ...... ______ 01096-7 8.00
Principles of Data Processing, Morrison ...... ______ 04268-0 7.50
Psychology: A Graduate Review, Ozehosky & Polz ...... ______ 04136-6 10.00
Real Estate License Examination, Gladstone ...... ______ 03755-5 6.00
Real Estate Mathematics Simplified, Shulman ...... ______ 04713-5 5.00
Refrigeration License Manual, Harfenist ...... ______ 02726-6 10.00
Resumes for Job Hunters, Shykind ...... ______ 03961-2 5.00
Resumes That Get Jobs, revised edition, Resume Service ...... ______ 03909-4 3.00
Simplify Legal Writing, Biskind ...... ______ 03801-2 5.00
Spanish for Nurses and Allied Health Science Students, Hernandez-Miyares & Alba ...... ______ 04127-7 10.00
Stationary Engineer and Fireman ...... ______ 00070-8 8.00
Structural Design ...... ______ 04549-3 10.00
The Test of English as a Foreign Language (TOEFL), Moreno, Babin & Cordes ...... ______ 04450-0 8.00
TOEFL Listening Comprehension Cassette ...... ______ 04667-8 7.95
Veterinary College Admissions ...... ______ 04147-1 10.00
Your Resume—Key to a Better Job, Corwen ...... ______ 03733-4 4.00

ADVANCED GRE SERIES

Biology: Advanced Test for the G.R.E., Solomon ...... ______ 04310-5 4.95
Business: Advanced Test for the G.R.E., Berman, Malea & Yearwood ...... ______ 01599-3 6.95
Chemistry: Advanced Test for the G.R.E., Weiss ...... ______ 01069-X 4.95
Economics: Advanced Test for the G.R.E., Zabrenski & Heydari-Darafshian ...... ______ 04548-5 5.95
Education: Advanced Test for the G.R.E., ... ______ 04117-3
Engineering: Advanced Test for the G.R.E., Ingham & Nesbitt ...... ______ 01604-3
French: Advanced Test for the G.R.E., Dethierry ...... ______ 01070-3
Geography: Advanced Test for the G.R.E., White ...... ______ 01710-4
Geology: Advanced Test for the G.R.E., Dolgoff ...... ______ 01071-1
History: Advanced Test for the G.R.E., ... ______ 04414-4
Literature: Advanced Test for the G.R.E. ...... ______ 01073-8
Mathematics: Advanced Test for the G.R.E., Bramson ...... ______ 04264-8
Music: Advanced Test for the G.R.E., Murphy ...... ______ 01471-7
Philosophy: Advanced Test for the G.R.E., Steiner ...... ______ 01472-5
Physical Education: Advanced Test for the G.R.E., Rubinger ...... ______ 01609-4
Physics: Advanced Test for the G.R.E., Bruenn ...... ______ 01074-6
Political Science: Advanced Test for the G.R.E., Meador & Stewart ...... ______ 01459-8
Psychology: Advanced Test for the G.R.E., Millman & Nisbett ...... ______ 01145-9
Sociology: Advanced Test for the G.R.E., ... ______ 04547-7
Spanish: Advanced Test for the G.R.E., Jassey ...... ______ 01075-4
Speech: Advanced Test for the G.R.E., Graham ...... ______ 01526-8

GRADUATE FOREIGN LANGUAGE TESTS

Graduate School Foreign Language Test: French, Kretschmer ...... ______ 01461-X
Graduate School Foreign Language Test: German, Goldberg ...... ______ 01460-1
Graduate School Foreign Language Test: Spanish, Hampares & Jassey ...... ______ 01874-7

PROFESSIONAL ENGINEER EXAMINATIONS

Chemical Engineering, Coren ...... ______ 01256-0
Civil Engineering Technician ...... ______ 04267-2
Electrical Engineering Technician ...... ______ 04149-8
Engineer in Training Examination (EIT), Morrison ...... ______ 04009-2
Engineering Fundamentals ...... ______ 04273-7
Fundamentals of Engineering, Home Study Program, (3 Vols.) ...... ______ 04302-4
Fundamentals of Engineering (Vol. I), Morrison ...... ______ 04234-6
Fundamentals of Engineering (Vol. II), Morrison ...... ______ 04240-0
Fundamentals of Engineering (2 vols.) ...... ______ 04243-5
Industrial Engineering Technician ...... ______ 04154-4
Mechanical Engineering Technician ...... ______ 04274-5
Principles and Practice of Electrical Engineering Examination, Morrison ...... ______ 04031-9
Professional Engineer (Civil) State Board Examination Review, Packer et al ...... ______ 03637-0
Professional Engineering Registration: Problems and Solutions ...... ______ 04269-9
Solid Mechanics, Morrison ...... ______ 04409-8

NATIONAL TEACHER AREA EXAMS

Early Childhood Education: Teaching Area Exam for the National Teacher Examination ...... ______ 01637-X
Education in the Elementary School: Teaching Area Exam for the National Teacher Examination ...... ______ 01318-4
English Language and Literature: Teaching Area Exam for the National Teacher Examination ...... ______ 01319-2
Mathematics: Teaching Area Exam for the National Teacher Examination ...... ______ 01639-6
National Teacher Examination ...... ______ 00823-7